STATEMENT CONCERNING PUBLICATIONS OF RUSSELL SAGE FOUNDATION

Russell Sage Foundation was established in 1907 by Mrs. Russell Sage "for the improvement of social and living conditions in the United States of America." While the general responsibility for management of the Foundation is vested in the Board of Trustees, the responsibility for facts, conclusions, and interpretations in its publications rests with the authors and not upon the Foundation, its Trustees, or its staff. Publication under the imprint of the Foundation does not imply agreement by the organization with all opinions or interpretations expressed. It does imply that care has been taken that the work on which a manuscript is based has been thoroughly done.

HUMAN PROBLEMS
in Technological Change

A CASEBOOK

Edited by EDWARD H. SPICER

RUSSELL SAGE FOUNDATION
New York , , , *1952*

Copyright, 1952, by
RUSSELL SAGE FOUNDATION
Printed in the United States
of America

*Library of Congress
Catalog Card Number: 52–11862*

WM. F. FELL CO., PRINTERS
PHILADELPHIA, PA.

THE CONTRIBUTORS

JOHN ADAIR, Associate Professor of Anthropology, Cornell University

ANACLETO APODACA, Agricultural Extension Officer, Institute of Inter-American Affairs

WESLEY L. BLISS, Wenner-Gren Fellow in Anthropology, University of Arizona

HENRY F. DOBYNS, Graduate Assistant in Cornell Field Seminar in Applied Anthropology

ALLAN R. HOLMBERG, Associate Professor of Anthropology, Cornell University

MARGARET LANTIS, Social Anthropologist, Harvard University

ALEXANDER H. LEIGHTON, Professor of Sociology and Anthropology, Cornell University

ALLISTER MACMILLAN, Research Associate, Cornell University

MORRIS EDWARD OPLER, Professor of Anthropology, Cornell University

TOM TAKETO SASAKI, Deputy Field Director, Southwestern Field Station, Department of Sociology and Anthropology, Cornell University

LAURISTON SHARP, Professor of Anthropology, Cornell University

RUDRA DATT SINGH, formerly Rural Life Analyst, Uttar Pradesh Government, India; Research Associate, Cornell University

EDWARD H. SPICER, Professor of Anthropology and Sociology, University of Arizona

JOHN USEEM, Professor of Sociology and Anthropology, Michigan State College

6430

ACKNOWLEDGMENTS

The original conception of this casebook came from Alexander H. Leighton, and was evolved in the course of working out teaching methods for Cornell University seminars in applied anthropology. The idea was further developed in discussions among John Adair, Henry F. Dobyns, Allan R. Holmberg, Morris Edward Opler, Lauriston Sharp, Alexander H. Leighton, and the editor.

The contributors to the volume have allowed the editor great license in organizing their data, and they have given much help in preparing their cases for publication.

Besides those who have contributed cases, there are others who have given aid in reading manuscript and offering suggestions. The following have been especially helpful: Carroll Barber, Solon T. Kimball, Clyde Kluckhohn, John L. Schweitzer, Katherine Spencer, and Robert K. Thomas.

To all of these the editor wishes to express his gratitude.

E. H. S.

Tucson,
September, 1952

CONTENTS

FOREWORD BY ALEXANDER H. LEIGHTON   9

INTRODUCTION BY THE EDITOR   13
  Change in the Modern World   13
  The Fabric of Human Culture   16
  Human Responses to Change   17
  Purpose of This Casebook   18

PART I. THE DISCOVERY OF HUMAN PROBLEMS

CASE 1. In the Wake of the Wheel   23
         Introduction of the Wagon to the Papago
         Indians of Southern Arizona
         BY WESLEY L. BLISS

SUGGESTIONS FOR STUDY—The Formulation of Questions   33

CASE 2. Corn and Custom   35
         Introduction of Hybrid Corn to Spanish
         American Farmers in New Mexico
         BY ANACLETO APODACA

CASE 3. Reluctant Cotton-Pickers   41
         Incentive to Work in a Japanese Relocation
         Center
         BY E. H. SPICER

CASE 4. The Village Level   55
         An Introduction of Green Manuring in
         Rural India
         BY RUDRA DATT SINGH

CASE 5. Steel Axes for Stone Age Australians   69
         BY LAURISTON SHARP

SUGGESTIONS FOR STUDY—A Checklist of Questions   91

5

PART II. THE ANALYSIS OF HUMAN SITUATIONS

SUGGESTIONS FOR STUDY—Roles   95

CASE 6.   New Land to Farm   97
           Agricultural Practices Among the Navaho
           Indians of New Mexico
           BY TOM SASAKI AND JOHN ADAIR

CASE 7.   The Wells That Failed   113
           An Attempt to Establish a Stable Water
           Supply in Viru Valley, Peru
           BY ALLAN R. HOLMBERG

SUGGESTIONS FOR STUDY—Interviewing   125

CASE 8.   Eskimo Herdsmen   127
           Introduction of Reindeer Herding to the
           Natives of Alaska
           BY MARGARET LANTIS

CASE 9.   South Sea Island Strike   149
           Labor-Management Relations in the
           Caroline Islands, Micronesia
           BY JOHN USEEM

CASE 10.   The Creek "Town" and the Problem of Creek
           Indian Political Reorganization   165
           BY MORRIS EDWARD OPLER

PART III. TYPES OF HUMAN PROBLEMS

SUGGESTIONS FOR STUDY—Finding Common Elements   183

CASE 11.   Sheepmen and Technicians   185
           A Program of Soil Conservation on the Navajo
           Indian Reservation
           BY E. H. SPICER WITH COMMENT BY JOHN COLLIER

Case 12. Experiment in Conservation 209
Erosion Control and Forage Production on
the Papago Indian Reservations in Arizona
by Henry F. Dobyns

Case 13. People of the Hinterland 225
Community Interrelations in a Maritime
Province of Canada
by Allister Macmillan and Alexander
H. Leighton

Case 14. Resistance to Freedom 245
Resettlement from the Japanese Relocation
Centers during World War II
by E. H. Spicer

Case 15. Democracy in Process 261
The Development of Democratic Leadership
in the Micronesian Islands
by John Useem

Suggestions for Study—Recurrent Groups of Problems 281

PART IV. CONCEPTUAL TOOLS FOR SOLVING HUMAN PROBLEMS 283

INDEX 297

FOREWORD

This book takes origin from Cornell's program for research and training in culture and applied science. Developed in the Department of Sociology and Anthropology since World War II, and supported primarily by the Carnegie Corporation of New York, the program is addressed to the question of facilitating the introduction of modern agriculture, industry, and medicine to areas that are deficient in these technologies. Of central concern is the fact that technological innovations are apt to have consequences ranging from hostility toward the innovator to extensive disruption and crisis in the society. Our program is concerned, therefore, not so much with technologies as such, as with the social and cultural dynamics that are involved.

By means of field stations in the American Southwest, India, Peru, and Thailand, research is going forward regarding the processes of culture and regarding methods for introducing new technologies. Training is carried out partly at the field stations and partly on the campus, and includes both social science students and those professionally trained in technological fields. In the case of the latter, an effort has been made to render the teaching as relevant as possible to the needs of a practical operator. Consequently, there has been emphasis on problems, or cases, as a base to which one can relate the findings of cultural anthropology, social psychology, and similar fields.

In such a context the present book evolved. Edward H. Spicer, of the University of Arizona, having participated during a number of seasons in Cornell's summer field training seminar in the Southwest, contributed largely to its development. When Russell Sage Foundation commissioned the production of the casebook, we were fortunate to secure his services as editor.

So much for development. If we look now at the fundamental idea which underlies the Cornell program, and hence this book, namely, the desirability of using social science as an aid to technology, there seems little need to justify the proposition so far as practicability is concerned. While social science embraces no

9

guarantees of success, enough experience has been accumulated to show that it can be of considerable help. A more significant question is the morality of attempting to manipulate human beings. Should anyone try to change peoples' ways? Should anyone utilize psychological and cultural knowledge in order to maneuver others toward goals they do not desire—for if they desired the goals, what need would there be of applied anthropology and psychology?

These are serious issues and reflect a well-founded fear that applied social science, like other technical developments, can be abused, can be employed by a few to control and exploit the rest of mankind.

Our work is founded on four major premises:

1. Millions of men, women, and children all over the world desire more freedom than they now possess from starvation, disease, and physical insecurity.

2. These people under stress, together with others who are more fortunate, are aware of the technological power and efficiency of the West and would like to have some, if not all, of these advantages.

3. The people who desire such improvements have little perception of the complex human difficulties involved. They want change, but have very incomplete ideas of the cost to their way of life.

4. The members of western society who introduce the changes are also incompletely aware of consequences.

It seems justifiable to assume, therefore, that the technological experts in public health, land improvement, industrialization, and similar fields (together with the administrators of such programs) have some responsibility for the human relations involved in their work. For instance, although the people of a society may want to be free of disease, they may have to be led to appreciate many subgoals, such as cleanliness in the house, which are not in their original perception related to the main problem. On the other hand, they may also have to be led away from ruthless adoption of western sanitary regulations, which would be far more disruptive to their way of life than any gain they could possibly derive.

The only practicable way to deal with the dangers inherent in applied social science is through wide education on the subject so that people can recognize programs that are sound in human relations and be on their guard against manipulative tricks. To counsel, as some do, the abandonment of applied social science because of its danger, is to advocate both the impossible and the undesirable, just as it would be both impossible and undesirable to abandon applied physiology (medicine) because it can be used to manipulate and kill, as well as to heal.

We offer this book, therefore, in the hope that our audience will include not only those who sponsor innovations, but also the recipients.

A. H. L.

Cornell University,
September, 1952

INTRODUCTION

Changing peoples' customs is an even more delicate responsibility than surgery. When a surgeon takes up his instruments he assumes the responsibility for a human life. On his skill and judgment during each moment of an operation depends the future of one individual. If the surgeon is not aware of the possibilities for good and for harm that lie in his manipulation of the scalpel, he may work irreparable damage. On his knowledge, which is to say, on his awareness of the experiences of thousands of predecessors in the profession, and on his ability to apply that knowledge at every turn of events, rests the well-being and the happiness of his patient.

The administrator of a program of technological change carries a heavier responsibility. Whenever he seeks to alter a people's way of life, he is dealing not with one individual, but with the well-being and happiness of generations of men and women. If his skill is poor and his judgment bad, he can destroy cooperative human relations and create hatreds that will affect uncountable numbers of people. If, on the other hand, his skill is equal to the task, the possibility is open for creating cooperation where it did not exist and for bettering the lives of generations. The gravity of the responsibility need not overawe, but it must impress, each candidate in the profession with the necessity for the most careful training as a basis for every judgment.

CHANGE IN THE MODERN WORLD

Modern life is characterized by a great outpouring of energy on the part of some people who strive to "better the lives" of others. This activity takes many forms. Some are on an international scale, as for instance the attempts of the United States, through Point Four organization, to "export skills and techniques to underdeveloped areas." Other measures are confined to a single country, such as the work of the Cultural Missions in Mexico or the Extension Service of the Department of Agricul-

ture in the United States. Still others are on the small scale of
work within a single community, which may be concerned with
the spread of only a single practice, for example, contributing to
a blood-bank.

These activities, superficially often widely different, are all,
nevertheless, a reflection of the same fundamental condition in
modern life, namely, different rates of progress by different parts
of society.[1]

But let us consider a little more closely what is involved. Why
are different rates of progress so pervasive in the modern world?
Certainly a large part of the answer to this question lies in the fact
of specialization. Intensive specialization in medicine, in tool
manufacture, in transportation, in agricultural science, and in a
host of other fields has proceeded at breakneck pace during the
past hundred years. This has led to considerable stores of knowledge and tested practice in each of these specialties, but the new
ideas and the new ways of doing things have not, obviously,
spread immediately and automatically in smooth-flowing waves
from the specialists to the millions of persons over the world who
can profit from their use.

Instead, the process seems to be something like this: From the
specialists who make the discoveries, the new ideas move to "the
educated," that is, to persons who have (up to a certain point)
the same kind of schooling as the specialists. Communication is
relatively easy because all have learned to use printed words in the
same way and their world of values, strongly affected by a
similar kind of school and college training, is very much the
same. As the educated become aware of the findings of the
specialists, they usually realize how much better off the new
knowledge would make thousands of poverty-stricken or disease-
ridden people, if only ways could be found to get them to use it.
Out of such vision have grown programs toward betterment on
dozens of fronts, but whether the program is that of a home
demonstration agent in rural United States or of a government
irrigation engineer in Iraq, the work rests on that widespread

[1] For one view in this regard, see Ogburn, William Fielding, *Social Change*. The
Viking Press, New York, rev. 1950.

realization of the difference between what is and what might be, which characterizes the modern world.

This situation has given rise to a new kind of specialist, namely, the specialist in spreading knowledge and practice beyond the small world of the college-educated. It is a kind of work that has increased greatly in importance in the past generation and may be expected to continue as intercommunication grows among all parts of the world. At the same time the need to bridge the gap between technological specialization and the web of human problems is becoming more and more clearly felt.

The extension worker and the public health nurse both attempt to alter traditional ways by demonstrating the advantages of the new. As a result they consciously and unconsciously direct changes in peoples' customs and beliefs. They are, moreover (and this is a fundamental point for understanding the essential nature of their problems), working across certain barriers. These barriers are differing language, belief, and custom. Coming out of the world of the highly literate, the technologist has a way of talking, acting, and thinking which is ordinarily sharply different from that of the people among whom his work is cast. It is this throwing together of two different cultural backgrounds that gives rise to the special group of problems that confront workers in these fields.

The situation in which such workers find themselves has been called "cross-cultural." It is a useful term for thinking about, let us say, Europeans from modern industrialized Belgium who work with Africans in the agricultural Congo and try to raise the native standard of living. The term emphasizes the strongly contrasting backgrounds of the two peoples and the fact that ideas and techniques are transferred across from one to the other of these different cultures. But the term "cross-cultural" is equally applicable to the efforts of a public health worker in Illinois, for example, who is engaged in persuading people in a rural neighborhood to screen their houses against flies. While the language barrier, although present, is less formidable in Illinois than in the Congo, there is still a cultural gulf between the highly trained, urbanized health worker and the rural farm people. The viewpoint of this casebook is that such apparently widely different situations have many fundamental features in common and that the problems which arise in them yield to basically similar treatment.

THE FABRIC OF HUMAN CULTURE

Let us look briefly at some aspects of the life habits that any technologically trained person is likely to bring into contact with another people's way of life in a cross-cultural situation. He has learned to separate, carefully, different aspects of experience in order to pay special attention to them. For example, he might be much aware of the chemical, as distinguished from the mechanical, effects of a certain kind of diet on the alimentary tract. He might be accustomed to think not in terms of foods, but rather in terms of certain selected qualities of foods, such as calories and vitamins. A viewpoint of this sort results from long discipline in making distinctions; it is a habit of mind essential in the acquisition of specialized knowledge.

Such a view of things is not likely, however, to characterize the people among whom work has been undertaken. They are not prone to think of food or crops in such analytical terms, but more probably connect them with supernatural beings or perhaps with their own moral behavior. It is easy to classify such beliefs as superstitions and to assume an attitude of disapproval, or even contempt, toward them, but the fact remains that the people do make such connections. The universe, for them, is not divided into the compartments (physical, chemical, biological) in terms of which the specialist has learned to think. Problems in the *application* of knowledge begin to be solvable only when the specialist recognizes the existence of the other culture and starts to compare it carefully with his own. It is then that he is in a position to recognize the materials with which he must work.

There is a strange artificiality about modern specialism as a standpoint from which to view the practical problems of dealing with human beings in cross-cultural situations. Everyone knows how, in solving his own personal problems, categories such as psychology, sociology, and economics refuse to remain separate. One has to balance considerations of family ties, for example, against falling in love, and the latter against financial realities. Economic security, family solidarity, and psychobiological drives, in other words, have to be considered together because there are very real connections among them. The compartmentalization of the laboratory, so neat and manageable, rarely appears in situations of practical decision. The lives of people in any society do not exist separated into the aspects in which scientists have analyzed them.

It is realization of this linkage of the different aspects of life that constitutes a beginning point for discovering the nature of the human problems with which one has to deal in changing peoples' customs and beliefs. When the horse was introduced to the North American Indians of the Plains, it transformed their way of life within two generations. After centuries as fairly peaceful farmers, they gave up agriculture and rapidly became warlike raiders.

During the past two centuries, all over the world we have seen similar sweeping reorganizations of peoples' lives as a result of the introduction of new means of subsistence, new tools, and also (as among the Indians of New Mexico) new ideas, in this instance, religious ideas. Such transformations are not queer accidents. They are the result of the working of the basic principle that customs and beliefs are linked into a whole and that changes in one aspect of life will have repercussions on other aspects. This interdependence is really the elementary fact from which the analysis of each case in this book proceeds and to which each returns.

HUMAN RESPONSES TO CHANGE

It has become something of a commonplace to say, "People resist change," but a generalization that has many more facts to support it is the opposite: "People accept change." The notion that people tend to resist rather than accept change may be a special idea of our era, formulated by those who are especially conscious of cultural differences or by those who are engaged in trying to bring about change. To the latter, certainly, the fact of resistance is more striking than acceptance. The truth is, however, that people everywhere constantly change their ways. Language, domestic animal breeds, tools, ways of growing crops, methods of curing, and forms of political organization have changed steadily through the centuries, not only among Europeans, but also among the Congolese, the Japanese, the Chinese, and all the other peoples of the earth. No generation seems to behave precisely like a former generation. Rates of change, comparing one people with another or one aspect of culture with another, show great differences, but the outstanding fact of constant change nevertheless remains.

Understanding that change is a process which people are undergoing all the time, gives us a vantage point from which to view conscious efforts to alter culture. We begin to see resistance as a symptom of something wrong in the cross-cultural situation, perhaps of the real impracticality of the proposed change, perhaps of unsatisfactory relations between the worker and the people. Once resistance is seen as a symptom of special conditions rather than as a constant element, it becomes possible, through the study of cases in which resistance appears, to discover causes of success and failure.

It seems possible, for instance, despite our ignorance, to support the following generalizations: people resist changes that appear to threaten basic securities; they resist proposed changes they do not understand; they resist being forced to change. It is partly for the purpose of illustrating such general propositions that the casebook has been prepared, but also to provide material in which students may see for themselves the outlines of principles not as yet clearly formulated by others.

PURPOSE OF THIS CASEBOOK

This is a book of concrete instances, not a treatise on the principles of technological and social change. Almost every case offers an actual example of an effort to bring about a change in some culture. Both successful and unsuccessful attempts are included. We have tried to select cases for which there is enough detailed record to indicate all the factors of practical importance and to make the results fully intelligible. In some, all available data are presented; in others, this procedure has not been necessary, since much of the material is accessible in the literature. It is hoped that a feeling for the whole reality of each situation will be evoked by what is given.

We have set the cases up as problems, in the belief that thinking through the question before the outcome is known will deepen the experience of studying the case and will parallel the real-life situations which the worker must face. Most of the cases are therefore organized along the following lines. After stating the *Problem* we introduce a chronological account of what led up to this situation, called *The Course of Events;* then follows *Relevant Factors*, which sets forth details concerning the nature of the change, the culture of the people, and the features of the cross-cultural situation. These sections should provide in each instance enough material for solving the *Problem*. It is hoped that after considering the *Relevant Factors*, the student will attempt to answer the questions posed in the *Problem*. This may involve a prediction of the ultimate outcome of the case or may consist of an explanation of why events proceeded as they did. Whichever is called for, an analytical discussion of the whole situation, showing how the different factors are related, will be necessary.

Only after the student has worked out his answers to the problem should he turn to the sections called *The Outcome* and the *Analysis*, which complete the exposition. The *Analysis* given is by the writer of the case, who ordinarily has had firsthand contact with the situation. His interpretation provides a critical standpoint from which to view the solutions offered by different students. However, it is not thought that the authors' conclusions are necessarily the ultimate truth. They are rather a challenge to the students to work out fuller and sounder analyses.

The cases have been arranged in an order that approximates progress from simple to complex. The first five, constituting Part I, are simple in the sense that either a single factor seems to have been decisive in bringing about the outcome, or the relations among several factors are easily seen. They are also designed to illustrate the commonest types of human problems that arise in cross-cultural change.

Part II consists of five cases illustrating the same kinds of problems (together with some additional types), but they are also regarded as being of somewhat greater complexity. There are more factors involved and the relations among them are not so readily seen as in the first cases.

In Part III, five cases deal with the kinds of problems that have already been illustrated, but they are again still more complicated. The interrelationships of factors are harder to discover and to demonstrate.

Parallel with the presentation of cases, an effort is made to acquaint the student with some elementary techniques for analyzing human problems. The *Suggestions for Study*, given in the different parts of the casebook, are designed to start him using basic, simple methods of question formulation, role analysis, interviewing, and role-playing with the case material as he goes along. It is hoped that through this means a viewpoint toward the material and a feeling for its nature will be developed simultaneously with the acquisition of information about specific instances.

The casebook does not give rules for solving human problems. It is designed rather to open paths for finding them.

PART I

THE DISCOVERY OF HUMAN PROBLEMS

Case 1

IN THE WAKE OF THE WHEEL: Introduction of the Wagon to the Papago Indians of Southern Arizona

by Wesley L. Bliss

1. THE PROBLEM

Like other American Indians, the Papagos of southern Arizona knew nothing of the wheel and its uses until the white men came. Relatively isolated in desert country, they did not begin to make much use of wheeled vehicles until shortly before 1900. Their adoption came about partly as the result of a deliberate program of the United States Bureau of Indian Affairs. The program was successful and had far-reaching effects on the simple routine of life in the desert villages.

The Indian agents correctly predicted that the Papagos would find uses for wagons but, so far as is known, no official anticipated the whole train of effects on Papago life. Hence, the introduction of the wagon was not integrated with other plans for the Indians.

What immediate changes in the life of a desert Indian village would you expect from the introduction of a wagon about the year 1900?

2. THE COURSE OF EVENTS

1. Spanish missionaries first came into contact with the Papago Indians in 1687. The missionaries, and the soldiers and few colonists who followed them, brought metal tools, cattle, horses, wheat and other European seeds, as well as Christianity and some ideas of political and military organization. The horses were used for riding and pack animals; but if wheeled vehicles were introduced, the fact is not recorded.

2. For almost 200 years following the first intensive contact with the Jesuit missionaries, the Papagos continued to live at the extreme margin of Spanish influence in the New World. The effects of this contact were not at all like those farther south, in

23

Mexico. Spaniards were little interested in the desert country and their influence was felt chiefly along the southern and eastern edges of Papago territory. Here Papagos moved into the villages around the mission churches for longer or shorter periods and learned something of new agricultural techniques and products. In the main, life in the desert villages continued very much as it had for hundreds of years.

3. About the middle of the nineteenth century, with the coming of Anglo Americans to southern Arizona after the close of the Mexican War, a new era began for the Papagos. They joined as allies with the Americans against their old enemies, the Apaches, and rendered effective service in pacifying the Apache frontier.

4. The agents of the Bureau of Indian Affairs who first came in contact with the Papagos in the 1860's expressed deep concern for the "poverty-stricken Indians," and efforts were made to help them. Impressed with the Papagos' lack of possessions, the agents undertook as one of their first acts the free distribution of knives, shovels, hoes, and other agricultural implements.

5. Later, a plan was put into effect for giving a farm-wagon to everyone who would agree to build a house in the Mexican adobe style, in place of the brush types traditional among Papagos. Many families in the village where the Indian agent had settled, at the eastern margin of Papago territory, responded during the next few years and received new farm-wagons.

6. The majority of Papagos lived far to the west of the agent's village and were not reached by this first program, so that it was only in the eastern villages that wagons came into use.

By the 1890's the program had been changed. A man did not have to build a Mexican-style house; he could obtain a wagon by applying to the agent. Payment could be made at leisure.

7. Three brothers of the headman of the village of Choulik, 60 miles west of the agent's village, had obtained work at various times as laborers on track construction for the Southern Pacific Railroad. They were thus thrown into rather close contact with Anglo Americans and their vehicles in the towns that had grown up along the railroad route.

8. When the brothers heard of the Indian agent's offer, they persuaded the headman to ask for a wagon. About a year after the request, the agent sent word that one was ready. The headman rode to the agency and was supplied with a heavy farmwagon and harness for a team of horses. He drove the wagon back to his home village.

9. The wagon was put into immediate service and continued in use for several years, until it wore out. It was the beginning of a successful introduction of wagons to all villages in the area neighboring Choulik.

3. RELEVANT FACTORS

The Papago pattern of life rested on a combination of hunting and gathering of wild food (cactus fruits and mesquite beans) with very small-scale flood farming along the intermittent streams. The introduction of cattle by the Spanish added something to Papago subsistence; the Indians allowed the animals to run wherever they could find forage and then hunted them like wild game. Although relatively few horses and mules were brought into the region, the horses multiplied through the years. At first they were sometimes used for food but, by 1900, were commonly employed as pack and riding animals.

Papagos had their own methods of packing. They made saddles of two cylindrical bundles of wheat straw or grass tied together with leather thongs and slung so that one rested on each side of the horse's back. Goods to be transported were put in panniers, made of fiber or rawhide nets, which were slung over the strawpack saddles. A man always rode a loaded animal. Most villages in the vicinity of Choulik had, by 1900, at least a small string of horses, usually one or two for each family.

The Indians customarily changed their residence with the season. During the winter months they lived in the mountains, where there were permanent supplies of water in the form of springs. In the summer they moved down into the valleys to plant and harvest crops of corn, beans, and wheat. The winter and summer villages were from 6 or 8 to 15 or 20 miles apart. Often during the winter in ordinary years, and always in drought years, family groups sought jobs in the Mexican villages of Sonora, among the Pima Indians on the Gila River, or among the newly arrived English-speaking migrants, who were establishing mines and cattle ranches in southern Arizona. The village of Choulik was some 60 miles from the nearest non-Papago settlement and over a hundred from more thickly populated areas like the Gila Valley to the north or the Alter Valley to the south.

Trading expeditions were frequently organized by the Papagos for the purpose of obtaining seeds to plant. Such trips were usually planned by all the males of a village, who would decide on types and quantity of seeds and select several men to go out with pack horses to secure them. Buckskin, grass rope, large baskets, and pottery ollas were the usual trade goods. Papago traders sometimes went as far as 250 miles on such expeditions— reaching Bisbee, Arizona, and Hermosillo, Sonora. Families also traveled annually or every other year to Magdalena, Sonora, on religious pilgrimages to visit the famous image of San Francisco.

Papago villages were small, rarely consisting of more than a hundred people, and were organized as land-using, political units, laying claim to some permanent water supply in the mountains and to an area of arable fields in the valley. Usually a *charco*, a large dirt-banked reservoir, held the domestic water supply for a field village during the summer months.

The 7 to 20 families of a village recognized the leadership of a headman. He, working closely with a council of all the adult men, planned and carried out communal enterprises, such as building water-spreading dams for the fields or repairing the *charco*. Usually all, or nearly all, of the families in a village were related in a patrilineal system. In village meetings, which might be held as frequently as every night, all males attended and addressed each other during proceedings by kinship terms. The village was consequently a closely knit social unit, recognizing communal property in fields, water supply, and wild food resources.

Hardly any surplus was produced in the desert villages, and there was no full-time specialization of labor. All the men, including even the curing and diagnosing shamans, worked in the fields. They took care of the horses and managed their packing, and most men could engage in the simple crafts of leather- and woodworking. Women, besides cooking and performing other household duties, were part-time specialists in pottery-making and basketry. The older boys and girls gathered wood from round about the village, armload by armload, and also carried the water in ollas from the *charcos* or springs to the houses.

REFERENCES FOR FURTHER STUDY

Joseph, Alice, Rosamond B. Spicer, and Jane Chesky, *The Desert People:* A Study of the Papago Indians of Southern Arizona. University of Chicago Press, Chicago, 1949.

Underhill, Ruth M., *Social Organization of the Papago Indians.* Columbia Contributions to Anthropology, vol. 30. Columbia University Press, New York, 1939.

Answer Question Presented in the Problem
Before Reading the Rest of the Case.

4. THE OUTCOME

The wagon was a desirable and nondisruptive innovation from the Papago point of view. Its use resulted, nevertheless, in a long series of small changes and new adjustments which affected everyone in the village. Some of these were of minor importance from any point of view and some were of far-reaching significance.

The men of Choulik quickly trained their horses to pull the wagon. The rawhide tugs which they had been using in plowing were not transferred to the wagon. Instead, manufactured harness, introduced simultaneously with the wagon, was kept in repair, and new harness was bought when the old wore out. The wagon itself was slightly modified by the addition of a simple wooden frame to support blankets as a shade for riders.

Within a few months one of the men of the village learned how to work iron by heating and hammering. He became capable of shoeing horses and keeping the metal parts of the wagon in repair.

The wagon was used intensively from the start, eliminating most of the packing on individual horses. Within a few years the net panniers and pack saddles ceased to be made.

There was also an important effect on another craft. Almost immediately the wagon was turned to use for carrying water from the *charcos* to the households. The only large water containers used up to this time had been the ollas made by the women, and these were easily broken. Following the example of white ranchers, wooden barrels were introduced. They were not very practicable, however, in the dry climate of the Arizona desert, since they dried out rapidly and fell apart. The Papagos turned then to metal barrels, which were unbreakable and unaffected by the dryness. These steadily replaced ollas both for hauling water and for storing it in the houses. The water supply on hand increased, and the number of ollas required by a household decreased. The latter were used only for drinking-water, which remained cooler and sweeter in ollas than in barrels. The making of ollas declined as a craft, with the result that less time of the women was used.

In order to use the wagon for transportation from the summer to the winter village, it became necessary to construct a road. This involved clearing and grading in order to get the wagon over the extremely rough terrain up the mountain to the winter village site. Some engineering skill was developed and a new form of group labor was introduced in which all the men participated.

When the question of moving from the summer to the winter village first arose after the wagon was introduced, the village council met and decided that all seven families of Choulik would use the vehicle in turn. The family that was prepared first, moved first, and was followed by the others as they were ready.

Treating the wagon as a common resource of the village was apparent in other ways. Trading journeys, such as those to procure seeds, were now made by wagon. Since only one or two men, instead of several, were assigned to make the trips, face-to-face contacts with Mexicans on the southern border of the Papago country declined.

Uses to which pack horses had not been put developed for the wagon. In addition to the regular hauling of water, it was also employed for carrying large supplies of firewood. Cutting wood on a large scale by the men of the family, instead of piecemeal gathering by women and children, became a new pattern. Soon this practice led to hauling loads of wood for sale to the nearest towns, as for instance, Tucson. An additional natural resource was thus developed, and Choulik entered the cash economy of the surrounding society in a new way. Villagers began also to be interested in raising a little corn and wheat for sale as the wagon offered an easier means of getting a few sacks to town.

The use of the wagon as a resource of the whole village led to increased cooperation and interaction of the officials of the village government. The management of transportation called for meetings to plan trading expeditions, to assign the wagon for wood and water hauling, and for all the uses to which it was put. In addition, the building and maintenance of roads constituted a new communal activity, which had to be planned and directed by the village council.

5. ANALYSIS

This summary of the first stage in the introduction of the wagon to pack-animal users suggests the complications of a relatively simple technical innovation even in a society well prepared for it. The case is only carried to the point where more than one wagon was acquired by the village. From there on, many other important innovations arrived, and it is less easy to trace the effects of wagon-use alone.

Although the effects of the one introduction require several pages to list, the explanation for each consequent change is fairly simple. The connections between the changes and the primary innovation are clear enough. The point of emphasis is that such connections must be anticipated in any technological introduction, if there is to be an attempt to guide the change. Foreseeing at least some of the interrelations of tools and customs is fundamental.

In the Papago case little or no conscious control of the innovation was exercised by the Indian agent. Interest in the wagon on the part of Choulik people arose from the headman's brothers having seen it used in towns, when they were working for the railroad. Furthermore, it was accident rather than planning that placed the first wagon in the hands of the headman of Choulik. We are not able, with the data at hand, to prove that his position in the village influenced the course of events, but it seems reasonable to infer that the development of communal use was related to that fact. If the wagon had come first into the hands of a person without the status of headman, other results certainly would have been possible, including disrupting shifts in leadership patterns.

The effects on Choulik technology were considerable. Panniers and pack saddles fell into disuse, those specific articles being replaced, as we should expect, by the wagon. The necessity for repairing the wagon led to the creation of a new specialty—blacksmithing. A third readily predictable effect was the introduction of roads and road-building techniques. All of these might have occurred to anyone who did advance thinking.

Other effects were not so obvious. It would have been difficult to say positively in advance that the time spent in pottery-making by women would be reduced, but it might have appeared as a possibility if the nature of the wagon had been reviewed in detail in relation to all the transportation activities of Papagos. Similarly, the changes in wood-gathering might have been anticipated, together with the consequent shift in the division of labor in household economy, involving increased participation of adult males in activities formerly confined to children and, to some extent, women.

Changes in the total economy that took place were probably of the type the Indian agent desired, although there is no record that he foresaw the specific direction they would take. The growth of needs for manufactured harness, metal wagon parts, and for metal barrels linked Papagos with the general American economy in new ways. Of these, the first, as directly connected with the form of the wagon itself, might have easily been predicted; the second, as an indirect result, might have been foreseen only as a possibility.

The development of firewood as a cash resource might have been foreseen as a result of a detailed review of the growing needs of the new towns at the edges of Papago territory, as might also the stimulus which the wagon gave to production of agricultural surpluses.

Acceptance of the wagon as a resource of the whole village under joint management was surely not a part of the expectation of the Indian agent. He probably thought in terms of individual ownership. What happened was an adjustment to the existing social organization and property concepts of the Papagos. The village headman brought the wagon into the culture as a unique resource, like the land, the use of which must be shared. This sharing led to the new group activity of road-building, in accordance with the same pattern as land improvements. Sharing the wagon as a means of trade led to modifications of the trading customs, with consequent effects on the frequency and mode of contact with outsiders. Through the period that we have discussed, the wagon may be regarded as reinforcing the community ties which already existed. Hence, its effects on the social life of the people were as important as those on the technology.

Thus, we see that the introduction of the wagon, simple as the initial event was, had broad repercussions on the Papago way of life. It not only displaced some parts of the technology and established new techniques and specialties; it also resulted in important shifts in the division of labor, had far-reaching effects on the economy, became for a period a strong factor for greater community solidarity, and influenced the relations of Papagos with surrounding peoples.

SUGGESTIONS FOR STUDY: The Formulation of Questions

The first case shows in fairly elementary fashion how different aspects of a culture are linked with one another. It shows how the introduction of one material item—the wagon—brought about changes in the social life of the people, as well as in their stock of tools and ways of making a living. The case suggests that the wise handling of an introduction calls for knowledge of how the different traditional ways of doing things are linked together and how the new trait may affect this linkage. For example, much could have been foreseen if the Indian agent had asked: "What will the wagon be used for? Who will use it? Will that mean any change in work habits of men and women?" Or more generally: "What is the division of labor among the Papagos? Where will a change in transportation affect that division?"

From asking such questions comes the acquisition of information necessary to the intelligent management of change. It is suggested that at this point the student begin to formulate a list of questions as he proceeds with the analysis of the next cases. The questions should be those that the field worker could ask of the people among whom he is working, and should be aimed at the systematic uncovering of facts necessary for the solution of the problems presented.

Case 2

CORN AND CUSTOM: The Introduction of Hybrid Corn to Spanish American Farmers in New Mexico

by Anacleto Apodaca

1. THE PROBLEM

For generations Spanish American farmers in the Rio Grande Valley of New Mexico have grown corn as an important crop. As compared with midwestern United States farmers their yields are very low, and the quality of the corn is poor by any ordinary standards. In one community recently, a county extension agent of the United States Department of Agriculture succeeded in introducing hybrid corn which gave about three times the yield of that grown traditionally. Once the results of the new seed were seen, a majority of the growers adopted the hybrid variety. Four years after the first introduction, however, nearly all the farmers had ceased to plant the hybrid and were again using the old corn. Why did a seemingly successful introduction not ensure the establishment of an improved seed? What factors had the county agent failed to take into consideration?

2. THE COURSE OF EVENTS

1. In 1946 the county extension agent in . . . County, New Mexico, decided to try hybrid seed corn as a way of improving the corn yield of farmers in his jurisdiction.

2. He persuaded leaders in one village to allow him to present information concerning a hybrid variety. Discussions with the farmers proved more successful than he had hoped. Forty of the 84 growers in the village planted small amounts of the hybrid and doubled the production per acre of the preceding year.

3. The following year 60 growers planted hybrid corn, and the county agent felt that the introduction had been successful.

4. In 1948, however, although the high yield had continued, only 30 farmers planted hybrid. The other 30 who had planted it the year before went back to the traditional variety.

5. In 1949 the decline in number of farmers planting the hybrid was even greater. Only three in the whole village planted it. They were farmers whom the county agent had long regarded as progressive. All the rest were growing the old corn, and the planting of hybrid had not spread to any other village.

3. RELEVANT FACTORS

Originally borrowed from the Indians, corn has long been a staple crop among Spanish American farmers of . . . County. They grow it for their own consumption, selling none of it outside the villages. Formerly, like the Indian women of the region, the Spanish American women ground the corn on stone slabs. Now it is made into meal at local mills. From the meal thin, round cakes, called tortillas, are prepared which serve as a major item in the diet. Also when crops are relatively abundant, corn is fed to the stock, and the stalks are used as roughage for the animals.

The corn grown prior to 1946 is a variety developed locally, which the farmers call "Indian corn." It attains medium height, producing a minimum of roughage. Its average yield is 25 bushels to the acre and the farmers save their own seed from year to year, mostly without benefit of selection. The corn is planted in small irrigated fields, for which there is usually a plentiful supply of water.

The county agent's relations with the farmers were good. He spoke Spanish in the same manner, was familiar with their background and agricultural practices, and had served as agent for several years immediately preceding this venture. The seed corn, he felt, had degenerated and he suspected that this was an important factor in keeping production low. He decided to introduce a hybrid seed that was known for high yield and proceeded carefully, consulting with the college agronomist, who selected a variety—Hybrid U.S. 30—that had been tested in the immediate area. It was considered disease-resistant and capable of producing a good growth, averaging 100 bushels to the acre.

Then the agent discussed the problem of low corn yields with the leaders of the village, having chosen this particular community as a likely place for a good response. The men readily recognized the need for better production and were willing to think that, perhaps, their seed strain was weakening after long continuous propagation.

The soils of the fields used by this village were tested and found to be of good fertility, since here, as elsewhere in the area, it had been customary to use some manure yearly. After discussion with the leaders of the various problems involved, a meeting was called in order to present the county agent's plan.

Everyone in the village was invited to the meeting. The agent showed movies of the hybrid corn and cartoons to enliven the demonstration. Then the leaders took over the meeting and explained in their own words the plan for introducing hybrid corn. All those present seemed to agree that the new seed was the answer to many of their problems and that they would be well able to afford the price of the seed, once it was available locally.

By special arrangement with a grower of seed, the new hybrid was furnished in exchange for the old seed. A demonstration plot which clearly showed a tripled crop was set up near the village, with the result that 40 farmers planted hybrid and each doubled his production the first year.

The whole procedure seemed to have been soundly based and to have got unusually rapid results. There was confirmation of this, when, in the following year, the county agent was able to report that 60 farmers, about three-fourths of all the growers in the village, had accepted the new seed. The seed was producing admirably; it was within their means and seemed a very profitable innovation.

REFERENCES FOR FURTHER STUDY

Harper, Allan G., Andrew R. Cordova, and Kalervo Oberg, *Man and Resources in the Middle Rio Grande Valley*. University of New Mexico Press, Albuquerque, 1943.

Leonard, Olen, and C. P. Loomis, *Culture of a Contemporary Rural Community, El Cerrito, New Mexico*. Rural Life Studies: 1. United States Department of Agriculture, Washington, 1941.

Sanchez, George I., *Forgotten People: A Study of New Mexicans*. University of New Mexico Press, Albuquerque, 1940.

Answer Questions Presented in the Problem
Before Reading the Rest of the Case.

4. THE OUTCOME

Inquiry during 1949, after nearly all the farmers had gone back to planting "Indian corn," revealed the reasons for their rejecting the hybrid. The feeling of need for better yields was still strongly present. No one complained of lack of market for surpluses, which the extension agent had feared might be a factor. There had not, in fact, been any real surplus over the requirements of people and livestock. No one had had any particular difficulty in producing the new crop. All those who had grown it were still much impressed with the large yields, and some said it confirmed their belief that their own seed had become weakened through generations of in-breeding. Owing to increased production, there had been no difficulty in obtaining seed.

Gradually the agent secured responses to direct questions as to why those who had tried hybrid had not continued to plant it. The answer was simple. As one farmer said, "My wife doesn't like that hybrid, that's all." He and others explained that the new corn had not been popular from the first harvest. All the wives had complained. Some did not like its texture; it did not hang together well for tortillas; the tortillas were not the color of nixtamal (the corn flour dough to which they were accustomed). Few had cared for the flavor, but the farmers who persisted in planting it after the first year had hoped that they would get used to it. It made abundant food for the stock and they were reluctant to drop it for that reason. However, after three years they had not become accustomed to the flavor or texture, and their wives were up in arms.

5. ANALYSIS

This is an instance of careful procedure, up to a point, in the best tradition of agricultural extension in the United States. The agent moved slowly and carefully, and then only after a considerable period of observation and analysis of the specific local situation. He examined all the technical aspects of soil, growing conditions, and existing practices. A real need was felt for the new crop and he was able to induce farmers to formulate that need among themselves. He utilized local leadership and made no start until the people thoroughly understood what was to be done. He demonstrated procedure and results. It cannot be said that he ignored any of the well-tried, and often reiterated, rules of extension procedure.

Nevertheless, the agent's exploration of the context of the change sought did not go quite far enough. He had paid attention to the relations between the agricultural technology and the environmental conditions, and to those between farming practices and the social organization of the community. He failed, however, to inquire into the food habits and their influence on the selection of crops. By experiment, as it were, he found that food habits could not be ignored. He learned that the interests and wishes of the village women had to be taken into account as an important factor in the agricultural economy. Finally, he found that in the system of values of the community, corn quality was more important than corn quantity.

The agent had proceeded on the belief that increased farm production was the only important factor involved. He had not gone into the uses of the crop, nor had he tested it as a food prepared by the farmers in the usual manner.

He failed also to make allowance for the customary courtesy of the people, who were not used to correcting "experts" or to expressing themselves freely in the presence of the latter. On reflection the agent realized that some of the farmers had had doubts about the introduction, but had not felt that they should discourage his efforts.

It is probable that a successful procedure would have included the following steps:

1. Trial of several varieties of hybrid corn and the selection of one
2. More thorough testing of the corn to see how it fitted into the culture patterns
3. Continued demonstration of the advantages of the new seed
4. Close contact with the growers to detect any difficulties and to make modifications in the plan as needed

By these means the taste problem might have been detected earlier and met through the use of a more suitable type of hybrid.

Case 3

RELUCTANT COTTON-PICKERS: Incentive to Work in a Japanese Relocation Center

by E. H. Spicer

1. THE PROBLEM

In the Colorado River Relocation Center, a settlement of involuntary wartime evacuees which had been recently formed in Arizona, people refused, when given the opportunity, to go outside the Center to pick cotton at current piecework rates. The income derivable far exceeded what they were receiving in token wages from the government. Was the failure to accept the opportunity due to lack of individual incentive, resulting from a plan for pooling the earnings in a common trust fund, to antagonism to the United States war effort on the part of these people of Japanese ancestry, to some other factors, or to a combination of these?

2. THE COURSE OF EVENTS

1. In October, 1942, farmers in the Parker Valley, Arizona, where the Colorado River Relocation Center was situated, sent urgent word to the administrators of the Center that the usual migratory labor on whom they counted to pick their cotton had not appeared. They said they were faced with loss of almost their entire crop unless evacuees would pick it. From among the 17,000 persons in the newly established Center there should be enough labor to do the job.

2. The administrators talked the request over in staff meeting and decided that the evacuees should be given the opportunity to pick the cotton. They believed it would be to the evacuees' advantage in several ways. Not only would it bring more money into the Center, it would also improve the public relations of the evacuees with the local farmers and with the United States public at large. It would be a demonstration of the readiness of the Japanese Americans to participate in the United States war effort

41

and thereby help to reduce the suspicion that had been aroused concerning them as a result of the evacuation.

3. The administrators also decided that indiscriminate recruiting by Parker farmers might disrupt the operation of the Center and that opportunities to make large sums by individuals would upset the framework of Center life, which was based on almost equal income for evacuees. Therefore, they proposed to present the request to evacuee leaders and urge a plan for turning what was earned by individuals into a Community Trust Fund, which would be used for community improvement.

4. Evacuee leaders and administrators came together in an especially called meeting. The evacuees concurred with the administrators in their view of the benefits and accepted, after some discussion, the proposal for a Community Trust Fund. They, too, believed that it would disrupt the pattern of life developing in the community if some individuals were permitted to make large earnings, while others continued to subsist on only the $12 to $19 a month paid to evacuee workers by the government.

5. The evacuee leaders presented and discussed the whole matter in block meetings in the Center. It was announced and advertised in various ways, until leaders were convinced that the plan was widely known.

6. Dates were set for the start of cotton-picking and members of the evacuee Community Council and the Issei Advisory Board and Block Managers (the three important over-all community organizations) themselves turned out to pick. However, only a very few evacuees, other than these officials, responded. Administrative staff and evacuee leaders were deeply discouraged.

What were the causes of the almost complete lack of response? With Parker Valley farmers ready to interpret it as disloyalty to the United States, what could be done to get a reasonable number of evacuees out to pick cotton?

3. RELEVANT FACTORS

At the beginning of World War II all persons of Japanese ancestry living on the West Coast of the United States were evacuated by the War Department and placed in "Relocation Centers" in inland wilderness areas. The Poston Relocation Center, situated in the Parker Valley on the Colorado River Indian Reservation in western Arizona, had a population of some 17,000 Japanese Americans.

The evacuation and incarceration of Japanese was an emergency war measure, described by officials responsible for it as required by military necessity. However, the relocation centers were placed in charge of an especially created government agency, the War Relocation Authority, which operated on the policy that the evacuees were in great majority not proved disloyal to the United States and that they might therefore be resettled outside the West Coast military zone. Temporary, and some permanent, resettlement of evacuees from the relocation centers had begun at the time of the cotton-picking issue in Poston.

Japanese Americans, in general, deeply resented the evacuation from their homes and businesses in California, Oregon, and Washington, which they had developed over a forty-year period. Different segments of the Japanese population reacted in different ways. A few believed that they might be better off in relocation centers for the duration of the war, thereby safe from any outbursts of anti-Japanese feeling on the West Coast as the war developed. Many older people, who had never been allowed by law to become United States citizens and were still Japanese nationals, regarded this enforced neutral position as perhaps safest. However, most of the older people were concerned chiefly about economic losses caused by evacuation. They resented these and also strongly resented the refusal of the government to treat their children as other United States citizens were treated. Older people also tended to regard the evacuation as foolish policy and scoffed at the idea that they could in any way interfere with the United States war effort if left in their homes on the West Coast.

The great majority of younger men and women, born in the United States and regarding themselves as Americans, felt up against a blank wall in the relocation centers. Frustrated in their plans, resentful of treatment not accorded to any other citizens, many spoke of having lost faith in the United States. Some, however, persisted in seeking positive ways to "demonstrate their loyalty," writing to the War Department to open Selective Service to them and favoring such projects as the introduction of camouflage net factories into the relocation centers, in which they could work on the production of war materials. A smaller number, often young men who had received some of their education in Japan (the Kibei), objected strongly to doing anything that would help the United States war effort and expressed loyalty to Japanese cultural traditions and national aims.

People of all sorts of backgrounds composed the population of the Poston Relocation Center. A majority had owned, managed, or worked on farms, but nearly as many had been shopkeepers, small businessmen, or members of the professions in Los Angeles and other southern California cities. Those with agricultural background had grown truck crops, such as celery, melons, lettuce, or strawberries. A relatively small number, chiefly elderly bachelors, were harvest laborers, fruit and vegetable pickers, and of these only a very few had ever picked cotton. However, there were no strongly crystallized attitudes toward cotton-picking, despite some tendency to look down on it as the occupation of "Okies" (derogatory name for migrant workers from Oklahoma or Texas).

At the time the Parker Valley farmers asked for cotton-pickers, Poston had been in existence for about five months. People had settled with no overt resistance into a very dusty, barren, and extremely hot Army camp in the bottomlands of the Colorado River. Families had taken up residence in the wooden, tar-paper-covered barracks, usually one family to an unpartitioned room 20 by 20 feet. The barracks were arranged in blocks, with populations of some 300 each. Every block contained a common mess-hall at which all families ate their meals, a common laundry room, and common latrines. The pattern of communal life thus established by the War Relocation Authority was not accepted cheerfully by the evacuees. They continually objected to the overcrowding and they denounced the mess-halls as threats to wholesome family life. Resentment against the government for these conditions was strong at the time of the cotton-picking episode.

The Center was organized under regulations set up by the War Department and the War Relocation Authority. There were three geographically separate sections, of which we shall describe Unit I, having a population of about 9,000. The 36 blocks of this unit were patrolled at their border by military police in Army uniforms. In the area a civil service government employee, called project director, was the ultimate local authority, within the framework of the Authority as set up in Washington. He was assisted by a staff of civil service employees, who had charge of the distribution of food to the mess-halls, the organization of agricultural work in the Center, the medical services, and other aspects of Center life. Below the level of the civil service employees, evacuees were hired as assistants at the monthly wage of $12, $14, or $19.

During June and July the War Relocation Authority announced plans for "self-government" within the Center. A Community Council consisting of elected individuals was set up as advisory to the project director and his staff. By War Relocation Authority regulation this Council was limited to young men and women, the Nisei, who, through birth in the United States, were citizens. In addition, an Advisory Board composed of Issei (men and women born in Japan and by United States law ineligible for citizenship) was in operation. Members of the Board, which functioned in an advisory capacity to the Community Council, were also elected. The basis of representation was the block, each block thus having both an Issei and a Nisei representative in the over-all organization.

The political structure that had developed by October also included Councils in each block, in which no distinction was made between Issei and Nisei. Members of the Block Councils were elected at large from the block. Weekly meetings were held, at which all kinds of local and community affairs were discussed. There were two topics that came up most frequently in the early months of the Center. One of these was the mess-hall and its management, and the other was block gardens and block beautification programs.

As the political structure had grown, there had at the same time developed other types of organization. Church groups had formed immediately on arrival of the evacuees in the Center. The various Buddhist sects had been assigned barracks in which to hold their services and meetings, and within each there was at least one recognized minister who had taken charge of affairs. Subgroups within the Buddhist organization had also taken form, such as women's groups (*Fujinkai*) and young peoples' groups (*Seinendan*). Similar developments had taken place in the four Christian sects represented in the population, and there was a proliferation of small social and athletic clubs.

Within this setting Community Council, Issei Advisory Board, and Block Councils had begun to be the scene of discussion, either directly or indirectly, of a number of basic issues. These issues were formulated in terms of the experience of the Japanese Americans as a minority group in the United States during the past forty years and had particular meaning and emotional content growing out of the evacuation from their homes. One of the subjects that the Japanese tended to keep more or less hidden from the administrators, lest their positions on it be misunderstood, was their relation to the United States war effort. The people of Poston were split in a number of ways on this question. One influential viewpoint maintained by many of the older men was that the evacuees must be careful to maintain a neutral position and must not allow themselves to be brought into any activities that directly furthered the United States war effort against Japan. They maintained that their status should be officially that of prisoners of war. In line with this position they opposed the introduction of camouflage net factories into the Center. Many other older men held that the neutrality position was probably the safest for Issei citizens of Japan, but that Nisei as citizens of the United States should have the opportunity to engage in the manufacture of camouflage nets and in other war production. The Nisei position on the issue ranged from a willingness to do anything their fathers said in order to maintain the last social unit left to them—their families—to vigorous denunciation of the neutrality position and aggressive espousal of opportunities for positive demonstration of loyalty to the United States.

Another question, which was for many not wholly separate from the neutrality problem, consisted in the over-all plan for life in the Center. Here again, as would be expected from the heterogeneity of the evacuees, there were many positions and shades of conviction and feeling. The essential issue involved may probably be stated as follows: Shall we as evacuees settle down in the Center to a peaceful, cooperative life for the duration of the war, unified in the aim of creating an ideal community? Such an objective fitted the views of most Issei regardless of their beliefs about relations to Japan and the United States as nations at war. It involved the concept of waiting quietly until the war was over and a basis existed for thinking about the future.

For many Nisei, however, it was not acceptable because it ignored the most important question on their minds: What will our future in the United States be? For them, the Center had to be tied into the life of the United States and there was no waiting for the future; the future was being decided momentarily. Some Nisei, however, accepted their parents' view that "we are all Japanese together" as a result of the evacuation. For them, waiting, and meanwhile living peacefully with one's family in the blocks, seemed the only course open.

These issues of neutrality and the cooperative ideal community were the matrix of much discussion in all formal and informal groups in the Center. Such matters as exclusive Nisei representation on the Community Council and the crops to be raised in block gardens were frequently considered within the sentiment systems which grew up around these matters.

The Poston administrators at the time of the request for cotton-pickers were hardly aware of this state of affairs. The complexity of the Issei position in relation to the war was not understood, and aspects of it that came to their attention were usually interpreted in rather black and white terms of loyalty and disloyalty in an ordinary American community. Administrative understanding of the issues concerning the nature of the Center as a framework for life was much better. In fact, differences of opinion on this matter among administrators often paralleled those among the evacuees.

On the matter of cotton-picking the administrators took the position from the start that it would be beneficial to the evacuees in a number of ways: (1) If the evacuees saved the crop of the Parker Valley farmers, good will toward them would be stimulated locally and, consequently, public relations in the Parker area would be improved. (2) Participation in the salvage of a crop of some wartime importance would demonstrate to the people of the United States generally that the Japanese Americans were not all saboteurs. (3) The influx of cash into the Center would supplement the small amounts paid to the evacuees as wages and thereby help to ease some of the tension resulting from the frustration of confinement. It was on this basis that they presented the matter to the evacuee community leaders.

There was, however, one aspect of the problem which the administrators regarded as difficult. The Center had been set up by government regulation on the basis of approximate equality of income for evacuees. The income derivable from cotton-picking would vary greatly among individuals and many families would probably, for diverse reasons, be unable to send any member out to pick. Furthermore, if large numbers rushed out immediately to the work, as the administrators thought was possible, the routine operation of the Center might be seriously disrupted for weeks. With these matters in mind, the administrators conceived the idea of a Community Trust Fund, into which all wages would go for later disbursement as evacuee community leaders might determine.

The administrators, in short, believed that uncontrolled recruiting of cotton-pickers by the Parker Valley farmers would be disruptive and, hence, they decided that the whole matter would have to be presented to the community leaders who could, in turn, present it to the people of the Center. This plan was followed, and a special meeting of the community leaders was called for discussion of the farmers' proposal and the administration's plan for a Community Trust Fund. The importance of the cotton-picking as a community affair affecting evacuee public relations and as an opportunity for bettering the general welfare by increased funds was stressed in the administrators' presentation.

The evacuee leadership reacted in a variety of ways. Some councilmen and some Issei Advisory Board members wanted to have nothing to do with it—probably thinking of that segment of local public opinion which opposed any participation in United States war effort. Some were immediately enthusiastic, among both Issei and Nisei, and accepted the whole view of the administrators. Some professed to be surprised at what they called the administration's "socialistic proposal" for handling the wages as a trust fund. Discussion, however, resulted in a general acceptance of the administration's position by the evacuee leaders. Issei Board members in particular strongly espoused the idea of a Community Trust Fund, holding that all had been leveled in the process of evacuation and that the injection of individual differences in wage receipts would threaten the basis of solidarity in the Center.

Community councilmen and Issei Board members presented the matter to meetings in their respective blocks and it became a widespread subject of discussion for several days. In almost all blocks the community leaders stressed the opportunity for added income and better relations with Parker Valley farmers but did not mention the third reason emphasized by the administration. Demonstration of loyalty to the United States by means of picking cotton while confined in relocation centers was not regarded by those leaders who were closest to their constituents as a point that would have weight; on the contrary, they seemed to feel that mention of it would be likely to rouse opposition.

Community leaders, both Nisei and Issei, turned out to pick cotton on the days set for beginning the work, but a bare handful of other evacuees joined them. The general reaction seemed to be apathetic. The evacuee leaders, as well as the administrative staff, were surprised and dismayed. Among both groups there was a tendency to interpret the failure to respond as a result of anti-government feeling and some began to believe that it was a definite demonstration of disloyal attitude toward the United States. On the other hand, some among both groups were convinced that the basic reason for lack of response was the absence of individual incentive in the form of wages paid directly to the cotton-pickers. Within a few days, however, a change was made in the arrangements and large numbers of evacuees began to go out to pick cotton. What sort of change would bring about such results?

REFERENCES FOR FURTHER STUDY

Bloom, Leonard, *A Controlled Attitude-Tension Survey*. University of California Press, Berkeley, 1948.

Leighton, Alexander H., *The Governing of Men:* General Principles and Recommendations Based on Experience at a Japanese Relocation Camp. Princeton University Press, Princeton, N. J., 1945.

Thomas, Dorothy S., and Richard S. Nishimoto, *The Spoilage*. University of California Press, Berkeley, 1947.

Answer Questions Presented in the Problem
Before Reading the Rest of the Case.

4. THE OUTCOME

Here and there over the community, as councilmen presented the trust fund idea in block meetings, residents proposed a different approach. A few insisted that only individual wage receipts would result in bringing any number of persons out to pick cotton. In one block it was proposed that the money earned go, not into an over-all community fund, but into a block trust fund which would be used for improvements in the mess-hall, for block parties, and for other purposes of a strictly local character. Similar proposals came up in other blocks.

It was also proposed in block meetings that members of various church groups or social clubs put their wages into trust funds for the use of their organizations.

Gradually these proposals were taken up throughout the Center. Leaders saw many possible uses for block funds and they obtained approval from the administration for the establishment of such funds. They also developed methods for bringing the pressure of block public opinion to bear on individuals. Bulletin boards began to blossom with lists of individuals who would go or had gone out to pick cotton. People in the blocks began to talk about those who went out and those who did not go. Over a period of a few days the numbers picking cotton quadrupled.

It appeared that all who were going out, did so in response to the block, social club, or church fund arrangement. Steadily the belief that most evacuees were opposed to the United States war effort disappeared among the community leaders and the War Relocation Authority staff. A few blocks were turning out a majority of their able-bodied man and woman power. Young people became enthusiastic for cotton-picking as a relief from the dullness of Center routine. Statements praising evacuees as workers and loyal Americans began to be made at farmers' meetings in the Parker Valley. Totals in the various block funds began to be known throughout the Center. Some competitive spirit in working for one's block developed.

The Community Trust Fund idea was discarded by the Board and interest in cotton-picking steadily increased until the War Department prohibited movement of evacuees out of the Center.

5. ANALYSIS

This case illustrates the strength of local group or neighborhood as a social unit focusing the interests and activities of its members. It demonstrates the greater strength of the local group over that collection of local groups which constituted a community. It demonstrates that in a newly forming community of heterogeneous population the neighborhood tends to emerge first as the effective social unit. Its solidarity may appear in so short a time as four or five months. On the other hand, solidarity for the community as a whole (even when stresses are great for promoting the latter and when there is vigorous leadership for over-all community interests) may lag very far behind neighborhood, or face-to-face group, solidarity.

The opportunity for cotton-picking was recognized by some staff members and most evacuee leaders as raising delicate issues, given the circumstances of existence in the Center. The staff, nevertheless, believed the matter worth pushing because of the great improvement in public relations for evacuees if the cotton were picked. They stressed, correctly, this aspect of the work along with that of its being an aid to the United States war effort. They did not believe the latter alone sufficient motivation in view of governmental action up to that point against the evacuees. The staff also wisely placed the matter in the hands of evacuee leaders for presentation rather than attempting individual recruiting on their own initiative. In doing so they were acting in accordance with their policy of building the conglomeration of uprooted people into a community and as nearly as possible in accordance with general public opinion existing at that time in the Center.

The presentation by the evacuee community leaders was in line with their own positions and with the policy of promoting community cooperation which they were formulating at the time. In advancing the trust fund proposal they were giving leadership consistent with the defined conditions of Center life. They showed that they recognized fundamental needs which the people felt, namely, the opportunity for variation in Center routine and for some participation in the life outside, as well as the need for supplementation of income. The community leaders also showed some understanding of the developing organization of the Center by carrying their proposal back for presentation in block meetings. Further, they demonstrated, as well as expressed verbally, their point of view by going out themselves to pick cotton. In addition, they showed recognition of the prevailing ambivalent attitudes toward the government and the United States war effort, by stressing Center community welfare in their appeals to the block people rather than assistance to the war effort which the administrators tended to emphasize.

All this, good as it was, was not enough. The staff and community leaders obviously overestimated the solidarity at this point of the 9,000 people of Unit I. Thinking in terms of their own organization, the Community Council, they attempted to motivate the people with reference to the whole unit. The result was a general lack of interest. Besides themselves, only a handful of men and women, chiefly a few who were in contact with the administration and who were long since convinced of the importance of "demonstrating loyalty to the U. S.," responded by picking cotton. It is clear in view of what happened later that for the vast majority of persons in the Center, the "community as a whole" had little meaning.

What were the community interests? For what would money in a general trust fund be spent? Who would control its use: the administrators? councilmen from distant blocks whom one did not know? To give one's wages into a Community Trust Fund was like casting them away on a wind at sea.

Fortunately, at this point, the community leaders were no more rigid in their views than the new structure of which they were a part. Out of the blocks to which they had taken their idea came proposals that had clear-cut meaning for the people. If the money could be spent for improving the kitchen and dining hall, for making the barren blocks more habitable, for parties to relieve the monotony, for equipment in an athletic club, or for a church, if it would be spent by men with whom one sat down to dinner and whom one saw and could make suggestions to every day, then the trust fund idea had real meaning.

To be sure, there were men and women in the blocks who held that any improvement in the kitchens ought to be paid for by the government which had evacuated them and placed them in these unpleasant circumstances, but even such people could not expect the government to pay for block parties. They realized they would have to do that themselves and here was a means for achieving such pleasures. Thus, despite differences of opinion in the blocks, arising from the complications of the Center situation, there could be some common ground on which people might accept the idea of a block or a church trust fund. The idea of a fund for a small local group grew rapidly as an expression of the kind of social organization which had developed up to that point in the centers. The community began to function in response to the outside stimulus, not as a single unified organization of 9,000 people but as a number of neighborhoods with similar interests and aims. The neighborhood leadership and neighborhood gossip began to push people out to pick cotton in response to the needs that almost everyone felt and saw about them in the drab and dusty blocks of barracks.

Case 4

THE VILLAGE LEVEL: An Introduction of Green Manuring in Rural India

by Rudra Datt Singh

1. THE PROBLEM

The average farmer in India has not accepted improved agricultural practices, more efficient implements, or the use of better seeds even though they have been on the scheduled program of the Departments of Agriculture, central and provincial, for a long time.

This problem has come into sharper focus since the "Grow More Food" campaign was launched in 1942 during World War II. It became still more acute at the time of the Bengal famine in 1943 and again when large surplus food areas were lost to the Indian Republic during the partition in 1947. Consequently, India feels pressure to obtain maximum productivity from all the lands within her present borders, and responsible persons have been increasingly asking why the farmers have not improved their crop yield by adopting new methods. The question remains: Can new approaches be developed to induce the Indian farmers to take advantage of existing scientific knowledge about agriculture?

2. THE COURSE OF EVENTS

1. The government of India had its first Department of Agriculture as early as 1871. The provinces organized their separate departments in 1882 on the recommendation of the Famine Inquiry Commission of 1880. The Famine Commission of 1901 recommended the appointment of experts capable of applying scientific methods to the improvement of agriculture. Under Lord Curzon, the Department of Agriculture was reorganized in 1905. A Central Research Institute was established at Pusa in Bihar with an agricultural farm and college.

2. After the Government of India Act in 1919, the responsibility for agricultural development was placed upon the provincial departments. The central government reserved the right to promote research. Later, in 1928, on the recommendation of the Royal Commission on Agriculture, an Imperial Council of Agricultural Research was established to stimulate and to coordinate research and extension activities of the agricultural departments. Sir John Russell in 1937, after a review of the work of the Imperial Council, recommended that the Council stimulate extension work by the departments and delegate the research work to the universities.

3. The agricultural departments were reorganized in order to bring the results of the agricultural research laboratories and experimental farms to the villages. They still have agricultural schools and colleges and research institutes as one aspect of their work, but their major activity is the support of village field demonstrators and village cooperative stores, which distribute seed and agricultural implements to the farmers. In the course of this work improved methods of agriculture are being studied. Interesting results have been obtained in regard to different crops in the research laboratories and on experimental farms. But the extension of this knowledge to the villages has been very slow.

4. Experiments in research institutes and government farms to test the usefulness of green manuring as a means of increasing yields of various crops have been going on in India for years. Some of the results in support of green manuring quoted at the second meeting of the Crops and Soil Wing of the Board of Agriculture in 1937 are given below. Only one crop, wheat, has been selected for illustration here.

Year	No Green Manuring	After Green Manuring (San-hemp)
1929–30	688 lbs. per acre	982 lbs. per acre
1932–33	827 " " "	1,456 " " "
1933–34	790 " " "	1,335 " " "

During the discussion it was maintained by one authority that green manuring by turning under a standing crop of san-hemp might very well be considered the most economical way of supplying organic materials to the soil in canal areas.

5. Because of the encouraging results obtained in the research institutes, plans were formulated to carry the new knowledge to the villagers. Distribution of san-seed was arranged through the central seed stores. One of these was situated in an area which will be the center of our attention. It was here that in 1948 the Etawah Pilot Project was organized for purposes of action-research, aimed at changing the habits and attitudes of the people. The original plan also provided for carrying on field demonstrations in the villages by the employees of the Agriculture Department.

6. An inquiry in the field about the traditional attitude toward green manuring in our area, and specifically about the progress of the program introduced by the government, revealed that the farmers have known vaguely for a long time about the beneficial results of plowing under parts of leguminous plants. In their indigenous system of crop rotation, legumes have an important place. Scattered cases where farmers have used leaves and branches of mature indigo for enriching the soil have also been reported. Since the introduction of the new extension program, a few farmers have used the scientifically tested method for green manuring by turning under sanai or san-hemp when the plants are three or four feet high. On the whole, however, the Pilot Development Project has resulted in almost no green manuring.

7. It was discovered that the local government seed store had been carrying san-seed for a number of years, but that, although according to the records, the proper amount of seed was being distributed, it was not being used for the intended purpose. Since, in order to popularize the practice of green manuring, the government was subsidizing the seed, it was being sold at a lower price than the prevailing market rate. As a result, persons who were not farmers, as well as farmers, bought the seed. Even the farmers often used it for purposes other than green manuring.

8. Much of the projected agricultural extension work in India had been interrupted owing to programs connected with the war.

Afterward India was partitioned and a large section of the surplus food-producing area became part of Pakistan. Foreseeing an imminent and continuous deficit in the supply of food, unless effective steps were taken, the Indian government planned to carry out some programs of action-research with the objective of discovering efficient methods of inducing the farmers to accept new agricultural practices.

9. On the invitation of the government of Uttar Pradesh, Albert Mayer of New York organized an action-research Pilot Project in our district of Etawah. Mr. Mayer was assisted in the planning and carrying out of the project by an agricultural extension expert, an agricultural engineer, an administrator, and a social scientist. The members of the team supervised the progress of the work in the field, helped the field workers, checked results, and modified the plan according to the needs of the situation.

10. The Pilot Project planners decided to introduce green manuring on a large scale in their area. A supply of seed was arranged for and a vigorous campaign was carried on to educate the farmers. During the campaign the workers returned with high expectations to Mahewa, the village where the administrative center of the area was located. They thought that the farmers were completely convinced, since they had not rejected the arguments in favor of green manuring put forward by the village level workers of the project.

11. Day after day passed and the supervisor, who was in charge of the cooperative store, waited for the expected customers, but very few farmers arrived to buy the seed. Of those who came, a large number were inhabitants of the villages close to the center. There were almost no customers from villages that were only a little farther than a mile from the center.

12. What had been confidently expected was not happening. It caused the Pilot Project workers to ponder. They knew many of the farmers who had promised to experiment at least with green manuring in one of their plots and it was puzzling to discover that they had not come to the center to obtain the seed. Finally, after much discussion, it was suggested that, rather than

wait for the farmers to come, the seed would be carried to them and delivered to their very doors.

13. The supervisor immediately objected. He said that in the government regulations it is clearly stated that seed can only be distributed and collected at the seed store. He claimed that he was not authorized, therefore, to deliver the seed to the doors of the farmers. Silence fell on the group that had been discussing what was to be done.

14. Some of the project workers expressed resentment against the hidebound system and bitterly complained that they could never make any progress in such an organization. The question arose: Would any official present feel strong enough to get the seed to the farmers without overconcern about minute regulations, and without previous sanction of the government? The upshot was that the district development officer authorized the removal of the seed from the seed store, thus risking the possibility of censure from above and mismanagement by subordinates who were legally not responsible.

15. Immediately seed was carried by the project workers on bicycles, bullock carts, and trucks to the different villages of the area. It was supplied to individual farmers who were willing to buy it. Others were offered the opportunity to take it on any day of the week and at any time of the day convenient for them. This was accomplished by leaving some seed in every village with one of the respectable and responsible villagers. The seed store thus distributed nearly 130 maunds (about 175 bushels). The workers kept check on the seed till it was sown in the fields.

16. At the proper time the standing green crop was turned under to decompose and to be absorbed in the soil. The winter crop was sown and, as expected, the yield was much more than the farmers had been accustomed to getting from their plots of land. In his Fortnightly Demi-Official (F.D.O.) Report of June 24, 1950, the district development officer said:

> The total increase in yield treated with green manure and sown with PB 591 (an improved variety of wheat) is 68.51%, out of which nearly 40% can be attributed to sanai green manuring.

The development and coordination adviser to the government of Uttar Pradesh wrote the following in his Interim Report and Appraisal of June 27, 1950:

> Last year a little over a hundred maunds of sanai were distributed and turned under with spectacular success in the rabi crop. . . . Our demonstrations with this and improved seed resulted in a yield increase of over 60% of wheat production.

3. RELEVANT FACTORS

The District of Etawah is situated between Ganga (the Ganges) and Jamuna (the Jumna) rivers in the south central section of the state of Uttar Pradesh. The Pilot Project area is thickly settled with villages and hamlets, consisting of big and small clusters of houses. Its southern section is heavily eroded, some of the ravines being as much as 100 feet deep. The northern part is flat, agricultural land irrigated by canals. The transportation and communication facilities are poor everywhere, but worse in the south than in the north.

The farmers live in communities of 200 to 2,000 persons. Almost all the inhabitants have lived in this area since birth, as did their ancestors. Everyone knows everyone else in his community and many have friends and acquaintances among the inhabitants of surrounding communities. The activities of most of the people are confined to a limited region surrounding their villages. Dealings with others are chiefly on a personal basis; they quickly characterize individuals known to them as good or bad, reliable or unreliable, kind or cruel, and miserly or generous. Rumors about persons and events spread fast in these communities.

The social organization of many communities is intricately patterned. The total population is made up of a number of caste groups, which are interrelated according to traditional lines. The intercaste social and economic arrangements are formalized in an elaborate manner. Nevertheless, for the most part, it is the informal group consisting of individuals and families who come together on the basis of personal knowledge, family tradition, and common problems, that influences the thinking and the action of the individuals in their day-to-day living.

An outside organization with which the villagers have had contact for a long time is the government. A villager's picture of the government (*sarkar*) has been formed by the activities of the police officers (*thanadar*) and the tax collectors (*tahsildar*) and all that is associated with them. The village watchman (*chowkidar*) and the village accountant (*patwari*), local representatives of the police and revenue departments, live in the village. The villagers have therefore always been conscious of the presence of government at their doors. Most of their experiences with it have been unpleasant and costly. It is no wonder that they have developed a strong attitude of avoidance.

Most of the government representatives for their part have always assumed an authoritative, paternalistic attitude toward the villagers. As government employees they kept themselves aloof. The maintenance of a respectable distance from the ruled has frequently been considered by officialdom one of the important methods of perpetuating control over them. When the representatives of the nation-building departments (Education, Public Health, Agriculture) appeared on the scene, they followed in the footsteps of the police and the tax collector in their behavior and attitude toward the villagers.

The presence of exceptionally sympathetic, humanitarian, and efficient individual officers and workers in the departments cannot be denied. But on the whole the picture drawn here of the bureaucratic organization and of the behavior and attitude of its personnel is realistic. This came out very clearly in interviews with the various officers. The gap between the government representatives and the villagers was never closed.

Another significant feature of the administrative machinery was its extreme centralization. Policies and plans were made at the top of the official hierarchy, with little participation by the men in the field. Once the plans were drawn up, the execution was the responsibility of the highest executive. Orders were passed down and the men in the field were expected to show results. Targets and steps were not modified in accordance with the local situation. Since no allowance was made for genuine difficulties in the field, exaggerated claims were often made. The goal of the worker was the satisfaction of the superior officer. Actual achievements were of secondary importance.

The local worker was given little opportunity for initiative, and, since the plans he had to execute often had no logical relationship to the local situation, he found it difficult to achieve the target set for him. Faced with the threat to his security, he took recourse to manipulation of results to save himself from censure and to protect his position. Once the records in the register were straight, the worker felt secure. It was not considered necessary to follow a program to the field and to check the final results.

Therefore, despite the considerable length of time over which agricultural research and experimental farms have developed in India, little of the new knowledge has percolated to the villages. Often the gains obtained in one year have been lost in the next because of the failure on the part of the departmental workers to follow up results and the ignorance of the farmers who do not know how to make proper use of the government agencies. On the whole, it is fair to say that no reliable and profitable functioning relationship has been established between the farmers and the agencies.

The Pilot Project planners decided to recruit as few government employees as possible. Therefore, the personnel of the project came to the job with none of the stereotypes about themselves and the villagers that are often present in the minds of government officers. Almost all the field workers were young graduates, fresh from schools and colleges. In making the selection much emphasis was laid on their aptitude for the job and their understanding of village life. Familiarity with the habits, attitudes, and thinking of the village people, which they had derived from their own rural background, was an important factor in their selection.

Those who were chosen were initiated into their new role through an orientation program lasting nearly three weeks. The plan of the project, its pioneering character, and its significance for the future development of rural India were very thoroughly explained and discussed. The role of the field workers and their immense responsibility in making the experiment successful were impressed on them. They were helped to picture themselves as pioneers forging new methods of approach which might prove of great significance in the rebuilding of India. They were quick to respond to the ideal, and the spirit generated in this manner at the outset continued to inspire their work. Great emphasis was laid during the orientation period on the problem of approach. Their real training, however, was begun on the job. The experienced officers kept moving from worker to worker in the field, helping each in the solution of his problems. Sometimes the difficulties faced by the workers were technical, but more often they had to do with human relations. Most of the instruction in connection with on-the-job training of the workers was given on an interpersonal basis. The workers were also encouraged to cultivate the friendship of individual inhabitants; and they were urged to participate in the social functions of the farmers, to get into their inner circle, and to try to be accepted as one of them.

The farmers in India are very badly off economically, most of them living from hand to mouth. Comparatively few are in a position to take any kind of risk. Experimentation with new methods of manuring involving expenditure of money, in this case for the seed, had to be carefully weighed before they would undertake it. How would an Indian farmer, illiterate or poorly educated and not analytical in the scientific sense, judge such an issue as the use of sanai for manuring?

The workers in the Etawah Pilot Project were a picked group, with native as well as cultivated sensibilities for humane and courteous behavior. It is true, under stress, they did flare up sometimes, but they sincerely regretted their action and tried to make amends. By disposition they were honest and sincere, and they made a good impression on the villagers. They were respectfully treated by their superior officers, something that is not very common in Indian official circles, and they reacted by treating others as equals.

The difference in approach between this attempt to introduce green manuring and previous attempts with generally similar objectives can perhaps best be indicated by excerpts from an article published in an Indian newspaper, *The Statesman*, under the heading "New Approach to Rural Development Problem."

The American-inspired Rural Development Pilot Project, covering a block of 100 villages in the Etawah District, is based on a new approach to an old problem. It is neatly summed up in the formula: "Help the villagers to help themselves." The four American experts and their Indian colleagues are happily free from authority to enforce their plans. Their only sanction is the good will of the villager, which has to be assiduously earned and retained. . . .

Improving the village, it was recognized, was easier than moulding the villager. The second operation is now considered in Etawah even more important than the first, for thus only are changes rendered permanent.

Securing the cooperation of the villager in all that is done is the primary object of the organizers. They do not think the villagers' initial resistance is either unnatural or even altogether undesirable. The Indian peasant, they say, is no more skeptical than his American counterpart. No one anywhere accepts suggestions from strangers unless they have proved their good intentions as well as the efficacy of their prescription. People who are not willing to demonstrate with their hands what they seek to teach are at an additional disadvantage in securing the friendship of the farmer.

Mr. X———, leader of the team, . . . has set the example. He spends days with farmers, eats with them and often sleeps on rough village beds, sharing his room with his many colleagues. The new spirit has caught on. The Etawah Project is an experiment in human relations between officers and subordinates and between members of the development team and villagers. . . .

Action is proceeding on two combined planes: human and physical. The first concerns itself with improvement of the people, by the people with the assistance of the development team. The second pertains to their surroundings, their lands, and their tools.

It has not been found necessary to saturate many villages with all the items on the development programme. The readiness of a village for a particular subject has to be taken into account. Only that service is offered which it agrees to accept. Thus different villages act as samples of different subjects.

REFERENCES FOR FURTHER STUDY

Converse, E., "Pilot Development Projects," *Far Eastern Survey*, vol. 20, February 7, 1951.

Opler, Morris, and Rudra Datt Singh, "The Division of Labor in an Indian Village," in *A Reader in General Anthropology*, edited by Carleton S. Coon. Henry Holt and Co., New York, 1948.

Answer Question Presented in the Problem
Before Reading the Rest of the Case.

4. THE OUTCOME

The next year at the time for the sowing of sanai, there was a great rush to the store for this seed. The rush started rather early for sanai sowing. The village level workers had not even started their campaign for green manuring, yet the farmers poured into the seed store, fearing that the stock of seed might be exhausted before they could obtain what they required.

The district development officer wrote in his report of June 24, 1950:

> *Sanai green manuring:* It was very remarkable that 293 maunds, 14 seers, and 5 Chhataks sanai seed have been sold during this fortnight, although it is just the beginning of the season. It is due to the success of our sanai demonstrations of last year which resulted in the increase in the yield of over 40%—last year we could sell only 128 maunds in the entire season, but this year more than twice as much has been sold out just in the beginning. Five hundred maunds of sanai seed have just arrived and it is expected that about 300 maunds of it will be sold out in the Pilot Development Project Area.

In his report dated August 7, 1950, there is the following item concerning the progress made in green manuring in the Pilot Project area:

> *Sanai green manuring:* 71 maunds, 13 seers of sanai were distributed during this fortnight. The total seed sold for sanai green manuring is about 560 maunds or 40 maunds below the target figure of 600 maunds.

It is obvious that a very high target figure was well on the way to being reached.

As an evidence of the continued success of the attitudes and methods which have been described, it might be mentioned that not long after this incident, at the time when there was an attempt to distribute pure wheat seed for winter cultivation, the operation was actually carried on in a number of villages rather than through the central seed store. This procedure played an important part in gaining the cooperation of the villagers in a program for saturating individual villages with one type of improved wheat seed.

5. ANALYSIS

In this endeavor to win over the villagers to experiment with green manuring for permanent adoption, the sincerity and good will of the Pilot Development Project workers moved the farmers a long way toward the goal. They dealt less in logic than in good will. They found that the farmer has the good sense to distinguish sincerity of purpose from mere efficiency. He may not know the refined and intricate legal code, but he understands the law of good will and fellow feeling. One has to be a real human being to convince him of a course of action. He has to be dealt with on the human plane before he is willing to take a risk.

Previous to the time for the distribution of the seed, the farmers had accepted the essential arguments of the Pilot Project workers, though not always without expressing a lively skepticism based on their past experiences with government projects and officials. As the matter stood at the time the seed was to be distributed, one might say that the amount of sacrifice the farmers thought they would have to make, in terms of the price of seed and the labor of carrying it to their homes, just about balanced the advantages they could envisage and the gratitude they would have liked to show the Pilot Project workers. Something of an equilibrium had been created. A small amount of activity this way or that would prove sufficient to tip the scales.

The decision of the Pilot Project workers to do something extra, to carry the seed to the homes of the farmers, was just what was needed at the critical moment. The village level worker proved his initiative by trusting villagers with the supply of seed. The rules with respect to the collection of costs, issue of receipts, and even the protection of the government seed were relaxed to the maximum for this occasion. Things were left to develop according to the drive and ability of the village level worker, who in turn demonstrated that he trusted villagers.

In summary, we can say that six essential factors were involved in the successful conclusion of this experiment:

1. An intelligent grasp of the situation on the part of the project workers, based on their knowledge of the people, of

their culture, and their psychology. The farmers, used to dealings on an interpersonal basis, responded favorably to the personal approach of the workers.

2. The cultivation of an atmosphere of understanding and willingness to cooperate. The project workers approached the farmers with this attitude and they were able to develop a similar response from the farmers by offering them repeated and satisfying opportunities for interaction. The practical results of this were particularly in evidence when the leading villagers themselves volunteered to take the responsibility of storing the seed and distributing it to others in their communities.

3. The high morale of the workers resulting from a democratic spirit in the organization. As a consequence everyone, whether of high or low rank, was willing to initiate action on his own responsibility.

4. The delegation of responsibility locally. When the seed was delivered to the village, the village level worker felt a responsibility for seeing that it was put to use; for, once it was in the village where he was supposed to stimulate increased agricultural productivity, it was impossible for him to shirk his function. Moreover, the fact that he had so important a part to play in the process gave him an enhanced feeling of status and worth, and to this he often responded by increased effort.

5. The courageous spirit of the district development officer which enabled him to instill a flexible element into an otherwise inflexible system.

6. Successful demonstration.

STEEL AXES FOR STONE AGE AUSTRALIANS
by Lauriston Sharp

1. THE PROBLEM

Like other Australian aboriginals, the Yir Yoront group at the mouth of the Coleman River on the west coast of tropical Cape York Peninsula originally had no knowledge of metals. Technologically their culture was of the old stone age or paleolithic type; they supported themselves by hunting and fishing, obtaining vegetable foods and needed materials from the bush by simple gathering techniques. Their only domesticated animal was the dog, and they had no domesticated plants of any kind. Unlike some other aboriginal groups, however, the Yir Yoront did have polished stone axes hafted in short handles, and these implements were most important in their economy.

Toward the end of the nineteenth century metal tools and other European artifacts began to filter into the Yir Yoront territory. The flow increased with the gradual expansion of the white frontier outward from southern and eastern Queensland. Of all the items of western technology thus made available, none was more acceptable, none more highly valued by aboriginals of all conditions than the hatchet or short-handled steel axe.

In the mid-1930's an American anthropologist was able to live alone in the bush among the Yir Yoront for thirteen months without seeing another white man. They were thus still relatively isolated and they continued an essentially independent economic life, supporting themselves entirely by means of their old stone-age techniques. Yet their polished stone axes were fast disappearing and were being replaced by steel axes, which came to them in considerable numbers directly or indirectly from various European sources to the south.

What changes in the life of the Yir Yoront still living under aboriginal conditions in the Australian bush could be expected as a result of their increasing possession and use of the steel axe?

2. THE COURSE OF EVENTS

1. In 1623 a Dutch expedition landed on the coasts now occupied by the Yir Yoront. All cultural items (although few in number) recorded in the Dutch log for the aboriginals they encountered were still in use among the Yir Yoront in 1935. To this inventory the Dutch added pieces of iron and beads in an effort to attract the frightened "Indians." They remained at this spot for two days, during which they were able to kidnap one and shoot another of a group of some hundred males. Today metal and beads have disappeared, as has any memory of this first encounter with whites.

2. The next recorded contact in this area occurred in 1864, and here there is more positive assurance that the natives concerned were the immediate ancestors of the Yir Yoront community. These aboriginals had the temerity to attack a party of cattlemen who were driving a small herd from southern Queensland through the whole length of the then unknown Cape York Peninsula to a newly established government station at the Peninsula's northern tip. As a result there occurred what became known as the "Battle of the Mitchell River," one of the rare instances in which Australian aboriginals stood up to European gunfire for any length of time. A diary kept by the cattlemen records the incident: ". . . ten carbines poured volley after volley into them from all directions, killing and wounding with every shot with very little return, nearly all their spears having already been expended. . . . About thirty being killed, the leader thought it prudent to hold his hand, and let the rest escape. Many more must have been wounded and probably drowned, for fifty-nine rounds were counted as discharged." The European party was in the Yir Yoront area for three days, then disappeared over the horizon to the north, not to return.

During the anthropological investigation some seventy years later, lasting almost three years, there was not one reference to this shocking contact with Europeans, nor anything that could be interpreted as a reference to it, in all the material of hundreds of free association interviews, in hundreds of dreams and myths, in genealogies, and eventually in hundreds of answers to direct and indirect questioning on just this particular matter.

3. The aboriginal accounts of their first remembered contact with whites begin with references to persons known to have had sporadic but lethal encounters with them beginning about 1900, and it may be noted that from that time on whites continued to remain on the southern periphery of Yir Yoront territory. With the establishment of cattle stations or ranches to the south, occasional excursions among the "wild blackfellows" were made by cattlemen wishing to inspect the country and abduct natives to be trained as cattle boys and "house girls." At least one such expedition reached the Coleman River, where a number of Yir Yoront men and women were shot, apparently on general principles. A stick of trade tobacco, the natives now claim, was left with each body; but this kindness was evidently unappreciated, for the leader of the excursion was eventually speared to death by a native fighting party.

4. It was about this time that the government was persuaded to sponsor the establishment of three mission stations along the seven hundred mile western coast of the Peninsula as an aid in regulating the treatment of natives. To further this purpose a strip of coastal territory was set aside as an aboriginal reserve and closed to further white settlement.

In 1915 an Anglican mission station was established near the mouth of the Mitchell River in the territory of a tribe neighboring the Yir Yoront on the south and about three days' march from the heart of the Yir Yoront country. Some of the Yir Yoront refused to have anything to do with the mission or to go near it, others visited it on occasion, while a few eventually settled more or less permanently in one of the three "villages" at the mission.

5. Thus, the majority of the Yir Yoront continued to live their old self-supporting life in the bush, protected until 1942 by the government reserve and the intervening mission from the cruder realities of the encroaching new order which had come up from the south. To the east was poor country, uninhabited. To the north were other bush tribes extending on along the coast to the

distant Archer River Presbyterian mission with which the Yir Yoront had no contact. Westward was the expanse of the shallow Gulf of Carpentaria, on which the natives saw only a mission lugger making its infrequent dry-season trips to the Mitchell River. In this protected environment for over a generation the Yir Yoront were able to recuperate from former shocks received at the hands of civilized society. During the 1930's their raiding and fighting, their trading and stealing of women, their evisceration and two- or three-year care of their dead, their totemic ceremonies continued apparently uninhibited by western influence. In 1931 they killed a European who wandered into their territory from the east, but the investigating police never approached the group whose members were responsible for the act. In 1934 the anthropologist observed a case of extra-tribal revenge cannibalism. The visitor among the bush Yir Yoront at this time found himself in the presence of times past, in an essentially paleolithic society which had been changed, to the casual eye, chiefly by the addition of oddments of European implements and goods put to a variety of uses.

6. As a direct result of the work of the Mitchell River mission, all Yir Yoront received a great many more western artifacts of all kinds than they ever had obtained before. As part of their plan for raising native living standards, the missionaries made it possible for aboriginals at the mission to earn some western goods, many of which were then given or traded out to natives still living under bush conditions; or they handed out gratis both to mission and to bush aboriginals certain useful articles which were in demand. They prevented guns, liquor, and damaging narcotics, as well as decimating diseases, from reaching the tribes of this area, while encouraging the introduction of goods they considered "improving." As has been noted, no item of western technology that was available, with the possible exception of trade tobacco, was in greater demand among all groups of aboriginals than the short-handled steel axe. A good supply of this type of axe was therefore always kept in stock at the mission for sale; and at Christmas parties or other mission festivals steel axes were given away to mission or visiting aboriginals indis-

criminately and in considerable numbers. In addition, some steel axes, as well as other European goods, were still traded in to the Yir Yoront by natives in contact with cattle stations established south of the missions. Indeed, such axes had probably come to the Yir Yoront along established lines of aboriginal trade long before any regular contact with whites had occurred.

3. RELEVANT FACTORS

If we concentrate our attention on Yir Yoront behavior centering about the original stone axe, rather than on the axe—the thing—we should get some conception of the role this implement played in aboriginal culture. This conception, in turn, should permit us to foresee with considerable accuracy some of the results of the displacement of stone axes by steel axes acquired directly or indirectly from Europeans by the Yir Yoront.

The production of a stone axe required a number of simple skills. With the idea of the axe in its various details well in mind, the adult men—and only the adult men—could set about producing it, a task not considered appropriate for women or children. First of all, a man had to know the location and properties of several natural resources found in his immediate environment: pliable wood, which could be doubled or bent over the axe head and bound tightly to form a handle; bark, which could be rolled into cord for the binding; and gum, with which the stone head could be firmly fixed in the haft. These materials had to be correctly gathered, stored, prepared, cut to size, and applied or manipulated. They were plentifully supplied by nature, and could be taken by a man from anyone's property without special permission. Postponing consideration of the stone head of the axe, we see that a simple knowledge of nature and of the technological skills involved, together with the possession of fire (for heating the gum) and a few simple cutting tools, which might be nothing more than the sharp shells of plentiful bivalves, all of which were available to everyone, were sufficient to enable any normal man to make a stone axe.

The use of the stone axe as a piece of capital equipment for the production of other goods indicates its very great importance in the subsistence economy of the aboriginal. Anyone—man, woman, or child—could use the axe; indeed, it was used more by women, for theirs was the onerous, daily task of obtaining sufficient wood to keep the campfire of each family burning all day for cooking or other purposes and all night against mosquitoes and cold (in July, winter temperature might drop below forty degrees). In a normal lifetime any woman would use the axe to cut or knock down literally tons of firewood. Men and women, and sometimes children, needed the axe to make other tools, or weapons, or a variety of material equipment required by the aboriginal in his daily life. The stone axe was essential in making the wet-season domed huts, which keep out some rain and some insects; or platforms, which provide dry storage; or shelters, which give shade when days are bright and hot. In hunting and fishing and in gathering vegetable or animal food the axe was also a necessary tool; and in this tropical culture without preservatives or other means of storage, the native spends more time obtaining food than in any other occupation except sleeping.

In only two instances was the use of the stone axe strictly limited to adult men: Wild honey, the most prized food known to the Yir Yoront, was gathered only by men who usually used the axe to get it; and only men could make the secret paraphernalia for ceremonies, an activity often requiring use of the axe. From this brief listing of some of the activities in which the axe was used, it is easy to understand why there was at least one stone axe in every camp, in every hunting or fighting party, in every group out on a "walk-about" in the bush.

While the stone axe helped relate men and women and often children to nature in technological behavior, in the transformation of natural into cultural equipment, it also was prominent in that aspect of behavior which may be called conduct, primarily directed toward persons. Yir Yoront men were dependent upon interpersonal relations for their stone axe heads, since the flat, geologically recent alluvial country over which they range, provides no stone from which axe heads can be made. The stone they used comes from known quarries four hundred miles to the south. It reached the Yir Yoront through long lines of male trading partners, some of these chains terminating with the Yir Yoront men, while others extended on farther north to other groups, having utilized Yir Yoront men as links. Almost every older adult man had one or more regular trading partners, some to the north and some to the south. His partner or partners in the south he provided with surplus spears, and particularly fighting spears tipped with the barbed spines of sting ray which snap into vicious fragments when they penetrate human flesh. For a dozen spears, some of which he may have obtained from a partner to the north, he would receive from a southern partner one stone axe head. Studies have shown that the sting ray spears become more and more valuable as they move south farther from the sea, being passed on in recent times from a native on one cattle station to a native on another where they are used during the wet season, when almost all aboriginal employees are thrust into the bush to shift for themselves until the next cattle-working dry season is at hand. A hundred and fifty miles south of the Yir Yoront one such spear may be exchanged for one stone axe head. Although actual investigations could not be made, presumably still farther south and nearer the quarries, one sting ray spear would bring several stone axe heads. It is apparent that links in the middle of the chain who make neither spears nor axe heads receive both as a middleman's profit simply for passing them back and forth. While many other objects may move along these chains of trading partners, they are still characterized by both bush and station aboriginals as lines along which spears move south and axes move north. Thus trading relations, which may extend the individual's personal relationships out beyond the boundaries of his own group, are associated with two of the most important items in a man's equipment, spears and axes, whether the latter are of stone or steel. Finally, most of the exchanges between partners take place during the dry season at times when the great aboriginal fiestas occur, which center about initiation rites or other totemic ceremonials that attract hundreds and are the occasion for much exciting activity besides trading.

Returning to the Yir Yoront, we find that not only was it adult men alone who obtained axe heads and produced finished axes, but it was adult males who retained the axes, keeping them with other parts of their equipment in camp, or carrying them at the back slipped through a human hair belt when traveling. Thus, every woman or child who wanted to use an axe—and this might be frequently during the day—must get one from some man, use it promptly, and return it to the man in good condition. While a man might speak of "my axe," a woman or child could not; for them it was always "your axe," addressing a male, or "his axe."

This necessary and constant borrowing of axes from older men by women and children was done according to regular patterns of kinship behavior. A woman on good terms with her husband would expect to use his axe unless he were using it; a husband on good terms with his wives would let any one of them use his axe without question. If a woman was unmarried or her husband was absent, she would go first to her older brother or to her father for an axe. Only in extraordinary circumstances would she seek a stone axe from a mother's brother or certain other male kin with whom she had to be most circumspect. A girl, a boy, or a young man would look to a father or an older brother to provide an axe for her or his use, but would never approach a mother's brother, who would be at the same time a potential father-in-law, with such a request. Older men, too, would follow similar rules if they had to borrow an axe.

It will be noted that these social relationships in which the stone axe had a place are all pair relationships and that the use of the axe helped define and maintain the character of the relationships and the roles of the two individual participants. Every active relationship among the Yir Yoront involved a definite and accepted status of superordination or subordination. A person could have no dealings with any other on exactly equal terms. Women and children were dependent on, or subordinate to, older males in every action in which the axe entered. Among the men, the younger was dependent on the older or on certain kinds of kin. The nearest approach to equality was between brothers, although the older was always superordinate to the younger.

Since the exchange of goods in a trading relationship involved a mutual reciprocity, trading partners were usually a kind of brother to each other or stood in a brotherly type of relationship, although one was always classified as older than the other and would have some advantage in case of dispute. It can be seen that repeated and widespread conduct centering on the axe helped to generalize and standardize throughout the society these sex, age, and kinship roles, both in their normal benevolent and in exceptional malevolent aspects, and helped to build up expectancies regarding the conduct of others defined as having a particular status.

The status of any individual Yir Yoront was determined not only by sex, age, and extended kin relationships, but also by membership in one of two dozen patrilineal totemic clans into which the entire community was divided. A person's names, rights in particular areas of land, and, in the case of a man, his roles in the totemic ceremonies (from which women are excluded) were all a function of belonging to one clan rather than another. Each clan had literally hundreds of totems, one or two of which gave the clan its name, and from any of which the personal names of clan members were derived. These totems included not only natural species or phenomena like the sun, stars, and daybreak, but also cultural "species": imagined ghosts, rainbow serpents, heroic ancestors; such eternal cultural verities as fires, spears, huts; and such human activities, conditions, or attributes as eating, vomiting, swimming, fighting, babies and corpses, milk and blood, lips and loins. While individual members of such totemic classes or species might disappear or be destroyed, the class itself was obviously ever present and indestructible. The totems therefore lent permanence and stability to the clans, to the groupings of human individuals who generation after generation were each associated with one set of totems that distinguished one clan from another.

Among the many totems of the Sunlit Cloud Iguana clan, and important among them, was the stone axe. The names of many members of this clan referred to the axe itself, or to activities like trading or wild honey gathering in which the axe played a vital part, or to the clan's mythical ancestors with whom the axe was prominently associated. When it was necessary to represent the stone axe in totemic ceremonies, it was only men of this clan who exhibited it or pantomimed its use. In secular life the axe could be made by any man and used by all; but in the sacred realm of the totems it belonged exclusively to the Sunlit Cloud Iguana people.

Supporting those aspects of cultural behavior which we have called technology and conduct is a third area of culture, including ideas, sentiments, and values. These are most difficult to deal with, for they are latent and covert or even unconscious and must be deduced from overt actions and language or other communicating behavior. In this aspect of the culture lies the "meaning" of the stone axe, its significance to the Yir Yoront and to their cultural way of life. The ideal conception of the axe, the knowledge of how to produce it (apart from the purely muscular habits used in its production) are part of the Yir Yoront adult masculine role, just as ideas regarding its technical use are included in the feminine role. These technical ideas constitute a kind of "science" regarding the axe which may be more important in relation to behavioral change than are the neurophysiological patterns drilled into the body by years of practice. Similarly there are normative ideas regarding the part played by the axe in conduct which constitute a kind of "morality" of the axe, and which again may be more important than the overt habits of social interaction in determining the role of the axe in social relationships. More than ideas regarding technology, ideas regarding conduct are likely to be closely associated, or "charged," with sentiment or value. Ideas and sentiments help guide and inform overt behavior; in turn, overt behavior helps support and validate ideas and sentiments.

The stone axe was an important symbol of masculinity among the Yir Yoront (just as pants or pipes are among ourselves). By a complicated set of ideas which we would label "ownership" the axe was defined as "belonging" to males. Everyone in the society (except untrained infants) accepted these ideas. Similarly spears, spear throwers, and fire-making sticks were associated with males, were owned only by them, and were symbols of masculinity. But the masculine values represented by the stone axe were constantly being impressed on all members of society by the fact that non-males had to use the axe and had to go to males for it, whereas they never borrowed other masculine artifacts. Thus, the axe stood for an important theme that ran all through Yir Yoront culture: the superiority and rightful dominance of the male, and the greater value of his concerns and of all things associated with him. We should call this androcentrism rather than patriarchy, or paternal rule. It is the recognition by all that the values of the man (*andros*) take precedence over feminine values, an idea backed by very strong sentiments among the Yir Yoront. Since the axe had to be borrowed also by the younger from the older, it also represented the prestige of age, another important theme running all through Yir Yoront behavior.

Important for an understanding of the Yir Yoront culture is a system of ideas, which may be called their totemic ideology. A fundamental belief of the aboriginal divided time into two great epochs, a distant and sacred period at the beginning of the world, when the earth was peopled by mildly marvelous ancestral beings or culture heroes who in a special sense are the forebears of the clans; and a second period, when the old was succeeded by a new order that includes the present. Originally there was no anticipation of another era supplanting the present; the future would simply be an eternal continuation and reproduction of the present, which itself had remained unchanged since the epochal revolution of ancestral times.

The mythical sacred world of the ancestors with which time began turns out on investigation to be a detailed reproduction of the present aboriginal world of nature, man, and culture altered by phantasy. In short, the idea system expressed in the mythology regarding the ancestral epoch was directly derived from Yir Yoront behavior patterns—normal and abnormal, actual and ideal, conscious and unconscious. The important thing to note, however, is that the native believed it was just the other way around, that the present world, as a natural and cultural environment, was and should be simply a detailed reproduction of the world of the ancestors. He believed that the entire universe "is now as it was in the beginning" when it was established and left by the ancestors. The ordinary cultural life of the ancestors became the daily life of the Yir Yoront camps, and the extraordinary life of the ancestors remained extant in the recurring symbolic pantomimes and paraphernalia found only in the most sacred atmosphere of the totemic rites.

Such beliefs, accordingly, opened up the way for ideas of what *should be* (because it supposedly *was*) to influence or help determine what actually *is*. Dog-chases-iguana-up-a-tree-and-barks-at-him-all-night had that and other names because, so he believed, his ancestral alter ego had these same names; he was a member of the Sunlit Cloud Iguana clan because his ancestor was; he was associated with particular countries and totems of this same ancestor; during an initiation he played the role of a dog and symbolically attacked and killed certain members of other clans because his ancestor (conveniently either anthropomorphic or kynomorphic) really did the same to the ancestral alter egos of these men; and he would avoid his mother-in-law, joke with a distant mother's brother, and make spears in a certain way because his and other people's ancestors did these things. His behavior in these rather than in other ways was outlined for him, and to that extent determined, by a set of ideas concerning the past and the relation of the present to the past.

But when we are informed that Dog-chases . . . had two wives from the Spear Black Duck clan and one from the Native Companion clan with such and such names, one of them being blind; that he had four children with such and such names; that he had a broken wrist and was left-handed, all because his ancestor had exactly these same attributes, then we know (though he apparently did not) that the present has influenced the past, that the mythical world has been somewhat adjusted to meet the exigencies and accidents of the inescapably real present.

There was thus in Yir Yoront ideology a nice balance in which the mythical world was adjusted in part to the real world, the real world in part to the ideal preexisting mythical world, the adjustments occurring to maintain a fundamental tenet of native faith that the present must be a mirror of the past. Thus, the stone axe in all its aspects, uses, and associations was integrated into the context of Yir Yoront technology and conduct because a myth, a set of ideas, had put it there.

REFERENCES FOR FURTHER STUDY

Sharp, Lauriston, "The Social Organization of the Yir Yoront Tribe, Cape York Peninsula"; "Ritual Life and Economics of the Yir Yoront," *Oceania*, vol. 4, June, 1934, pp. 404–431; vol. 5, September, 1934, pp. 19–42.

————, "Tribes and Totemism in Northeast Australia," *Oceania*, vol. 9, March and June, 1939, pp. 254–275, 439–461.

Warner, W. Lloyd, *A Black Civilization*. Harper and Bros., New York, 1937.

Answer Question Presented in the Problem
Before Reading the Rest of the Case.

4. ANALYSIS

The introduction of the steel axe indiscriminately and in large numbers into the Yir Yoront technology was only one of many changes occurring at the same time. It is therefore impossible to factor out all the results of this single innovation alone. Nevertheless, a number of specific effects of the change from stone axes to steel axes may be noted; and the steel axe may be used as an epitome of the European goods and implements received by the aboriginals in increasing quantity and of their general influence on the native culture. The use of the steel axe to illustrate such influences would seem to be justified, for it was one of the first European artifacts to be adopted for regular use by the Yir Yoront; and the axe, whether of stone or steel, was clearly one of the most important items of cultural equipment they possessed.

The shift from stone to steel axes provided no major technological difficulties. While the aboriginals themselves could not manufacture steel axe heads, a steady supply from outside continued; and broken wooden axe handles could easily be replaced from bush timbers with aboriginal tools. Among the Yir Yoront the new axe never acquired all the uses it had on mission or cattle stations (carpentry work, pounding tent pegs, use as a hammer, and so on); and, indeed, it was used for little more than the stone axe had been, so that it had no practical effect in improving the native standard of living. It did some jobs better, and could be used longer without breakage; and these factors were sufficient to make it of value to the native. But the assumption of the white man (based in part on a realization that a shift from steel to stone axe in his case would be a definite regression) that his axe was much more efficient, that its use would save time, and that it therefore represented technical "progress" toward goals which he had set for the native was hardly borne out in aboriginal practice. Any leisure time the Yir Yoront might gain by using steel axes or other western tools was invested, not in "improving the conditions of life," and certainly not in developing aesthetic activities, but in sleep, an art they had thoroughly mastered.

Having acquired an axe head through regular trading partners of whom he knew what to expect, a man wanting a stone axe was then dependent solely upon a known and an adequate nature and upon his own skills or easily acquired techniques. A man wanting a steel axe, however, was in no such self-reliant position. While he might acquire one through trade, he now had the new alternative of dispensing with technological behavior in relation with a predictable nature and conduct in relation with a predictable trading partner and of turning instead to conduct alone in relation with a highly erratic missionary. If he attended one of the mission festivals when steel axes were handed out as gifts, he might receive one simply by chance or if he had happened somehow to impress upon the mission staff that he was one of the "better" bush aboriginals (their definition of "better" being quite different from that of his bush fellows). Or he might—but again almost by pure chance—be given some brief job in connection with the mission which would enable him to earn a steel axe. In either case, for older men a preference for the steel axe helped create a situation of dependence in place of a situation of self-reliance and a behavior shift from situations in technology or conduct which were well structured or defined to situations in conduct alone which were ill defined. It was particularly the older ones among the men, whose earlier experience or knowledge of the white man's harshness in any event made them suspicious, who would avoid having any relations with the mission at all, and who thus excluded themselves from acquiring steel axes directly from that source.

The steel axe was the root of psychological stress among the Yir Yoront even more significantly in other aspects of social relations. This was the result of new factors which the missionary considered all to the good: the simple numerical increase in axes per capita as a result of mission distribution; and distribution from the mission directly to younger men, women, and even children. By winning the favor of the mission staff, a woman might be given a steel axe. This was clearly intended to be hers. The situation was quite different from that involved in borrowing an axe from a male relative, with the result that a woman called such an axe "my" steel axe, a possessive form she never used for a stone axe. (Lexically, the steel axe was differentiated from the stone by an adjectival suffix signifying "metal," the element "axe" remaining identical.) Furthermore, young men or even boys might also obtain steel axes directly from the mission. A result was that older men no longer had a complete monopoly of all the axes in the bush community. Indeed, an old man might have only a stone axe, while his wives and sons had steel axes which they considered their own and which he might even desire to borrow. All this led to a revolutionary confusion of sex, age, and kinship roles, with a major gain in independence and loss of subordination on the part of those able now to acquire steel axes when they had been unable to possess stone axes before.

The trading partner relationship was also affected by the new situation. A Yir Yoront might have a trading partner in a tribe to the south whom he defined as a younger brother, and on whom as an older brother he would therefore have an edge. But if the partner were in contact with the mission or had other easier access to steel axes, his subordination to his bush colleague was obviously decreased. Indeed, under the new dispensation he might prefer to give his axe to a bush "sweetheart" in return for favors or otherwise dispose of it outside regular trade channels, since many steel axes were so distributed between natives in new ways. Among other things, this took some of the excitement away from the fiesta-like tribal gatherings centering around initiations during the dry season. These had traditionally been the climactic annual occasions for exchanges between trading partners, when a man might seek to acquire a whole year's supply of stone axe heads. Now he might find himself prostituting his wife to almost total strangers in return for steel axes or other white men's goods. With trading partnerships weakened, there was less reason to attend the fiestas, and less fun for those who did. A decline in one of the important social activities which had symbolized these great gatherings created a lessening of interest in the other social aspects of these events.

Not only did an increase in steel axes and their distribution to women change the character of the relations between individual and individual, the paired relationships that have been noted, but a new type of relationship, hitherto practically unknown among the Yir Yoront, was created in their axe-acquiring conduct with whites. In the aboriginal society there were almost no occasions outside the immediate family when one individual would initiate action to several other people at once. For in any average group, while a person in accordance with the kinship system might be superordinate to several people to whom he could suggest or command action, at the same time he was also subordinate to several others, in relation with whom such behavior would be tabu. There was thus no over-all chieftainship or authoritarian leadership of any kind. Such complicated operations as grass-burning, animal drives, or totemic ceremonies could be carried out smoothly because each person knew his roles both in technology and conduct.

On both mission and cattle stations, however, the whites imposed upon the aboriginals their conception of leadership roles, with one person in a controlling relationship with a subordinate group. Aboriginals called together to receive gifts, including axes, at a mission Christmas party found themselves facing one or two whites who sought to control their behavior for the occasion, who disregarded the age, sex, and kinship variables among them of which they were so conscious, and who considered them all at one subordinate level. Or the white might impose similar patterns on a working party. (But if he placed an aboriginal in charge of a mixed group of post hole diggers, for example, half of the group, those subordinate to the "boss," would work while the other half, who were superordinate to him, would sleep.) The steel axe, together, of course, with other European goods, came to symbolize for the aboriginal this new and uncomfortable form of social organization, the leader-group relationship.

The most disturbing effects of the steel axe, operating in conjunction with other elements also being introduced from the white man's several subcultures, developed in the realm of traditional ideas, sentiments, and values. These were undermined at a rapidly mounting rate, without new conceptions being defined to replace them. The result was a mental and moral void which foreshadowed the collapse and destruction of all Yir Yoront culture, if not, indeed, the extinction of the biological group itself.

From what has been said it should be clear how changes in overt behavior, in technology and conduct, weakened the values inherent in a reliance on nature, in androcentrism or the prestige of masculinity, in age prestige, and in the various kinship relations. A scene was set in which a wife or young son, his initiation perhaps not even yet completed, need no longer bow to the husband or father, who was left confused and insecure as he asked to borrow a steel axe from them. For the woman and boy the steel axe helped establish a new degree of freedom which was accepted readily as an escape from the unconscious stress of the old patterns, but which left them also confused and insecure. Ownership became less well defined, so that stealing and trespass were introduced into technology and conduct. Some of the excitement surrounding the great ceremonies evaporated, so that the only fiestas the people had became less festive, less interesting. Indeed, life itself became less interesting, although this did not lead the Yir Yoront to invent suicide, a concept foreign to them.

The whole process may be most specifically illustrated in terms of the totemic system, and this will also illustrate the significant role which a system of ideas, in this case a totemic ideology, may play in the breakdown of a culture.

In the first place, under pre-European aboriginal conditions in which the native culture has become adjusted to a relatively stable environment in which there can occur few, if any, unheard of or catastrophic crises, it is clear that the totemic system must serve very effectively to inhibit radical cultural changes. The closed system of totemic ideas, explaining and categorizing a well-known universe as it was fixed at the beginning of time, presents a considerable obstacle to the adoption of new or the dropping of old culture traits. The obstacle is not insurmountable and the system allows for the minor variations which occur about the norms of daily life, but the inception of major changes cannot easily take place.

Among the bush Yir Yoront the only means of water transport is a light wood log, to which they cling in their constant swimming of rivers, salt creeks, and tidal inlets. These natives know that forty-five miles north of them are tribes who have a bark canoe. They know these northern tribes can thus fish from midstream or out at sea, instead of clinging to the river banks and beaches, and can cross coastal waters infested with crocodiles, sharks, sting rays, and Portuguese-men-of-war without the recurring mortality, pain, or anxiety to which they themselves are constantly subjected. They know they lack any magic to do for them what the canoe could do. They know the materials of which the canoe is made are present in their own environment. But they also know, as they say, that their own mythical ancestors lacked the canoe, and therefore they lack it, while they assume that the canoe was part of the ancestral universe of the northern tribes. For them, then, the adoption of the canoe would not be simply a matter of learning a number of new behavioral skills for its manufacture and use. The adoption would require at the same time a much more difficult procedure, the acceptance by the entire society of a myth, either locally developed or borrowed, which would explain the presence of the canoe, associate it with some one or more of the several hundred mythical ancestors (and how decide which?), and thus establish it as an accepted totem of one of the clans ready to be used by the whole community. The Yir Yoront have not made this adjustment, and in this case we can only say that ideas have for the time being at least won out over very real pressures for technological change. In the elaborateness and explicitness of the totemic ideologies we seem to have one explanation for the notorious stability of Australian cultures under aboriginal conditions, an explanation which gives due weight to the importance of ideas in determining human behavior.

At a later stage of the contact situation, as has been indicated, phenomena unaccounted for by the totemic ideological system begin to appear with regularity and frequency and remain within the range of native experience. Accordingly, they cannot be ignored (as the "Battle of the Mitchell River" was apparently ignored), and an attempt is made to assimilate them and account for them along the lines of principles inherent in the ideology. The bush Yir Yoront of the mid-1930's represent this stage of the acculturation process. Still trying to maintain their aboriginal definition of the situation, they accept European artifacts and behavior patterns, but fit them into their totemic system, assigning them as totems to various clans on a par with original totems. There is an attempt to have the myth-making process keep up with these cultural changes so that the idea system can continue to support the rest of the culture. But analysis of overt behavior, of dreams, and of some of the new myths indicates that this arrangement is not entirely satisfactory; that the native clings to his totemic system with intellectual loyalty, lacking any substitute ideology; but that associated sentiments and values are weakened. His attitudes toward his own and toward European culture are found to be highly ambivalent.

All ghosts are totems of the Head-to-the-East Corpse clan. They are thought of as white, and are, of course, closely associated with death. The white man, too, is white and was closely associated with death, so that he and all things pertaining to him are naturally assigned to the Corpse clan as totems. The steel axe, as a totem, was thus associated with the Corpse clan. But it is an "axe," and is clearly linked with the stone axe, which is a totem of the Sunlit Cloud Iguana clan. Moreover, the steel axe, like most European goods, has no distinctive origin myth, nor are mythical ancestors associated with it. Can anyone, sitting of an afternoon in the shade of a ti tree, create a myth to resolve this confusion? No one has, and the horrid suspicion arises that perhaps the origin myths are wrong, which took into account so little of this vast new universe of the white man. The steel axe, shifting hopelessly between one clan and the other, is not only replacing the stone axe physically, but is hacking at the supports of the entire cultural system.

The aboriginals to the south of the Yir Yoront have clearly passed beyond this stage. They are engulfed by European culture, in this area by either the mission or cattle station subcultures, or for some natives a baffling, paradoxical combination of both incongruent varieties. The totemic ideology can no longer support the inrushing mass of foreign culture traits and the myth-making process in its native form breaks down completely. Both intellectually and emotionally a saturation point is reached, so that the myriad new traits which can neither be ignored nor any longer assimilated simply force the aboriginal to abandon his totemic system. With the collapse of this system of ideas, which is so closely related with so many other aspects of the native culture, there follows an appallingly sudden and complete cultural disintegration and a demoralization of the individual such as has seldom been recorded for areas other than Australia. Without the support of a system of ideas well devised to provide cultural stability in a stable environment but admittedly too rigid for the new realities pressing in from outside, native behavior and native sentiments and values are simply dead. Apathy reigns. The aboriginal has passed beyond the reach of any outsider who might wish to do him well or ill.

Returning from the broken natives huddled on cattle stations or on the fringes of frontier towns to the ambivalent but still lively aboriginals settled on the Mitchell River mission, we note one further devious result of the introduction of European artifacts. During a wet season stay at the mission, the anthropologist discovered that his supply of tooth paste was being depleted at an alarming rate. Investigation showed that it was being taken by old men for use in a new tooth paste cult. Old materials of magic having failed, new materials were being tried out in a malevolent magic directed toward the mission staff and some of the younger aboriginal men. Old males, largely ignored by the missionaries, were seeking to regain some of their lost power and prestige. This mild aggression proved hardly effective, but perhaps only because confidence in any kind of magic on the mission was by this time at a low ebb.

For the Yir Yoront still in the bush a time could be predicted when personal deprivation and frustration in a confused culture would produce an overload of anxiety. The mythical past of the totemic ancestors would disappear as a guarantee of a present of which the future was supposed to be a stable continuation. Without the past, the present would be meaningless and the future unstructured and uncertain. Insecurities would be inevitable. Reaction to this stress might be some form of symbolic aggression, or withdrawal and apathy, or some more realistic approach. In such a situation the missionary with understanding of the processes going on about him would find his opportunity to introduce religion and to help create the constitution of a new cultural universe.

SUGGESTIONS FOR STUDY: A Checklist of Questions

The questions which have been set down up to this point by the student probably are of a rather specific type, applicable only to the actual situations which have been analyzed. Nevertheless, it will be found, as they are compared, that they fall into certain types and that, for example, the ground covered by the questions asked in Case 2 is much the same as that covered in Case 1. In other words, there is material here for making a master list of questions to be used in any problem of guided cross-cultural change. If such a general schedule of questions has not already been worked out by the student, he may find it profitable to do so at this point.

We present here an example of one such master checklist which might be used for gathering information in a wide variety of situations. It could, of course, be developed further in any number of directions, depending on the needs in a particular problem.

1. What, if anything, will the introduced trait replace?
2. What other tools and techniques are likely to be modified as a result of the introduction?
3. What other tools and techniques will have to be modified if the new trait is accepted?
4. For what new tools and techniques is there likely to be a demand as a result of the introduction?
5. Who in the society will have to abandon or change their occupations, if there is replacement? Who will be likely to modify their occupations and who will be given new occupations?
6. Who within the society will benefit immediately from the introduction? Will the benefits be in terms of economic advantage, increased prestige, or what?
7. Who, if anyone, is likely to suffer immediately? In terms of real or fancied threat to economic security? In terms of social status?

8. Will shifts in occupation affect the division of labor between men and women?

9. What are the formal and informal social organizations in
which those affected participate?

10. How are these social organizations likely to be affected?
Will their power or social position be enhanced or lowered?

11. Is there a possibility of the introduction opening up new
forms of cooperation? Of conflict?

12. Do the individuals and group leaders affected understand
the nature of the introduction?

13. Who has participated in the planning of the change? Who
has not participated?

14. What customs, other than the technology, are likely to be
affected? Food habits? Relations of young and old? Marriage customs? Ceremonials? Religious beliefs? Major
values?

15. Does the change reinforce these customs or conflict with
them?

16. What are the attitudes toward the innovator (the field
worker) as a person? Toward the ethnic group of which he
is a member?

17. What is the recent history of the relations between the
introducing group and the people?

18. What is the history of similar introductions to this group?

PART II
THE ANALYSIS OF HUMAN SITUATIONS

SUGGESTIONS FOR STUDY: Roles

The first step in discovering the human problems that face the cross-cultural worker is knowing what kinds of questions to ask. Each field situation is unique and needs to be studied on the ground. Such a study consists in acquiring information about the main aspects of the total situation, a process which may be systematic to the extent that one has available a well-thought-out checklist of questions.

The way the questions are used is also an important problem. They cannot be applied successfully in haphazard fashion to just anyone who comes along. Therefore, a second step is to determine of whom the different questions ought to be asked. This calls for recognition of the different roles that people play in any society. If the introduced item is something that women are going to use, as in the case of the hybrid corn in New Mexico, then it is important to discuss it with the women themselves. From them one can discover best what they think and feel about both the old and the new trait. From the people in the Relocation Center blocks, rather than from their representatives on the Community Council, one could discover how people felt about a Community Trust Fund. The formulation of questions, then, is the beginning; but the questions may not be very revealing unless they are asked of the people who can give the best answers.

It is suggested that the student practice analyzing the situations described in the following cases in terms of the roles played by different people, including the cross-cultural worker. Who, in the situation described, would be likely to give one type of information needed and who another? From what points of view would various people see this introduction or proposed change? What interests give rise to such different points of view? Try to define as many roles as you can in each of the following situations and review the five simpler cases of Part I in order to define the roles evident there.

Case 6

NEW LAND TO FARM: Agricultural Practices Among the Navaho Indians of New Mexico

by Tom Sasaki and John Adair

1. THE PROBLEM

Navaho Indian farmers who live on an irrigated tract along the San Juan River in northern New Mexico are making ineffective use of valuable farmland. In 1942 the gross yield per acre cropped was $28, as compared to $128 per acre among Mormon farmers living just across the river. Yields have improved since, but are still far below those of the white farmers. The soil conditions on both sides of the river are comparable. The Navaho farmers have the advantage of a carefully engineered irrigation system superior to the old ditches of the white farmers.

The Fruitland Irrigation Project, where these Navahos live, was established fifteen years before the writing of this case by the United States Bureau of Indian Affairs. It was part of a large-scale plan for bringing about a better adjustment between natural resources and the 55,000 Indians living on the Navajo[1] Indian Reservation in Arizona and New Mexico. It consisted in the development of water resources to provide more farm land and the settlement of Indians, who are traditionally sheepherders and dry farmers, on these irrigated tracts.

The Navahos who have settled on the Fruitland Project have had some help from Indian Service extension agents since the beginning of the project. Moreover, there is the example before them of thriving farms owned and managed by the Mormons. Why do the Navahos, in the face of these advantages, remain so backward in their agricultural practices?

[1] The official spelling by the United States Office of Indian Affairs is "Navajo." However, the common nongovernmental usage is to spell the word as pronounced, "Navaho." We follow the latter in this book except when employing governmental names.

2. THE COURSE OF EVENTS

1. In the early 1930's the Navajo Service of the United States Bureau of Indian Affairs determined to put into effect a broad program of soil conservation and development of natural and human resources on the Navajo Indian Reservation. This included irrigated farm tracts and the settlement of Indians on these tracts.

2. In October, 1933, engineers surveyed and staked out a 13-mile area along the south bank of the San Juan River at the northeast corner of the Reservation. This was to be the Fruitland Irrigation Project. The digging of the main canal began the following year, Navahos from the immediate vicinity as well as from other parts of the Reservation being employed in the work.

3. As building the canal began in 1934 the Navajo Service announced that each family settling on the project would receive 20 acres of farm land in exchange for those sheep, goats, and horses which they might possess in excess of the carrying capacity of the range and which they would have to surrender. It was generally understood that tracts of this size would enable the settlers to raise crops for cash sale.

4. The new land became available for distribution in 1936, but Navajo Service administrators had become convinced in the meantime that 20-acre tracts would be impracticable. Observation of Navaho farm practices at the neighboring project of Shiprock, and elsewhere on the Reservation, indicated that there would not be full utilization of farms as large as 20 acres. Furthermore, smaller tracts would permit the relocation of a greater number of families from the arid mesa lands. Accordingly, policy was announced to the effect that farms in the Fruitland Project would be limited to 10 acres. Many meetings were held with the farmers and the reasons for the smaller tracts were explained.

5. Between 1936 and the beginning of World War II many young men from different parts of the Reservation came to the Fruitland Project, took up 10-acre assignments, and began farming.

6. During the war years the administration of the Fruitland Project met with a number of reverses. First, a cut in Indian

Service appropriations by Congress necessitated a revamping of many projects. A school which had been built some years before the war and announced as an agricultural high school was finally set up as an elementary school. In addition, there was rapid turnover of personnel. Finally, an agricultural extension agent of Spanish-American background who had been popular with the Navahos left after a year's service and was not replaced.

7. By 1948 there were 205 farms assigned to 191 family units. Acreages ranged from 4.9 to 33, the larger plots belonging to farmers who had been in the area before the project and who had refused to give up their holdings. Fifty-two per cent of the tracts were of 10 acres or less. Also, by 1948 Fruitland and the neighboring community of Shiprock had become known to Navajo Service administrators as difficult communities, that is, as centers of resistance to government programs.

8. A development of major importance in the years since World War II has been off-reservation employment. During the war years Navahos worked off the Reservation in great numbers. After the war, demand for them continued in several different occupations: crop-picking on truck farms and in sugar-beet fields (activities which could be carried out by the whole family working as a unit), and track work on the railroad (in which men engaged without taking their families along). This off-reservation employment resulted in a constant shift of population in and out of the Fruitland Project.

3. RELEVANT FACTORS

The Navaho Indians have made a part of their living by agriculture for at least the four or five hundred years since they first settled in the southwestern part of what is now the United States. Since coming into contact with Spaniards in the 1500's they have added sheep-raising to their economy, but dry farming has remained an important source of subsistence.

This economy was supplemented by raiding the Spanish villages and the settlements of the Pueblo Indians. These raids for livestock, grain, and other booty became a menace to these colonists and to the "Anglos" who settled in towns and on ranches during the early territorial period. In 1863 the Navahos were all rounded up by United States troops and marched off to Fort Sumner, a military outpost several hundred miles to the east. They remained there in this "concentration camp" until 1868, when they were allowed to return to their homeland and a reservation was set aside for their use.

This early history is important, for it must not be forgotten that the Navahos have the psychology of a defeated people and in times of crisis the old feelings of hostility are revived. Such hostility to whites flared up during the stock reduction program when the Fruitland Project was just getting under way.

A great many of the Fruitland Navahos formerly lived at the southern end of District 13, in what is known as "Burnham's." The Navajo Service carried on vigorous recruitment for Fruitland land assignees in this area in an effort to relieve pressure on the badly overgrazed land.

In the vicinity of Burnham's the land settlement pattern, the social organization, and the economy of the Navahos are typical of life in other parts of the barren eastern edge of the Navaho country. The people live in scattered huts or "hogans," one family unit of mother, father, and children, with often a grandparent or two sharing the dwelling. Hogans are located in areas where soil and moisture conditions are the most favorable for agriculture and where browse for the sheep is not too distant. The best lands are situated near the courses of the intermittent streams. Whenever there is sufficient rain to fill the stream-beds, the water is diverted to the fields where it spreads out over the cultivated areas. Frequently there is little or no rain during a year, with consequent crop failure.

Corn is the main crop, with beans, squash, and potatoes next in importance. Horticultural methods follow a pattern proved through trial and error, and borrowed from the Pueblo Indians hundreds of years ago. The ruling principle is the conservation of every bit of moisture in the soil, and seed selection, plowing, planting, and cultivation are all carried on with reference to this aim. A highly drought-resistant variety of corn has been de-

veloped through centuries of seed selection. The corn is planted
in hills, six or eight kernels to each mound. The plants are low-
growing, with tremendously long root systems that require careful hand cultivation to avoid cutting.

The primary responsibility for crop production falls to the men,
but they are always assisted by the women and children during
the planting and harvesting seasons. The men do the heavy work
in preparing the ground for planting; yet, even then women
occasionally take a turn at the plow. During the busy seasons
adjoining families help each other in the fields. Such extended
families consist of conjugal groups related through the female line.
Sisters usually live in hogans within a radius of a mile or so, and
often, if the land is sufficiently good, a mother and her daughters
all have their hogans within shouting distance. The men married
into the families of such a group of women cooperate in farm
work, especially when new areas are being cleared of stones and
sagebrush and leveled before being planted for the first time. The
sisters, aided by their children, take over, once the crop is picked,
and have charge of husking, drying, and storage.

The children, especially the boys, are expected to take part in
the raising of crops, and in weeding and cultivating the fields.
After the corn has achieved a good stand and is five inches or so
above the ground, the adults frequently leave their homes for a
round of "squaw dances" (a type of summer religious ceremonial) which last for several days. The older children are left to
look after the crops on such occasions. Navaho boys are thus
steadily inducted by their parents into the techniques of agriculture, and by the time each male is ready for marriage, he is well
trained in all phases of crop production.

The Navaho men have rigorous duties in their religious life
which may require them to leave fields and flocks for extended
periods at various times during the growing season. Most of the
ceremonials, or "sings," are focused on curing and ensure good
health if properly carried out. The gods, however, control crops
as well. If the people maintain the favor of the deities, there will
be general well-being, including good crops, but disfavor brings
drought and crop failure.

The Navaho farmer had no knowledge of crop rotation or the use of fertilizer as a means of maintaining soil productivity. When one arable field dropped in yield, the family would abandon it and seek another nearby. The clearing and preparing of new fields was a recurrent feature of the Navaho agricultural economy. The movement of family groups in this manner over a period of years was, however, within a defined territory. The extended families who farmed and herded within such a territory recognized land-use rights of one another and maintained such rights against outsiders.

A number of related extended families of this sort is often referred to as an "outfit." What unity it has is based primarily on common land-use rights, but there is also an organization which, informal though it is, might be regarded as political. The collection of extended families usually recognizes some older man as ultimate authority in the case of disputes and as a spokesman for the whole group in dealings with neighboring Navaho outfits. The strongest ties within an outfit are those between conjugal families constituting an extended family. The relationship is traced through females and in terms of matrilineal clan groupings. The status of any person, man or woman, is determined by his mother's kinship affiliations. The female-linked extended families, then, constitute the basic social units which managed and used the land within an area over which members of an outfit ranged.

The people who have settled at Fruitland have this background of economic and social life. The Irrigation Project is divided into three fairly distinct geographical areas, which have become known as Units I, II, and III, in order from up to downstream. However, a few Navaho farmers had lived for many years prior to the establishment of the project in the areas of Units I and II, where crude irrigation ditches, built by Mormons just after 1900, carried water to farmland near the San Juan River.

Unit II has been occupied by Navahos for the longest time. Kinship ties and social organization are almost identical with those of the Navahos living in the Burnham's area. There is similar mutual cooperation among members of extended families and an identification beyond the extended family with the outfit. When the government built the big canal and began to lay out the farms, the families in the Unit II area simply formalized on paper what had been traditional land-use patterns. Few new families were relocated here, and the social organization remained cohesive. Furthermore these Navahos, who are the most successful farmers on the project, had an economic advantage over the newcomers in so far as pooling of land by conjugal families permitted some of the older males to farm as many as 50 acres.

The representative to the Tribal Council and formal leader of the whole District 13 of the Navajo Reservation is such a resident of Unit II and the most prosperous farmer of the Fruitland Project. The backing of his family and clanmates and wide influence among other residents of District 13 have served to keep him in this elected office for many years. As a delegate to the Council he has been very outspoken in criticism of the government stock reduction program and the land assignment system on the Fruitland Project. He has joined with other members of Unit II against a number of programs introduced by the Indian Service supervisor, thus gaining for himself and his colleagues the reputation of "agitators."

In the areas of both Units I and II there were, before the establishment of the Irrigation Project, organizations called "Chapters" which were recognized by the Indian Service. These were units of self-government which had developed from local groups. The Chapter in Unit I had served as an informal native version of a farm association and was active in the purchase of community-owned farm implements. However, after the reorganization of the Tribal Council in 1936, the Chapters ceased to be recognized by the Navajo Service administrators.

Before the opening of the big canal, the Navahos living in the areas of Units I and II were self-contained, geographically and socially. For instance, each area had its own water system and was in no way dependent on the other. After the installation of the canal they, along with Unit III, shared the same water supply. The government considered the whole enlarged irrigated area as a unified project and its personnel serviced all three Units. Today over-all community meetings are encouraged by the administrators to which Units I and II each send elected officers. Having had no Chapter organization, Unit III has no elected officer, but residents of the Unit do attend the meetings. Such meetings are held at irregular intervals and matters like canal cleaning, land assignments, livestock regulations, and grasshopper control are discussed. In recent years attendance at such meetings has been limited to a small number of the total residents.

The need for instructing the settlers on the Fruitland Project in irrigation farming practices was realized by the Navajo Service. An agricultural extension agent of the Indian Bureau was assigned with headquarters at Unit II. During his year of residence he made good progress in working with the men. But, as mentioned previously, the manpower shortage during the war prevented his remaining on the project, and he was not replaced owing to shortage of funds. Instead, agricultural extension became a secondary duty of the district supervisor, whose first responsibility was livestock management.

On occasion agricultural extension men from the central agency and from Shiprock called meetings at the school building on Unit II. Correct methods of irrigation, crop rotation, and fertilization were explained to the farmers, and sometimes films were shown. These meetings were conducted in English and interpreted by a Navaho to the older residents who do not understand the language of the administrators.

At Fruitland the annual agricultural cycle begins late in March or April, when the families return to the project from off-reservation employment, or from the Burnham's area, where many still retain homes. The first major operation is cleaning the canal, which is done as a return for water rights. Lateral ditches draw the water off from the main siphon to the farms, as many as twenty farms being irrigated from each lateral. When ditch cleaning is completed, water is let into the fields, which are then well soaked to assure sufficient ground moisture for planting. From this point on, during the growing season, there are persistent troubles with irrigation. Farms at the ends of the laterals

often suffer from lack of water, and there is constant protest that
the irrigation system is inadequate for the needs of the project.
There is also a great deal of erosion of fields, some farmers facing
the loss of much of their holdings within a few years.

In general, the handling of crops during the growing season is
far below the standard of the white farmers across the river,
and this is reflected in the relatively low yields already mentioned. It may be relevant to point out that the Mormon-owned
farms are on the average considerably larger than those of the
Indian.

By 1948, when the senior author of this case began the field
research, approximately 1,000 Navahos, comprising 191 households, had been established on 2,500 acres. All but a few hundred
acres of the land that could be brought under irrigation has been
subjugated. As a result, there is at present a shortage of tillable
soil, which has caused the Navajo Service to institute a policy of
enforcing land use by declaring that farms not under cultivation
are to revert for reassignment. This is a cause of anxiety. In the
words of one Navaho:

> This is not our land. It belongs to the government. . . . We don't
> know when the government is going to take the land away from us.
> It is just like what they did with our sheep. They gave them to us,
> but they took them away too.

Hostility toward Navajo Service has not been limited to the
Indians. From the first years of the Fruitland Project there has
been a great deal of hostility toward the Navajo Service on the
part of local whites, especially the traders, but shared by journal-
ists, lawyers, and others in the nearby town of Farmington. This
hostility may have its roots in deep-lying resentment and suspicion of central government, no matter what its political com-
plexion, which is one of the heritages of frontier life. However,
there was also specific cause. Stock reduction, as urged by the
Navajo Service, affected the interests of the traders and others
who were dependent on Navaho sheep products. The traders
have long been important in Navaho life. As men who to some

extent speak the language of the Indians, Navaho leaders have come to rely on them for information and guidance. Up to 1950 the hostility of the traders toward the Navajo Service had deepened rather than abated.

REFERENCES FOR FURTHER STUDY

Kluckhohn, Clyde, and Dorothea Leighton, *The Navaho*. Harvard University Press, Cambridge, 1946.

Sasaki, Tom Taketo, *Technological Change in a Navaho Indian Farming Community:* A Study of Social and Psychological Processes. Ph.D. Thesis, Cornell University, 1950.

Answer Question Presented in the Problem
Before Reading the Rest of the Case.

4. ANALYSIS

As noted in the beginning, the utilization of the new land falls far short of possibilities. That the resettlers have not improved their standard of living to a level commensurate with the opportunities is most clearly apparent in the poor farming practices of the Navahos. These may be listed as follows:

1. There is inefficient use of the irrigation system. This manifests itself in a number of ways. Those farmers who have fields along a single lateral of the ditch system have not worked out any plan of rotated irrigation. More often than not, they all open their gates at the same time. The result is that those whose fields are near the canal end of the lateral get sufficient water, but those at the far end do not, and consequently their crops suffer. Although it has been pointed out to them that scheduling would relieve the situation, they have put no such plan into operation. Along with this failure to employ a scheduled plan for irrigation goes a misuse of water, which results in the erosion of topsoil from the fields. A farmer who leaves his turn-gate open when the flow from the lateral is small may return to find that much of his field has been washed away because farmers farther up the lateral have closed their gates, with a consequent very great increase in flow. A further important feature of the misuse of the water is tied up with the habit of turning the care of fields over to children for considerable periods during the growing season, when parents are busy with ceremonials or other activities. All these practices add up to a serious loss of soil and low crop production.

2. There is failure to adapt to the requirements of intensive agriculture in the same fields year after year. Few Navahos have undertaken crop rotation, with the result that much of the alfalfa acreage and the adjoining cornfields show a diminishing yield each year. In addition, there is resistance to using fertilizer, either in the form of manure, which could be obtained from their own sheep, or of the commercial phosphates available at the local trading post.

3. The Navaho farmers are very lax in the control of insects. Some of the more experienced use hand sprays which they own, or a government-owned sprayer for community use; a few even hire the equipment owned by Mormon farmers across the river. Usually, however, nothing is done about bean beetles or grass-hoppers until they reach scourge proportions. Then sometimes an emergency call goes out to the Navajo Service for help.

Although the value of crops produced on the Fruitland Project has steadily increased during the past ten years, this reflects rising prices more than increased productivity. Agricultural practices such as those just described constitute a major (although not the only) factor in this condition. Any program of improvement must focus here.

A large part of the present condition of the Fruitland Navahos is due to lack of an educational program. That is to say, the Navahos do not have adequate access to the technical knowledge they need.

Even if a full-time extension worker had been on the project since its founding, it is likely he would have had little success if he had not taken into consideration that much of the attitude toward farming which characterized the dry-farm economy of the resettlers has persisted under the new situation. The concept of enriching fields through fertilization and crop rotation has not replaced the older concept of "move on when the land does not yield."

There is also a persistence of certain practices which are obvi-ously brought over from the dry-farm background and are ill-adapted to the new situation. One of these is the use of children during the growing season, children who are uninstructed in the new irrigation techniques.

What little extension work there has been, has ignored the im-portant role of the women and the children in farming. Even though the school was an elementary one, the program could have been furthered by working through the teachers and the children to the mothers in the hogans.

Demonstration on the farms might have been given for the whole Navaho farm family instead of for adult males only. Thus, older methods of sharing agricultural labor within the family might have been modified to fit the new environment.

The relation of the "bad practices" to specific features of Navaho economy, social structure, and religion may be clearly seen in these instances, but it is not enough merely to say that extension workers, if there are enough of them, should concentrate their efforts on these points. Why do Navahos who are noted for interfamily cooperation elsewhere on the Reservation fail to develop such a simple organization as would be required to effect rotation of irrigation along the laterals—one of the most serious needs in the new situation?

The answer here lies not in any persistence of older traits, but rather in their breakdown. The settlement of the project has included Navahos from all over the Reservation, especially in Units I and III. Outfit and kinship groups have been broken up, either before or after moving to Fruitland, and, except to some extent in Unit II, fail to provide a basis for cooperation among families. It is this condition which so far has blocked the growth of organization for management of the water supply, and has resulted in low productivity and the loss of acres of valuable topsoil. We thus see the influence both of persistence and loss of older culture traits in the present situation.

We have noted that when the old social organization persists, as it does to a large degree on Unit II, farming is carried on with greater efficiency: tools are bought and shared cooperatively, the land is tilled, and crops are harvested by the endeavor of related families. In planning for future resettlement Navajo Service might well profit from this experience at Fruitland by allowing the relocation of extended families onto contiguous tracts, thus preserving the cooperative work units.

The old Chapters which were incipient farm associations could have been of great value in extending scientific agriculture and in motivating the community to take a direct interest in the project. However, they were ignored by the administration rather than supported and encouraged.

The project was never envisaged by the Navahos as "theirs" but rather as belonging to the government. One reason for this was that the administrators did not make a distinction between an efficient administrative unit for maintaining the technical side of the project (that is, the irrigation system itself) and effective units for awakening community leadership. So we find that the administration's approach to the people was part and parcel of the maintenance of the irrigation system. They considered the community as one integral whole, just as they did the canal and lateral ditches; whereas in reality there were three separate communities, two of which had a basis of political organization, and a third which could have been patterned likewise. Poor attendance at meetings might have been overcome by calling together residents of the three units separately, thus taking advantage of their feeling of "belonging" to their respective units, a feeling that was not extended to the larger project.

When the Fruitland Project was first inaugurated in the mid-1930's, subsistence farming was in harmony with the over-all Navaho barter economy. However, the sharp acceleration of off-reservation employment ushered in cash economy. The inexperienced and untrained Fruitland farmers preferred to pick the crops of the corporation farmers or work at other types of off-reservation employment. Work on their own farms of small acreage and with minimal skills was less likely to net as great a cash income.

By 1940 it was quite apparent that the project could not offer more than a subsistence living secondary to wage work for those farmers holding only 10 acres. The administration could encourage the growing of crops which would yield a higher return than alfalfa, beans, and corn (the principal crops now being grown), but this could not be done without opening up markets in the vicinity for such crops. Certainly it would be more efficient to consolidate holdings at Fruitland so that each farmer had at least 20 acres, and preferably more. Increased acreage, with improved methods would bring a cash return more commensurate with off-reservation wages and with the income of the white farmers living across the river. In order to accomplish this, some of the farmers would have to be offered newly subjugated lands in return for their assigned plots.

It has been noted, in addition, that lack of personnel, frequent turnover, and sometimes unsuitable personnel in the Indian Service extension work have been important factors. It must be pointed out that faulty personnel management was not within the complete control of Navajo Service. The regulations providing for pay, tenure, upgrading, and so forth, conform to Civil Service regulations established in Washington and are not tailored to the needs of cross-cultural administration in an isolated area. Low pay and lack of the conveniences and the comforts that the civil servant is accustomed to in other parts of the United States tend to discourage Navajo Service employees who seek better jobs elsewhere.

But even if capable persons in sufficient numbers were retained at Fruitland, with knowledge of the lags and disorganization noted, would that be sufficient? The answer is doubtful.

It has been pointed out that the Navahos have the psychology of a defeated people. Their distrust of whites flares up during periods of tension and the Navajo Service becomes the scapegoat for all the wrongs of the past. Furthermore, programs designed for the aid of the Navaho are perceived by the Indians as being to their disadvantage. Alterations in policy, frequently due to shortage of funds, are construed as "broken promises." From the Navaho point of view the advantages of living on the Fruitland Project are outweighed by the disadvantages. The Navaho feeling of insecurity, as expressed in the quotation given previously, prevents the growth of attitudes toward the land which would encourage care of and investment in it.

It is evident that improved agricultural methods will take hold only when the Navaho perception of the innovators has been changed.

Case 7

THE WELLS THAT FAILED: An Attempt to Establish a Stable Water Supply in the Viru Valley, Peru

by Allan R. Holmberg

1. THE PROBLEM

In the village of Viru—a rural community of about 2,000 people which lies in a fertile valley of the same name on the coast of Peru 300 miles north of the capital city of Lima—intensive agriculture has been practiced for the past several thousand years. Because of peculiar geographic and climatic conditions on the coast of Peru, however, it does not rain in Viru, so that the farmers there must depend exclusively on irrigation to grow their crops. Water for this purpose comes from a small river which runs down the center of the valley and which swells periodically during the rainy season in the Andes (December until May). High in the valley which depends for its life on this small stream, the water is diverted into a complex network of irrigation ditches that run the length and breadth of the area. Consequently, little if any of the stream ever reaches the sea.

The supply of water in Viru, however, is neither great nor constant. The river is generally dry from May until December, and even during the rainy season in the Andes water does not always descend in quantities sufficient to irrigate all the fields. For this reason, yields are often diminished; sometimes crops fail completely. At best the farmer can hope to harvest but one crop a year even though the climate in which he lives is favorable, and the land on which he farms fertile enough, to raise two. The lack of an adequate and secure water supply, therefore, may be regarded as the principal drawback to economic security and to agricultural expansion in this valley.

Most of the farmers of Viru are too poor to undertake irrigation projects of their own. Through their political representatives, however, they had for years been soliciting the Peruvian government for aid. Many promises had been made, but few had ever been fulfilled. Nevertheless, in August, 1947, the government finally decided to drill six wells in strategic parts of the valley, the water of which was to be piped to the village for household needs and for a sewage system, as well as to augment the supply of water for irrigation at those times when the river would be dry. The offer was reciprocal in the sense that it entailed a certain amount of collaboration from people of the village in such matters as the building of trails, the removal of rock, and the digging of ditches—a collaboration that was promised by the *Junta Transitoria*, or Transitory Board, then in charge of municipal affairs.

In spite of the obvious advantages of this offer, which was immediately publicized by the *Junta* (by word of mouth), the people of the village displayed a marked lack of interest in, and in some cases outright opposition to, the project even before it began. Although the government made good its offer and one technically successful well was eventually drilled—under no few difficulties, to be sure—the project was later abandoned, largely for lack of favorable response from the very people who had for years voiced the loudest complaints about the scanty water supply.

Why, then, were the people of Viru reluctant to get behind a project so likely to fulfill a long-desired village need? And in view of the fact that nothing beneficial resulted—rather, that harm was done—what could have been done to enlist the support of the village so that the project might have been a success?

2. THE COURSE OF EVENTS

1. Before deciding to drill the wells, the Peruvian government sent a geological commission to survey the possibilities of ensuring the success of the venture. In company with the water commissioner of Viru, the geologists made a reconnaissance of the upper part of the valley near the village. Their report was favorable, and a number of sites most likely to yield water were selected and marked.

2. The one chosen for first drilling lay on private land near the main irrigation ditch about two miles up the valley from the village. Shortly thereafter, two technicians arrived and the well-drilling equipment was hauled into the village. Before operations could start, however, it was necessary to repair and widen a road which passed near the site and to open a trail from the main road to the spot where the first well was to be drilled. This was a community responsibility.

The *Junta* had trouble finding people who were willing to help, even though at this time of year (September) no agricultural work was going on. The harvest in Viru is generally in July and the farmer cannot again begin to prepare his fields for sowing until December, when there is some hope that water for irrigation will soon descend from the mountains. Moreover, there were no funds in the municipal treasury to hire the necessary workers. The *Junta* went into debt, therefore, to pay for the labor needed to widen and repair the road. Even then few people responded to the call. Finally, with great difficulty, the machinery was hauled to the site.

3. Meanwhile, the technicians themselves encountered trouble in finding a place to live or even a place to eat. Moreover, working at a distance of two miles from town with no way of getting out and back except on foot, it was both exhausting and uneconomical for them to return for lunch each midday; yet, at first, no one could be induced to send lunch to them or to pack it so they could eat at the site.

Nevertheless, they had a job to do and they began work at once. The drilling itself went smoothly enough because the technicians could carry out this operation with machinery alone.

4. While the well was being drilled, however, few people showed enough interest even to visit the site. Exceptions included the water commissioner (part of whose job it was), the man on whose property the operations were taking place, and some members of the *Junta*. In the village, reactions to the well were varied: a few were enthusiastic about it; some were skeptical of its possible success; and others knew nothing about it. Still others spoke openly against it, saying that it was all politics, that the geologists

and technicians did not know their business, that the site selected was a poor one, and that if water were struck the village would not benefit by it anyway. The technicians were somewhat surprised by such hostile attitudes and lack of interest, since the well was not costing the village a centavo, but they went about their work without seriously complaining until their first job was done —and a hard one it was, for it took them more than thirty days to drill through a hundred feet of solid rock. At this depth the well gave a constant flow that was considered adequate to justify the drilling of another. However, in view of the lack of sufficient help and favorable response from the villagers, both the engineer and the technicians recommended termination of the project.

5. On the part of the villagers the reaction to this conclusion was one of "I told you so." The technicians left, the equipment was withdrawn, and by April, 1948—the last time the writer visited the village—a pump had not even been installed on the well that had been drilled. Thus Viru, as far as its water supply was concerned, was in the same condition that it had been before the project was started. Meanwhile, hostility toward the national government had increased and thousands of dollars had been uselessly spent on a project that might have resulted in success.

3. RELEVANT FACTORS

In order to understand why events took the turn they did, it will be necessary to call attention to a few facts about the culture of Viru and to a few of the circumstances that existed at the time the well was being drilled.

In the first place, the village itself is made up largely of small landowners and sharecroppers. The majority of these are natives of the valley who depend for their subsistence on small plots of irrigated land from two to ten acres in size but some of whom, for commercial purposes, also sharecrop on large haciendas outside the village, paying as rent 25 per cent of the crop.

At the same time, the village contains a few large landowners not all of whom are native-born, but some of whom through unscrupulous practices and unfair dealings have managed to accumulate land holdings of considerable size. In some cases, for example, these large holdings include parcels which formerly belonged to the community and the church and which were secured through shady deals. As a result, the community is normally split along two main lines: on the one hand, there is a dichotomy between large and small landowners; on the other, between natives born in Viru and *forasteros* (people from the outside). Needless to say, members of these groups do not always see eye to eye, especially on serious matters. Moreover, outsiders in general have less status than the natives and the large landowners are more prestigeful than the small.

In the second place, national political conditions existing at the time bear considerable relevance to an understanding of the course of events. The political party then in power was the so-called liberal or APRA (Alianza Popular Revolucionaria Americana), one of the main planks of whose platform was to break up the large estates and wealthy power groups and to return the lands and the rule to the people. Being underdogs, the majority of small farmers and sharecroppers in Viru—that is to say, the bulk of the population—were either members of the liberal party or gave considerable lip service to it. On the other hand, certain power groups as represented by the larger landowners and the priest—some of whom were highly respected in the community—were violently opposed to the liberal party and thoroughly disapproved of its aims. The community was therefore further split along political lines, and rather widely so.

In the third place, municipal affairs were in the hands of a Transitory Board. Until this time local government had been the charge of a Municipal Council, the principal members of which had always been appointed by the prefect of the Political Department, who was himself an appointee of the national government in Lima. This system made for strong central government which had always been the policy of dictatorships in Peru. The liberal party planned to change all this; in fact, their congress was discussing a bill to legalize municipal elections for the first time in Peruvian history. But as a temporary measure and to give time to prepare rural areas for this change, Transitory Boards were set up (in the same way that Municipal Councils had been previously appointed) to govern at the local level. Because of a scarcity of enlightened liberal party leadership in the rural areas, however, the government was sometimes hard put to find educated local personnel to appoint to these boards. As a result, it was necessary either to make appointments from the outside or to be satisfied with inferior local personnel. In appointing the Board of Viru, a combination of these two alternatives was resorted to.

For a further understanding of this case, attention should be called to another cultural factor, namely, the status system. Positions of prestige in Viru are not assigned only to those of good family and wealth; they may be gained also by those of more humble birth and means. The principal channels for acquiring prestige in the community are wealth, education, the institutions of *compadrazco*, and the religious fiesta. Having reached the pinnacles of success in this system—as reflected by being a man of means, of some learning, the godfather to many children, and having been the first steward of the religious fiesta of the patron saint—one is in a position to assume the highest responsibilities of leadership and power as expressed by being appointed mayor of the Municipal Council. Under normal circumstances one cannot arrive at such a position, which takes a long period of time, without at least having been born in the village.

A final cultural factor to which some attention should be directed is that of the value system. Not long before the well was drilled, Viru was a relatively isolated village; actually, it was put in ready contact with the outside world only after 1939, when an asphalt highway connecting it with other coastal valleys in Peru was completed. Until that time ideas of change and progress, as typified by modern science and technology, had hardly entered the minds of most villagers; rather, their outlook on life, as typified by religion and magic, was essentially static and pessimistic. Lacking scientific knowledge and techniques to control their water supply, they had for years relied on religious beliefs to explain their lack of water and on magical means to ensure whatever supply they did enjoy. In other words, such natural phenomena as the water were thought to be controlled by supernatural forces—as represented by images of the Catholic saints—which could be influenced only by the observance of magico-religious rites, specifically by the celebration of the feast days of certain saints. In Viru, for example, the first water of the new agricultural year generally appears in the irrigation ditch soon after the celebration of the fiesta of the Virgin of Sorrow, which occurs on the twelfth of December. If the year is dry, it is believed that this fiesta has not been properly celebrated and that the Virgin is castigating the people. If the year continues to be dry, the image of St. Isidore, patron of farmers, may be taken out on a religious procession and worshipped at the river until water comes. If crops fail completely, people are being punished for their sins. On the other hand, if the year has been good and the harvest bountiful, it is attributed to the fact that the Catholic saints, who control the weather, the insect pests, and the water supply, have been abundantly honored by religious fiestas and are thus favorably disposed toward man. In this connection it is significant to remember that at the time the well was being drilled many of the people of Viru subscribed to these magico-religious ideas and practices with respect to the water supply.

Answer Questions Presented in the Problem
Before Reading the Rest of the Case.

4. ANALYSIS

We are now in a position to disclose a number of significant reasons for the failure of this project. In the first place, local people, many of whom knew a great deal about the water supply of the valley, were little consulted by the technical commission or the technical staff; in fact, they were almost completely ignored. One of these people, for instance, had had considerable experience in drilling wells on his own land and was thoroughly acquainted with water conditions in the valley; yet, he was bypassed by the technical commission. Moreover, he was a native of the village, with wealth, prestige, and power, and had formerly been a member of the Municipal Council. Actually at the time, he was the most powerful informal leader in the village. While strongly against the political party then in power, he opposed the project not so much on political grounds as on the grounds that he was not consulted in the planning stage and that he was slighted by the technical commission and even members of the Transitory Board, who regarded him as their political enemy. Consequently, he used none of his influence and prestige to support the project but spoke openly against it, saying that it was sure to fail.

In the second place, the site for drilling the first well fell on the property of a large landowner against whom—although he was a native of the village—there was considerable hostility on the part of some of the large landowners and many of the small ones. For this reason, many people suspected that the owner of the property alone would benefit from the drilling of the well. Moreover, some of the sites selected by the commission were located on public lands, so that the people thought that the first operation at least should have taken place on them. It should be mentioned, however, that the first site picked by the technical commission was in no way related to the question of whose land it was situated on; it was selected solely because of its likelihood of yielding an abundant supply of water and because of its proximity to the village. Nevertheless, many of the villagers believed otherwise and thought that they would never benefit from a well drilled on this particular site.

In the third place, the local governing body was transitory and its principal members were neither native-born Viruñeros nor representative of the real leadership of the community. The principal member of the Transitory Board, the mayor, did not even reside in the village but on a neighboring *hacienda*. He only rarely visited the village and delegated most of his duties to the lieutenant mayor. Although a resident of the village, he had been born in another part of Peru. He was besides a *curandero* (native medical practitioner), whose reputation for healing among many of the people was not high. In addition, he had the reputation of being a meddler and an opportunist who was generally insincere. A third member of the board, the secretary, although not an official of much importance, was a local boy and a member of an old family in Viru. But he was unmarried and was so young that he had not gained much prestige through the channels previously mentioned. Moreover, he typified the younger progressive members of the community, who were at this time far in the minority.

In the fourth place, members of the Transitory Board themselves showed a lack of interest in the project. Neither was there support from the prestige elements in the community, such as the priest, the director of the school, the public and lay-religious officials. For that matter, even the people of the village were little informed about what was going on and therefore became suspicious of the motives of the *Junta* and the activities of the technicians. As a result, malicious rumors about the project circulated freely and many people became hostile to it simply for a lack of accurate information.

Finally, quite a large group of prestigeful men in the village conceived of this operation, consciously or unconsciously, as a threat to an old way of life which they valued highly and which for some time they had been fighting to conserve. To be sure, it had been a losing battle ever since it began, for the termination of the asphalt highway had made possible a considerable flow of modern technology and new ideas, one of the results of which was that the old value system—as typified by the patriarchal family, the *compadrazgo* system, the religious fiesta, and the cult of the saints—had already begun to break down. Actually, a lack of water during the intervening years between the completion of the highway and the drilling of the well was explained by these people as the consequence of the waning of the customary religious practices. In fact, many members of this conservative element were heard to remark that before the coming of modern influences there seldom had been any lack of water in Viru because the cult of the saints had been strictly practiced. This idea, of course, received reinforcement from the priest, who bitterly railed against the increasing secularization that had accompanied the modernization process. Consequently, this group, while it did not openly oppose the project, gave it no support.

In view of the foregoing circumstances, what might have been done to have enhanced the chances for the success of this project? In an *ex post facto* analysis of this kind, of course, no one solution can be final. But a number of possibilities come to mind.

1. More advice should have been sought from local people, even though most of them knew little about the technical aspects of the potential water supply of the valley. Such a suggestion does not mean that the technical commission would have had to accept as final the decision of the villagers as to where to drill the well. But had the question been discussed with the local people (with a committee of leaders, at least)—not an unknown practice in Viru—it would have been possible to explain the objectives of the project and why it was necessary to select the sites exclusively with reference to their potential water supply. If such a meeting had been held during one of the important religious fiestas, for example, when almost everyone comes to town, it might have been possible to have broken down resistance to, and gained considerable support for, the project even before it began.

2. The first well should have been drilled on land other than that of a large landowner who was little respected in the community; particularly since good potential sites had already been located on public lands by the technical commission. Such a step would have helped to eliminate the suspicion of many people that the village as a whole would not benefit from the drilling of

the well, and it would have provided a sound basis for wide community participation.

3. The Transitory Board, since it did not represent the real leadership of the village, should not have been the only local group consulted. Every community contains informal leaders who are often more influential than the people actually holding office. In this instance, therefore, some attempt should have been made to find out who these leaders were and to gain their support for the project. As it happens, it would have been relatively easy to have enlisted the aid of the priest, the director of the school, members of the local sports club, and many farmers and merchants who were highly respected in the community. And if in gaining this support it was found impossible to work with the *Junta*, attempts should have been made to change its membership or by-pass it rather than to let the project fail.

4. The central institution of the religious fiesta itself, or the cult of the saints, might have been employed to publicize and dramatize the scientific techniques of drilling wells. Had the support of the priest and the lay-religious officials been gained, for example, the site could have received the proper religious blessing, or a religious procession could have been held to it, all of which would have helped to enlist the support of the conservative elements who later opposed the project.

These are but a few of the possibilities that could have been tried in order to enhance the likelihood of success in this venture. It happens that the gathering of data presented here was incidental to a larger study under preparation at the same time. But if a capable social scientist had been sent in beforehand specifically to investigate the factors likely to lead to success or failure in a project of this kind, the significant ones could have been discovered in a relatively short period of time—say, a month. And had such a course been adopted and had the social scientist's recommendations been taken into account in planning the project, there is every likelihood that Viru, after 400 years of suffering from lack of water, would have at least obtained a secure supply.

SUGGESTIONS FOR STUDY: Interviewing

It would be useful now to test the skill developed in distinguishing roles. One method of doing this is role-playing. Let students assume the different roles that appear in one of the cases and enact those roles while another student, who is attempting to solve the problem, questions them in an effort to obtain the information he needs. There should be enough data in the cases just given and in those to follow for the establishment of some roles in considerable detail.

To carry out role-playing profitably, students will require some knowledge of good interviewing technique. It is not our purpose to attempt giving instructions on interviewing,[1] but there are some points worth stressing that are particularly relevant to cross-cultural situations. Here there is need for the greatest possible degree of spontaneity and the least forcing of expression into a mold of the interviewer's making. Good results can rarely be achieved through a systematic question and answer procedure, wholly controlled by the interviewer. Rather, it requires the creation of a situation in which there is maximum opportunity for the interviewee to associate ideas in his own way and to follow his own interests. Under such circumstances, the interviewer in a cross-cultural situation is much more likely to get through to the ways of thinking and feeling really characteristic of the culture in which he is working.

The following procedure in connection with role-playing may prove useful. For each of the following cases, let a student prepare a checklist of questions and thoroughly familiarize himself with them, so that he knows them *without referring* to his notes. Then, after definition and assignment of roles to other students, let this student conduct a series of interviews with his questions merely in mind, not written out before him. It should be emphasized that he will have a very clear-cut, twofold problem, namely, the maintenance of a spontaneous interview, largely

[1] See Garrett, Annette, *Interviewing:* Its Principles and Methods. Family Service Association of America, New York, 1942.

guided by the interest of the interviewee, and at the same time the acquisition of information which has been systematically outlined in the checklist of questions. If the student visualizes the process of interviewing in the following way, it may help him deal with this twofold problem.

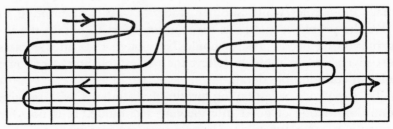

HYPOTHETICAL COURSE OF AN INTERVIEW

In the diagram the squares represent the items of information which the student has systematically determined that he needs for the solution of a problem. The curving line represents the course of the interview. It may not begin at the point the interviewer had expected, or disclose the items in the order in which he had thought of them. Perhaps a first interview, moreover, does not touch on all the items. Nevertheless, through skilfully keeping the interviewee talking along the lines of his own interest, and in his own way, answers to most of the questions can be obtained—perhaps to all those concerning which the interviewee has anything valuable to offer. Additional items of information may be obtained in a second interview or from interviews with other persons.

Case 8

ESKIMO HERDSMEN: Introduction of Reindeer Herding to the Natives of Alaska

by Margaret Lantis

1. THE PROBLEM

During the period 1892 to 1902, through public and private effort, reindeer were imported from Siberia for the benefit of Alaskan Eskimos. After the heavy slaughter of whales, walrus, and other sea mammals by the train-oil industry in the second half of the nineteenth century, the Eskimos needed a new source of food. Reindeer, like their relatives, the undomesticated American caribou, were especially useful since they provided not only food, but also skins for parkas, long sinews for thread and cord, and antlers for knife handles and other implements. Finally, there was a small market for the meat and it was hoped that the Eskimos could get needed cash income from its sale together with that of skins.

By the 1930's it was obvious, however, that the new native industry was not functioning as expected. There was inadequate control and use of the reindeer, which were thought to number many thousands and which by then had been distributed the full length of west Alaska. Also, since white men now had many deer, there was conflict over their ownership.

By 1938 the principal administrative policy problems were: (1) Should whites own reindeer? (2) Should individual ownership or associations (corporations) be encouraged among Eskimos? (3) Where and how should the reindeer be marketed? Or should they be used only for native consumption? (4) Were the herds in the most suitable locations? (5) What was the best system of herding? (6) What was the best system of marking the animals for identification or of allocating them so that ownership was undisputed?

After 1939–1940, when all reindeer owned by whites were purchased by the federal government to be returned to the native people for establishment of a solely native industry, the second question became the biggest problem. Did individual ownership, or communal ownership by each Eskimo village in some form of association, appeal more to the Eskimo? Which would work better in his culture and in his physical situation, and hence provide the best development and utilization of the herds? Should the associations that had been organized in some localities be abolished or extended?

2. THE COURSE OF EVENTS

1. A total of 1,280 reindeer, a few hundred at a time, were introduced at Teller, on Seward Peninsula west of Nome, and as they increased in size were gradually sent with Lapp and Eskimo herders to most of the large coastal communities from Point Barrow on the north to Kodiak, Umnak, and Atka Islands on the south. When this program was initiated in the 1890's, several church missions had an official connection with the Bureau of Education by means of which their missionaries were employed also as teachers in the federal school system. Reindeer, therefore, were entrusted to the mission schools (representing eight different denominations), as well as to the first secular schools, and both herds and herders were under the general supervision of the teachers. The following system of distributing deer locally was established. Individual Eskimos were lent 100 reindeer, provided they agreed to care for them, train apprentices, and repay at the end of five years the number of animals borrowed; they were permitted to keep whatever increase there was. For pay as a herder, the government gave an apprentice a specified small number of deer and an amount of supplies annually for four years, and allowed him two months' schooling each year. The last benefit usually was not achieved, however. When an apprentice's herd numbered 100, he engaged an apprentice himself; when 150, another apprentice, and so on, until he had four. Eskimos who received the original loans of deer had been especially trained at Teller by Lapps brought there for the purpose.

The Nome Gold Rush created a new demand for meat, and the price of reindeer doubled. After the rush subsided and, according to a ballad, "the miners left the country where they hadn't made a cent," the market for reindeer meat became small, but steady.

2. From 1915 on, deer came increasingly into possession of white men, although it was originally intended that they should be held only by or for the native peoples, whether Eskimo, Aleut, or Indian. The white owners had a different interest and objective: they sought to develop the large potential stateside market for reindeer meat, which tastes much like beef and a little like venison, though it is not so gamy. Since the reindeer through the 1930's were allowed to run in very large herds with a minimum of herding, the deer of various owners came together and mingled. Any one herd, especially on Seward Peninsula at the north side of Bering Sea, probably would contain reindeer belonging to individual Eskimo owners, Eskimo community associations, Lapps, and local white businessmen. In some places religious missions also owned reindeer that ran with the others.

3. The government Reindeer Service encouraged in Eskimo communities the formation of reindeer-owning associations. Most herd-owners in a village (in some communities, all owners) would contribute their animals as capital and would form a corporation. A board or council would be elected by the members to manage its affairs. In practice, all members were simply co-owners of herds in which they had reindeer. There was a minimum of formal organization and procedure. The manner in which members were credited with reindeer increase or profit will be explained later. Apparently, roundups were held and animals slaughtered at a time determined by the council, usually with the advice of the reindeer superintendent. The real day-to-day functioning of these associations has never been described, so far as the author has been able to ascertain.

4. The results of multiplication of ownership are not surprising: conflict between Eskimo and white owners, straying of animals, and decreasing interest on the part of the Eskimos. When they ceased trying to protect their herds, they no longer derived potential value from them, and the old need for food and cash income, especially the latter, continued.

5. In the late 1930's a Subcommittee of the Senate Committee on Indian Affairs held hearings in Nome and elsewhere on the reindeer industry and other problems pertaining to the welfare of native Alaskans. The Northwestern Livestock Corporation, dominated by a white family in Nome, largest owner and principal target of Eskimo charges of unfair practices, finally offered to sell its reindeer and slaughterhouses to the federal government. This offer, plus the findings of the Senate Subcommittee which were published in 1939, facilitated the Bureau of Indian Affairs' proposal to buy all nonnative-owned deer and to reestablish the industry as a solely native enterprise. In 1939, $750,000 was authorized for purchase of reindeer, abattoirs, and other equipment from 40 owners: individuals (including Lapps), missions, and companies.

6. Since evidently no thorough roundup and accurate tally had been made after 1923, it is not surprising that both the Reindeer Service and the private owners, especially the Livestock Corporation, steadily and excessively increased their estimates of the number of deer without adequate check. The Reindeer Service, for example, estimated 600,000 reindeer in Alaska, including native and nonnative ownership, based on a 1937 roundup and count of 175,000 animals, a count then thought to be quite incomplete. The Livestock Corporation, called locally the Lomen Company, had estimated its total number at 250,000 head, based on the known increase rate of reindeer but without adequate account of losses.

When the deer were at last rounded up in 1940 and counted with fair accuracy, the Livestock Corporation was found to have only 87,000 animals, of which 14,000 to 15,000 were on Nunivak Island in Bering Sea. The 1940 roundups, therefore, were an essential conclusion to the controversy between the Eskimos and the Lomens.

7. Very few condemnation suits were brought. Most owners sold to the government willingly, at prices ranging from $3.00 a head for most herds to $11 for the good herd on Nunivak Island. Average payment per head was $3.74. Total expenditure was less than the appropriation!

8. The four abattoirs owned by the Northwestern Livestock Corporation were closed—other white owners and Eskimos slaughtered their animals in the open—and a slaughterhouse in a new location, on Nunivak Island, was planned in order to get the herds away from the overgrazed areas.

9. New personnel was brought as rapidly as possible into the Reindeer Service, which now was under the Alaska Native Service, Alaska branch of the Bureau of Indian Affairs.

10. Before we unfold the further developments, let us look at the Eskimos' economic and community life, in both proto-historic times and as it has been developing since 1940. We must keep in mind that, although the chief problem posed here pertains to type of ownership of reindeer herds, the technical questions of herd management are as basic. Material needs of the animals, needs of the industry as a production system, and personal needs of the native people—all are "givens" that must be taken into account.

3. RELEVANT FACTORS

In their aboriginal hunting and fishing, Alaskan Eskimos had both individualistic and cooperative systems. In hunting the caribou, which formerly numbered several millions in the Territory, the people of northwest Alaska, e.g., on the Kobuk and Noatak Rivers, had large communal drives. One common method was to drive the deer into a lake where hunters, concealed in kayaks among reeds or bushes, could shoot the swimming or wading animals with bow and arrow. Women, children, everyone who could keep the pace, participated in such drives. In the Nunivak-Lower Kuskokwim River region and in the rugged mountainous area of southwest Alaska, apparently more often one family or two hunter-partners would stalk caribou, using various ruses. Mountain sheep, wolves, and other land animals customarily were trapped or hunted by one man, or a man and his close kin, or a man and his partner. When large seal-nets were set under the ice or large nets were used to take sea-birds on their cliff rookeries, at least two hunters naturally had to work together.

The most common type of hunting with projectiles, particularly with the harpoon, was the seal hunt, and in this the hunter was a complete unit, an individualistic competitor. The Aleuts had a system whereby individual kayak-men came together in a circle around a sea-otter in open water, and there were other variations from the individual-hunter formula. Yet, these involved only momentary cooperation, not a large or long-term association. The nearest to the latter was the whale-boat (umiak) crew which persisted throughout a season and might last several seasons. For whaling and walrus hunting, the boat-owner selected each man for his special skill and endurance.

A long-term association for work and ritual existed among the occupants of a men's ceremonial house. (This institution was more important on the coast than in the interior.) In a large village there would be two or more men's houses, each with a leader. As in the umiak crew, there were emotional and material rewards for identification with a strong, successful man.

Demonstration of individual skill, good sense or wisdom, possession of supernatural power, and persistence gained a man prestige. Important in securing a position of leadership and highest prestige was the additional trait of generosity. Individual effectiveness, in which skill and persistence were necessary and in which supernatural help was assumed to be present, was the over-all essential qualification. How can a man demonstrate his skill today? Herding reindeer is not nearly so spectacular as killing a walrus or a polar bear, moose, or mountain sheep.

Just before and during the time that whites entered the reindeer industry, the United States Bureau of Education sponsored Reindeer Fairs. In 1916 at Igloo, near Nome, representatives of ten villages competed in many contests to determine: the fastest sled deer, the best-trained deer for driving, who could catch and break a bull to drive most quickly, who could butcher and dress a carcass the cleanest and fastest. There were additional contests: in song writing about reindeer, shooting with bow and arrow and with rifle, snowshoe racing, and other sports. Sleds, harness, and clothing also were judged. The competitive emphasis on skill, the showing-off of fur clothing and other fine homemade possessions, the resourcefulness displayed in long travel by reindeer sled across strange country to reach Igloo—all fitted into the Eskimo system of individual prestige. During the rapid expansion of the private Livestock Corporation in the 1920's, however, the tone became one of big business rather than native festival.

One must consider also location of the communities and mobility of their inhabitants. Alaskan Eskimos, even in pre-European times, were not like Eskimos on the Arctic coasts of Canada. They did not travel in large arcs of migration, building a new snowhouse every night. (This was a slight exaggeration and a proto-historic rather than old prehistoric development even for most Canadian Eskimos.) The Alaskans lived in houses that were built as well as they could be with local materials (drift logs, whale bones, sod, mud, and hides from walrus and caribou). They were constantly on the move, it is true, but they were excursionists, making short trips in safe areas, since warfare was a real threat. As soon as possible, they returned to permanent habitations. Even though in the summer they might occupy tents, especially where influenced by either Athabaskan Indians or Siberian Chukchee, they still tried to erect these at some favorable spot on river, bay, or island where there were a few other people. At the same time a family was self-reliant enough to travel off wherever it had to go to obtain food. Necessity could always override preference.

When missions and Bureau of Education schools (later transferred to the Alaska Native Service) were established, when traders built stores, and when miners and trappers settled down to be sourdoughs, the Eskimos were encouraged to live in the larger villages the year round. Teachers were most anxious about the welfare of the children in this respect. Devastating epidemics of smallpox, measles, and diphtheria virtually wiped out many small settlements, and the few survivors moved to the remaining villages. Hence, the trend has been decrease in number of communities and increase in their population.

No matter whether ancestral Eskimos got most of their food from caribou or from seals—anthropologists argue this point— there is not much question that at the time the reindeer were introduced most Alaskan Eskimos were oriented more to the sea than to the interior. All of them, however, would hunt inland when animals were available. The combination of caribou or mountain-sheep hunting, fishing, bird hunting, and sea-mammal harpooning or netting required seasonal variation. One month a group would go upriver for fish, next month to the coast, getting seal-oil by trade or by catching seals under the new autumn ice. The shifts in movement, the trips here and there, depended upon rumor of good hunting, a desire to consult a shaman, a wish to visit a relative, or the depletion of food stored along one's trap-line. Since a herd of domestic animals, in contrast, must be moved more methodically, and must be watched at all times, an adjustment in economic habits was required.

In the early days of the reindeer business, the European system of "close herding" was used, with good results for the deer. This system means staying with the herd constantly, through blizzard, spring thaw, and summer mosquitoes, through holidays and hunting seasons. Long-term results for herd-owners might be good, but short-term effects were likely to be dispiriting or at least uninteresting.

To hold the reindeer together and to guard them every moment, which were the purposes of close herding, the size of each group had to be limited. Although unmanageable size was no problem up to about 1920, the deer seemed to multiply faster than man's knowledge and interest in managing them.

Before and especially during the period when the Eskimo community associations for reindeer management were sponsored by the Reindeer Service many problems developed, some of which continued into the new regime of the 1940's:

1. The necessary number of earmarks for identification increased confusingly. It was not easy to determine ownership from the slices, swallow-tail cuts, and other marks on the ears. And no other system has even yet been found satisfactory, such as hot-iron branding—the reindeer coat is much too heavy and the skin is too thin—or metal tags on the ears.

2. As the herds grew, it was more difficult to protect them from wolf, lynx, and other predator. Reindeer react much like sheep and are easily stampeded.

3. When the herds spread inland, they encountered the American caribou on their great migrations. Being closely related, the reindeer were often carried off by caribou unless alertly herded. It is as if the pioneers on the United States frontier had tried to herd half-domesticated bison, without fences, when the great bison migrations were moving north and south on the high plains.

4. Until large-scale commercial herding developed, a fawn was "marked to its mother," but when herders did not or could not know their animals, marking could not be done accurately and quarrels over ownership ensued.

5. Having to find their own forage during the long, hard winters, reindeer were likely to be weakened and to need protection, especially at fawning time. The lichens, on which the animals feed in winter, were being depleted, particularly on Seward Peninsula, where the deer were first introduced. As it requires twenty-five years or more to "bring back" thoroughly depleted lichens, careless herding engendered long-range as well as immediate problems.

6. There were the parasites: the bot-fly whose larvae infest the nose of the reindeer, weakening them, almost maddening them, and the warble-fly whose larvae burrow through the skin, decreasing the commercial value of the hides. These also can be combated by care in moving the herd from an infested range.

7. Without system or facilities for marketing meat, the associations could not get money to hire enough herders, to replace the original owner-herders.

During the period 1915 to 1930 some of the government reindeer superintendents were not strong leaders, did not understand the business, or did not have sufficient conviction of its value, and hence the Eskimos gradually stopped trying to make the system work. Certain range rules that were intended to solve the problems noted above reveal considerable ineptness in the Reindeer Service. In 1931 it issued new regulations that were quite complicated. These allocated a percentage of the annual increase of animals to each local co-owner of a herd and a smaller percentage to owners of strays from other herds. Moreover, these percentages varied according to the total percentage of increase each year, entailing still more figuring of the number of adult females and fawns. When, by such allocation and marking, an owner was "over" or "short" he was debited or credited reindeer. One can imagine how difficult it was to sort and mark fawns, tally accurately, and figure percentages in the terrific hurly-burly and noise of corralling several thousand terrified deer, often in bad weather. Moreover, it is doubtful whether the rules were accurately translated into the Eskimo language. At any rate, the marking never was accurate, and as a result every owner had "overs" or "shorts" each year until finally he did not know what his herd numbered.

Nevertheless, with the large numbers of reindeer of so many different owners running together, with fawns separated from their mothers, and with so many adult strays, some scheme for crediting animals to owners had to be used.

Let us turn from the beginning to the end of reindeer management, from identification of the fawn to disposal of the meat. In planning the marketing of meat and skins, the following factors must be considered:

1. There are no docks along Bering Sea or the Arctic Ocean where the herds are located; hence, there are lighterage charges to transport carcasses from shore to ship and equipment from ship to shore.

2. The freight charges of the few ships that have refrigerator space are high.

3. Ships can reach such places as Kotzebue and Derring for a very limited season and usually come on short notice when the weather happens to be good, making it difficult for herd-owner or manager to know when and how many animals to butcher, especially if he does not have much cold-storage space.

4. Although at a few fields cargo planes now can be used profitably, most village "fields" still cannot accommodate large enough aircraft for shipping the bulky carcasses in quantity. On the other hand, there are many more small airfields now than there were before the war, and the bush pilots, who carry both freight and passengers, fly more regularly and more often.

5. Public demands regarding meat condition are more rigorous than they were thirty years ago when the business first boomed commercially. Deer can no longer be butchered on the beach and fresh carcasses loaded on the ship to be refrigerated en route. They must now be hung (bled) and cleaned properly, cooled, frozen, and stored in deep-freeze, and sacked in stockinette or, as some of the Eskimos say, the deer must have on their underwear when they go traveling.

6. In the United States, the best markets for luxury meats are New York and other cities of the East, requiring another 3,000 miles of freight charges. Some states prohibit sale of reindeer meat, classifying it as game. Finally, there is no steady market, since most Americans prefer beef, no matter how good the reindeer may be.

7. Although Alaskan markets in communities along the large rivers can be reached by newly introduced shallow-draft refrigerator barges, many other potential markets, especially on islands, cannot be served with any regularity because of weather hazard.

Throughout the history of reindeer in Alaska, there has been a local market, among both Eskimos and whites, for skins to be made into parkas and boots. In the colder regions two parkas are worn, the inner one with the fur turned next to the skin. Eskimos also use the coarse, thick winter hide for a mattress and make lighter reindeer skins into sleeping bags.

During World War II an organization developed that was helpful to the reindeer industry of northwest Alaska as a whole, though it had little effect in the southwest part of the territory. The Nome Skin-sewers was formed to make fawnskin parkas and similar garments for the Air Force and other government agencies, and later for more general marketing through the Alaska Native Service. Eskimo women in and near Nome tanned and stitched the skins to order. The value of the Skin-sewers' product in 1946 (latest year for which we have figures) was $32,081. Organization of community stores was a more widespread development, although of less importance to the industry. These stores provided not only purchasing but also marketing facilities for clothing and other craft products.

World War I brought a few troops but not until World War II was there any large influx of people into central and west Alaska. By that time, that is, after 1942, there were no large slaughtering and marketing operations. The armed services could ship meat from the States more dependably and probably more cheaply than they could get it locally. Large construction projects and population growth in the 1940's did, however, facilitate a shift to a money economy, and this had indirect effects on the industry.

The war had some of the same results in northwest Alaska that it had in villages of the States: men and even whole families moved to the centers of war construction. Since native responsibility for the herds had been deteriorating throughout the 1920's and 1930's, the occurrence of a great war immediately after the Reindeer Service launched its new program was a serious obstacle to redevelopment or initiation of local responsibility. But again, good effects partially counterbalanced the bad. The war created a market for fawn-skin clothing.

Although this provided greater incentive for killing than for conserving animals, loss by excessive or indiscriminate slaughtering was not so great as loss (1) by mere straying, due chiefly to poor herding, and (2) by wolf depredations. The conflicts between whites and natives, the inappropriate policies of the Reindeer Service before the war, and the disruption caused by the war finally culminated in a serious decrease of animals, leaving less than a third of the number purchased by the government in 1939–1940.

Wolves were unusually numerous from 1946 through 1949. In the Shungnak herd, for example, they caused a known loss of 75 animals in a herd of about 770 deer during the winter and spring of 1947–1948, despite the herder's trapping of eight of them. The killing of four wolves around the Hooper Bay herd in the winter of 1947–1948 stopped molestation that season, but there already had been a reported loss of 107 head from a herd numbering fewer than 600. It looked as though this was too big a problem for local herders alone.

The competing attractions—and also hazards—of wage work, hunting, trapping, and reindeer ownership provided a much more complex situation than that in the 1890's, when reindeer were introduced.

The developments we have surveyed indicate the final big factor to be cited—acculturation. It is so comprehensive that "factor" is an inadequate designation. On the Arctic Coast from Seward Peninsula to Barrow at the topmost point, acculturation has gone further and more rapidly than in the deltas of the Kuskokwim and Yukon Rivers on Bering Sea between the Seward Peninsula and the Alaska Peninsula to the south. Below this area the Aleuts and the Eskimo-Aleut-Indian population on

Bristol Bay and the Alaska Peninsula have been thoroughly acculturated for more than a generation but the question of community association vs. individual control of herds was not involved. All herds but one in the region are government-owned, simply providing food and skins for local native consumption. St. Lawrence Island, in the northern part of Bering Sea, is a special case. Its people, who had a reindeer association, were isolated, yet "modernized" and well-to-do, largely because of good walrus-hunting, fox trapping, and a craft of walrus-ivory carving.

In the acculturation process, Eskimos have been learning simple accounting, pricing, and other aspects of trade. Also, they have been learning forage resources, range requirements of reindeer, and other aspects of their own environment that they could previously take for granted or disregard. Acculturation has affected the Eskimo value system, bringing to it approximately the same attitudes and needs that modern industrial American culture has brought to other parts of North America.

Given the above ecological and cultural conditions, what could the Reindeer Service do?

REFERENCES FOR FURTHER STUDY

"Alaska [including Reindeer]," Hearings Before a Subcommittee of the Committee on Indian Affairs, United States Senate, 74th Congress, 2d Session, Pt. 36, 1939.

Andrews, C. L., *The Eskimo and His Reindeer in Alaska*. Caxton Printers Ltd., Caldwell, Idaho, 1939.

Lantis, Margaret, "The Reindeer Industry in Alaska," *Arctic*, vol. 3, April, 1950, pp. 27–44.

Rainey, Froelich, "Native Economy and Survival in Arctic Alaska," *Applied Anthropology*, vol. 1, October–December, 1941, pp. 9–14.

Answer Questions Presented in the Problem
Before Reading the Rest of the Case.

4. THE OUTCOME

Implicit in the program developed by the Reindeer Service in the early 1940's was the assumption that these essential continuing functions belong to the government:

1. Predator and parasite control.

2. General supervision and regulation, as of any natural resource; for example, there must be law enforcement against poachers. (Neither Eskimos nor whites are blameless. In pre-white times and recently, some Eskimos have slaughtered animals unnecessarily, as well as poached.)

3. Maintenance of one slaughterhouse to provide meat for Alaska Native Service institutions, perhaps also to train Eskimos in proper butchering according to modern health and commercial standards.

4. Maintenance of a few government herds for emergency use and as a sort of revolving fund for loan of deer.

5. Loan program to help Eskimos start as small businessmen, thus ending the associations.

6. Protection of the industry against white encroachment to see whether it can prosper as a native industry. If it does not, then it can be opened to nonnatives.

7. Improvement of quality and size of herds by extension methods. This helps raise the prestige of herding, especially if there is emphasis on skill, and increases income.

Reorganization of the Reindeer Service was effected gradually. The personnel were almost entirely new. Some of them made unwise decisions because of ignorance, while others learned good management by traveling with Eskimo herders and observing the reindeer under routine conditions. Ranges were examined and allocated by a range specialist. The old slaughterhouses, located in areas of poor forage and straying deer, were abandoned and a new modern slaughterhouse was built on Nunivak Island. This began operation in 1945 and shipped 13,000 carcasses during its first three seasons. Some carcasses were sold commercially to pay expenses of the plant, others provided meat for Alaska Native Service institutions: hospitals and boarding schools. Nunivak Eskimos earned about $15,000 a season at this plant in 1946 and 1947. The slaughterhouse was not operated in 1948 or 1949, however, because of sudden and unexpected loss of deer from starvation, parasites, and wolves that had somehow reached the island. It was planned in 1950 to keep the herd down to about 3,000 to allow depleted ranges to recover and to keep the whole operation under better control. The Nunivak program, however, was apart and different from the main development.

To prevent straying and loss to wolves and other predators, a program of predator-control was started. This did not function vigorously until after the war, by which time wolves had become numerous. The principal method was to drop poisoned bait from airplanes onto the ridges where dog-teams and other animals would not be affected. Herders, trappers, and others also killed wolves for a bounty. In a larger and more highly organized industry like most of the livestock industries in the United States, a trade association of producers can perform some of the functions which the government must undertake for the small scattered producers in Alaska. But even in the States, the Bureau of Entomology, for example, still is needed.

The Fish and Wildlife Service and Public Health Service have cooperated by including reindeer and caribou in research on parasites of Alaskan animals. With stronger animals and hides not marred with holes made by warble-fly larvae, new markets for reindeer leather can be sought. When commercially tanned, the hide becomes a soft, heavy leather somewhat like pigskin and good for gloves.

Close herding was reinstituted except on the islands where there are no wolves and the reindeer cannot get away.

The big shapeless associations have been ended and their equally indefinite herds reassigned as a new plan has been developed. Terminating the associations obviated the elaborate system of "overs" and "shorts." There never were associations in all the villages (they were more numerous in northwestern than in southwestern Alaska), but as late as 1947 there still were seven. By 1949, however, there were only two.

The purpose of this action was to get the deer again into the possession of individual Eskimos who would be personally responsible for them. An Eskimo is lent a minimum of 500 deer, to be repaid in five years. For efficient herding, a man is encouraged to take 1,000 head. A borrower also receives supplies for the first year, in return accepting supervision and training. Under this system he has a strong interest in protecting his herd. For example, whereas in 1947 migrating caribou carried away three herds of government reindeer, an alert and capable owner in the Kotzebue area managed to get his herd into the corral before the caribou came by. This man now has 3,000 head from his original loan of 1,000, which he is repaying to the Alaska Native Service. It has been found again and again that a herd must be large enough to support a family and an extra herder or two, and to remain an economic unit even when a hundred deer are lost, but it should not be too large to hold together as a single group. The Alaska Native Service recommends 2,000 head as a safe number. Possibly 3,000 are not too many. The following exemplifies the opposite situation. A remnant of an association herd, the Point Hope, numbering 327 deer in July, 1947, was returned to the government by the borrower because the herd was too small to pay its way. A herder was hired, but when, in 1948, he left the deer to get supplies, the remaining 250 animals disappeared.

Regarding government herds other than that on Nunivak Island, one can report both successes and failures. (All government deer are supposed to have local herders if in an area where herding is necessary.) The entire Bethel herd strayed. The Hooper Bay herd suffered losses not adequately explained, but they were probably due chiefly to the Eskimos' efforts to hold the deer on depleted ranges near the village. The Escholtz herd, which was started in 1940 with 4,500 reindeer from the old Lomen herds, suffered a loss—chiefly from straying—of 1,500 head the first winter on its new range in the Kotzebue area but has held together well since 1942. From it have come several good herds now under private Eskimo management. During and immediately after the war when many Eskimo men were on construction jobs away from their villages or in the Alaska Scouts, little attention was given to several herds, with the results one might expect. Despite discouragement, the program of transferring reindeer from the associations and from government ownership to individual Eskimo ownership has been effected. In the summer of 1949, the Reindeer Service record was as follows:

Type of Ownership	Location	Number of Head
Association	Wainwright	270
	St. Lawrence Island	450
		720
Government	Escholtz Bay (Kotzebue)	3,500
	St. Michael (including former Egavik herd)	150
	Hooper Bay	400
	Nunivak Island	4,500
	Atka Island	1,700
	Umnak Island	1,400
	Pribilof Islands	700
		12,350
Individual	Barrow	750
	"	1,600
	"	650
	Kotzebue	1,500
	"	1,500
	Shungnak	400
	Selawik	1,500
	Noatak (new herd from Escholtz Bay)	1,100
	Wainwright	450
	Golovin	1,500
	Igloo (Seward Peninsula)	750
	Candle	650
	Alitak (Kodiak Island)	2,500
		14,850
	Total	27,920

Small, steady, local marketing by air and water transport has developed encouragingly, without much planning. For small herds, involving the sale of perhaps only 20 or 30 carcasses at a time, air freight is adequate and, for local hauls, not very expensive. There is a steady market for reindeer meat at towns like Nome, White Mountain, Kotzebue, and Barrow. When white men come into the industry expecting to make a big business of the reindeer, they must ship many hundreds or thousands of carcasses and must have, therefore, modern refrigerator ships, abattoirs, and other expensive facilities. The Eskimo owner can successfully limit his activities to the local market.

In regard to one important factor, there has been neither planning nor much accidental success, namely, recognition of the Eskimos' need for nonmaterial satisfaction. The white man assumes that possessiveness, economic independence, and other traits will function in Eskimo society exactly as in his own society. A few Eskimos in northwest Alaska who have been herd-owners for a long time have self-assurance and take pride in reindeer management. The income so derived is in most cases supplemented by income from other sources. Thus these owners have economic security. Most of the other owners, however, do not have enough stability, economic security, or prestige. Reindeer management still does not have the excitement and glamour of hunting mountain sheep, walrus, or bear. But when the only alternative is a routine job as a store clerk or maintenance man at a Civil Aeronautics station, herding may be more attractive. Although offering little physical comfort, it does offer the excitement of a personal contest with wolves and storms.

So much for government functions. The most important Eskimo function of 1950–1955 is to care for the reindeer so that the decrease will be halted and the herds will again multiply. Their next function is to supply local markets with good meat. Since meat prices always are high in north and west Alaska, price is only a minor problem. At the time of writing the prospect for the industry is mildly hopeful, but apparently reindeer will not be the chief source of income. About 20 native communities will have a dependable supply of meat and skins at hand, which most of the families in about 15 communities will have to buy since the deer will be privately owned. The owner-families in these villages will have cash income. Where there are government herds, occasional wage work and meat are obtainable. Although one cannot predict the exact size of population coming in or the rate of influx, the increase in defense activity in Alaska—such as construction of local radar stations—undoubtedly will bring greater demand for fresh meat. This may well induce more Eskimos to undertake reindeer herding.

It now seems likely that the reindeer industry will become a stable part of a complex economy. A combination of sources of income has been achieved by a few Eskimo families, and more will follow their example. A man, for example, can work in construction, a fish cannery, or mining in the summer while his family or perhaps an adolescent son and a hired herder travel with his herd. In the winter he can herd the deer himself, especially where trapping is not profitable. In many cases, a man is in no more difficult situation when watching a herd in the winter than when he follows a 40-mile trapline in 40-below-zero weather.

5. ANALYSIS

Seeing the aboriginal variation from region to region and from one hunting technique to another, one would find it difficult to say, on this alone, whether Alaskan Eskimos would find modern individual ownership or cooperative ownership of animals more compatible with their habits and values. More helpful in understanding Eskimo attitudes are the old sources of prestige. A man who had a cache of food and who could clothe his family in the more valuable furs was envied and admired, but beyond these useful possessions, mere possessiveness had little value. Generosity, as we have seen, was more admired. To have goods to give away, a man and his family had to be skilled, successful hunters and workmen. The distribution of gifts was, therefore, a display of the evidence of one's competence, hard work, and good fortune; the latter, in turn, a sign of supernatural approval. But how can a man get any satisfaction from giving away reindeer skins when all he can be certain of is that this year he has 8 per cent of a herd of 5,000 head, with an additional 1 per cent credited to him somehow? He does not know which individual animals belong to him and, therefore, cannot feel that they are products of his effort.

Not merely individual ownership, but what individual ownership facilitated in display of approved personal qualities was the important consideration. Possibly the associations could have been set up so that a person did not feel that his effort was submerged in the group effort, but this seems doubtful. The problem of incentive has appeared often in modern industry. When the worker knows that he has not designed the product or formed the organization to produce it, that he has not engineered the production line, that he has contributed only a small piece of the final product, that he cannot say how it shall be disposed of or at what price, he is not likely to identify himself with either the organization or its product. The Eskimos in their associations did have a voice in planning roundups, for example, but beyond this they became lost, especially when their associations were competing with white men's companies over which they had no power and which they probably did not understand.

A few young Eskimos apparently saw the politics of the associations as an opportunity to obtain authority and leadership. This was a white man's substitute for the older Eskimo men's leadership of whaling expeditions and their authority in the men's ceremonial house. The old sources of prestige were not entirely gone, however; so there was small need for an entirely new system. The question the administrator must ask, therefore, is not merely, What are the benefits of the proposed program? But rather, Can we get *more* benefits in another practicable way? In another system that is already functioning?

For some of the poorer or less ambitious Eskimos, security has been more appealing than leadership and prestige. Probably, for a person of this type, not reindeer associations but some entirely different occupation would be best. Or, if he wants to engage in the reindeer business, a good herd of his own might give the greatest feeling of security. The present period is difficult because neither the old nor the new economy is functioning fully; but as the new economy develops, there will be a variety of jobs, to suit different temperaments.

Economic organization can and probably will take different forms. For example, associations function better on islands, such as St. Lawrence Island. Here, all reindeer belong to an association, and there are apparently no conflicts over identification of animals and ownership, no problem of traveling with the herd and guarding it. Also, the people are experienced in managing a community store and other cooperative activities.

In summary, among the factors *unfavorable* to the Eskimo functions in developing or even maintaining this industry, some are old and some are new:

1. Continuation of hunting, especially sea-mammal hunting, which is needed to supply oil for food, heavy hides for kayak and umiak covers, and other raw materials, but which conflicts with herding.
2. Continuation of life habits that, whether good or bad, are difficult to break, and that are not amenable to "close herding."
3. Competition of herding with new wage work. A steady position as caterpillar tractor driver offers a more certain income than reindeer that may die in a hard winter. Some men would rather have the security, others would rather have the freedom of self-direction.
4. Increase of air freight from the States, bringing meat.

The *favorable* factors are the acculturative changes now occurring:

1. Increasing knowledge of forage, of government regulations, of probable income. This knowledge is not present in all localities, however.
2. Increasing division of labor in the male population.
3. Growth of a money economy, engendering greater need for cash income, hence an incentive.
4. Development of local markets, with growth of villages and government installations.
5. Greater ease of local shipping.
6. Some increase of possessiveness and individualism in the Eskimo value system.

Often, administration can be most helpful, it seems, by simply understanding and using the processes of general acculturation already under way rather than by introducing wholly new schemes, such as the elaborate one of allocating—on paper—

percentages of herds to individual owners. One should avoid complicated schemes which, though logical, are not locally practical. Eskimos are very alert and eager to learn new skills; they are sufficiently competitive and self-assured to handle the new occupation if the development of the economy is favorable. Nevertheless, the wisest administration is often the one that is modest in its plans and expectations.

Aside from acculturation, one must understand that a new industry exists as a dynamic entity in a changing context. What might have worked out satisfactorily from 1910 to 1915 will not necessarily work in 1950 to 1955. In northwest Alaska, Eskimos whose ancestors had lived in the interior might have returned there to develop a truly nomadic life centered in the reindeer. But now, when most Eskimos engage in at least seasonal wage work and in modern trade, the children must attend school so that they will not be at a disadvantage in economic competition. Hence, families cannot travel with the herds. In 1910, before United States businessmen acquired reindeer, that is, when the Eskimos had no competition except from a few Lapps, they might have evolved from their old communal arrangements for caribou drives a new communal system of herding and dividing reindeer —although this is doubtful. After 1930, however, the young Eskimo men had different examples to follow. They had then and have now the old prestige needs, but they also have progressively new concepts of themselves as businessmen.

As for the reindeer, they need care, not the predatory attitude of the hunter. When a man can identify with a specific herd, he may be motivated to be a good herdsman.

Case 9

SOUTH SEA ISLAND STRIKE: Labor-Management Relations in the Caroline Islands, Micronesia [1]

by John Useem

1. THE PROBLEM

On the island of Angaur in the Palaus following World War II, native workers who had at first refused to accept any compensation for their efforts became involved two years later in a sharp controversy over the adequacy of their wages. For a brief period the situation appeared ominous and work stopped. Drastic decisions were made. Phosphate was urgently needed for Japan's postwar agricultural rehabilitation and no prolonged interruption in output could be permitted. In the subsequent weeks tension was high. Then it seemed to disappear in the field of labor-management relations, but comparable controversies sporadically occurred in other areas.

Were the pertinent factors in this case well understood by those involved in economic transactions with Angaur people? Did the decision made with respect to the specific incident which precipitated the immediate problem provide the formula for working out other issues?

2. THE COURSE OF EVENTS

1. In 1944 the armed forces of the United States occupied the island of Angaur, in the Palau group of the Western Carolines. Most of the facilities, including the villages and the phosphate mining plants, were destroyed during the invasion. A military government fed, clothed, and sheltered the inhabitants who survived. Native workers were offered employment on nonmilitary installations. When asked whether they would accept, the leaders unanimously agreed, but stated that they could not take any money from those who had so generously aided them. These

[1] This case is drawn from a larger study by the author, *Power: A Study in Cross-Cultural Relations*, The Dryden Press, New York, 1952.

Angaur people were not unfamiliar with a modern economy, for they had been employed by the Germans and Japanese as wage-workers and prior to the war had experienced a fairly high level of living, based on foreign-purchased goods.

2. Following the termination of hostilities, a critical shortage of agricultural fertilizers in Japan led to the reestablishment of phosphate mining on Angaur. The administration entered into a contract with an American company in order to start operations as rapidly as possible. The company assigned to this task engineers from its regular staff and, in addition, recruited a number of skilled laborers from various West Coast cities. No preparatory training was given to the personnel for working in a cross-cultural situation. The company, however, hired a labor relations expert, whose task it was to make all necessary arrangements with the native workers and to serve as liaison between the company and the community. He had been chosen because of his experience with natives on the Burma Road, with Chamorros in Guam, and with Mexicans in the United States.

3. Enthusiasm among the islanders over the opening of the mines ran high. Everyone now would have an assured source of gainful employment, plus the security of knowing that Angaur had not been abandoned to shift for itself. Concern lest the loss of income force a lowering of living standards comparable to those of ancestral times disappeared. Working conditions were considered quite satisfactory. Schedules of hours and work routines were similar to those prevailing before the war; the jobs were familiar activities for most; and the supervision of the work gangs seemed fair. In comparison with neighboring islands, Angaur appeared fortunate. Not only were there to be ample employment opportunities, but also utilities and imported consumer durable goods were to be made available without charge or at nominal prices. There was no feeling of exploitation and the foreign managers were most welcome. A general expectancy of a promising future prevailed.

4. The expert in charge of the recruitment of local workers sought out the senior-ranking person on the island by asking for the "chief." The latter was instructed to select the men to be

hired and to pick a gang boss. The chief readily complied, choosing twenty workers and a boss who had had an excellent reputation with the Japanese as a reliable worker—nearly all belonged to his own in-group.

Soon thereafter, the expert discovered a former G.I. on the island who had married a native girl and had settled down as a permanent resident. He proved to be an able, congenial person. The expert informed the community that he and the former G.I. were like "brothers" and the latter would serve as his intermediary with the Angaur people. He asked the G.I. to recruit additional manpower, which he agreed to do. Most of those whom he recommended were suggested by his wife's clan. Natives hired through this arrangement were classified as skilled workers. Many of them were skilled but so were also some who had been employed as unskilled in the group previously hired by the chief. Hence, those who were recruited by the former G.I. received higher wages than did workers who had secured their jobs through the island chief. Members of the G.I.'s clan were quick to note the superior influence which he had with the foreigners. Rumors began to spread that his clan was now more powerful than that of the chief.

5. Stirred by the threat to his status, the chief called upon the labor gang boss (whom he had chosen) to institute negotiations to correct the impression and to alter the wage differentials between the two classes of workers created by the means of selection. This decision was reached late one night after much drinking and prolonged discussion. In the small hours of the morning, one of the higher officials of the company was awakened and a protest made to him. Not knowing what was going on and fearing an attack, the official hastily agreed to go further into the matter and the next day he called in the expert for advice. The expert informed him that this was the work of troublemakers and that such cases had to be dealt with firmly and promptly in order to let the natives know who was in control; otherwise, there might be further trouble.

In a state of panic the company officials asked for sidearms from the military forces to defend themselves and sent out an emergency call for help to the commanding officer of the Palau islands. The following day the senior-ranking military officer in Palau flew to Angaur. A brief hearing was held which was attended by company officials, the native chief, the labor boss, and several others. Following a terse interrogation of those present, the commanding officer announced his decision. The native labor boss who had lodged the complaint was deemed guilty of agitation and inciting to conflict and his punishment for the offense was banishment for six months to another island. The chief was warned sternly to avoid a repetition of subversive activity, else he, too, would be ordered to move, and also removed from office. The islanders were admonished to refrain from intervening in any way to help the offender, or they would receive similar sentences. The officer summarized the case in these words: "The gang boss was just trying to be a John L. Lewis out here. We won't stand for any troublemakers."

For a brief period there was considerable tension. The offender and his family were transported to Koror. Rumors circulated. One was that it would be wise for the chief to retire so that someone better able to deal with the Americans could take office. The supporters of the chief became apprehensive. Numerous private conferences were held by various groups to determine the implications of this crisis.

6. There were no subsequent management-labor conflicts over wages but intermittently other comparable crises occurred. Exemplifying these was a complaint by one faction to the civil affairs administration that there was insufficient land to raise food, which in their opinion was due to the progressive extension of the areas used for mining and to the loss of land occasioned by building the wartime airstrip. In one acrimonious quarrel the women of one village tore out the taro being grown by another. Conscientiously endeavoring to protect the interests of the inhabitants, the administration interrupted the mining operations so as to avoid any chance of the land resources being jeopardized. Studies were made which disclosed that there was no real lack of land for subsistence but there were differences in accessibility to it among the various groups. Each time a suitable settlement

on the distribution of the land and related issues seemed to be worked out by the administration and yet new disputes followed.

7. In the next few months the military officer in charge completed his tour of duty and left Palau. The company, unable to achieve its output quota, withdrew from the area and army engineers in collaboration with a new civil affairs staff assumed charge. There were no further wage controversies, although other unanticipated conflicts among the inhabitants have continued to arise from time to time.

3. RELEVANT FACTORS

Today Angaur has a population of about 250 and occupies a single village site. This is but a fraction of its former size. Before the coming of the foreigners there were 2,500 or more inhabitants and 30 villages; by 1870 the population had fallen to 50 persons residing in 4 villages.

The lands on which phosphate is located are confined to the northern portion of the island. The Japanese made a systematic survey of Angaur and reallocated land holdings with respect to use but not to legal ownership. This plan required the villagers in the north to move south and each household was assigned a proportionate share of land needed for every type of crop. No consideration was given to the effects of this decision on other social relationships. While compensation was given to the northerners for their loss, none was provided to the southerners for the encroachment of the northerners on their lands. Officially both native groups acquiesced to the move, but the arrangements were never legitimized in accord with native social rules.

Traditionally, each village on Angaur was autonomous, yet graded according to social rank and allied with certain others in a loose confederation. No functionary had the formal authority to act for the island as a whole even though a loose alliance did exist. The Germans initiated, and the Japanese completed, the creation of a political superstructure in which each island became a district headed by a "chief." This official faced the foreigners.

In purely native affairs, his authority was circumscribed and each village retained its own sovereignty.

The northern villages outranked the southern, yet were occupants on the latter's lands. Even though the northern villages had higher social status, they did not have authority over the southern villages. The northerners were invited to affiliate formally with the southern villages but declined to do so, for this would have made them social satellites or merely co-equals rather than social superiors. The foreign-created office of island chief was filled by the head of a prominent northern village. He was acceptable in varying degrees to rival villages as their representative in official transactions with foreigners but not as supreme in domestic affairs.

In addition to containing this vying for dominance between villages, the power structure in Palau is one in which there is acute competition among the elite ranking clans. In each community the clans are scaled in a hierarchy but the positions are subject to change. The clan into which the G.I. married had aspirations to advance to a higher station; the clan's members regarded the G.I. as an asset upon which they could capitalize by securing from the foreigners special concessions that would raise their prestige. The clan of the chief rated first in its own community but this seniority could be lost if the office passed to a competing clan, for the latter could try to use its new authority to alter the assigned positions.

During the war, Angaur became a military bastion. The Japanese offered to relocate the inhabitants on one of the other Palau islands and, after some hesitation, the offer was accepted. Not all of the natives were willing to leave and some were unable to do so before the American invasion. Those who remained behind became familiar with American ways and felt that the group that had been resettled and had stayed with the Japanese were not prepared to assume postwar leadership under the new rulers. This claim was ignored by the prewar leadership (including the foreign-facing chief and most of his supporters) that returned to Angaur determined to maintain dominance. There have been, consequently, various maneuvers to shift the balance of power away from the chief.

These cross-currents are not unusual for the culture. Rivalry has been institutionalized in Palau and is an established element in the social order. Since intergroup wars as a means of settling contests have been outlawed, other techniques which include intrigue and the manipulation of the foreigners have been accentuated. The islanders are masters of the craft of drawing the foreigners into their domestic controversies and using them to favor, unwittingly, one group over another. Limited knowledge of native patterns and language on the part of the foreigners has aided the inhabitants in achieving their ends.

Angaur has had a large foreign resident population in the past. Interaction with them has been, on the whole, amicable. The natives view the presence of the strangers as a distinct asset to their economic and social advancement. Continuing contact with foreigners has been accompanied by increasing wealth and by adoption of their ways of life. The American government was well received on the island. Relations from the outset have been characterized by cooperation and good feeling on both sides.

Following demobilization, there were insufficient civil affairs officers in the former Japanese mandates to permit the stationing of any trained personnel on Angaur. The center of military government was located on Koror, an island some distance from Angaur, and during the time of this case the staff was reduced to a single officer. He could not visit Angaur often, and, in the line of command, was under an aviation officer in charge of Palau. During the labor troubles on Angaur, the civil affairs officer was not informed of the conflict and not consulted on how to settle the dispute.

The Palau islands as a military base had its headquarters on the island of Peleliu, which is north of Angaur and south of Koror. The senior commander had no prior experience or training in dealing with natives and regarded his duty as one to be passed over as smoothly as possible. He was not hostile to natives but was disturbed over the many and complicated problems presented to him. In communicating with the islanders he was forced to rely on a young native who had a very limited knowledge of English. The governor was irritated by the role he was

called upon to play in the mediation of this case, which he regarded as an "unwarranted" dispute. He was eager to settle the
conflict promptly and avoid any recurrence of the trouble. This is
revealed in part from a reconstruction of the trial which proceeded somewhat as follows:

Officer: "Ask the chief what has happened on Angaur."

Chief: "I don't know." [This was merely a parrying reply, for the
chief is an astute political tactician who has been in office over
25 years and who has had prolonged experience in dissembling
with foreigners.]

Officer: "This is not private work but government work. Why are
you the cause of the strike?" [The interpreter had difficulty here
translating, for he did not know what was meant by a strike.]

Chief: "We don't know anything about a strike." [The chief had
heard vague references to strikes from the Japanese but thought
they meant some form of subversive revolution.]

Officer [to the gang boss]: "You planned a strike but you won't tell
it here." [Apparently at this point similar questions were put
again and the same answers were repeated.]

Officer [to the gang boss]: "You are causing a strike, since you tried
to raise the wages. It is your intention to overthrow the chief and
take power."

Gang Boss: "Why do you say this? I don't want to cause a strike or
become a chief." [Actually he is ineligible to become a local
headman under any line of inheritance.]

Company Expert: "The gang boss was trying to cause a strike by
asking for a raise in pay."

Officer [to the chief]: "Do you agree to the decision?"

Chief: "We do not know what to say about this. I don't know anything about the trouble he has been causing." [Palau authorities
are adroit at sidestepping personal responsibility and feigning
innocence in the presence of charges by foreign officials.]

The information available to the Americans on Palau was
rather extensive and there were current data about Angaur in
particular. Although the military government officer was conversant with what was known about Palau and sympathetic to
the natives, he was seldom consulted by his superior officer or by
the company. The officer in charge of Palau had not read any of

the publications, being neither greatly interested nor having the time to engage in much reading. No one in the mining company had examined any of the literature. The management assumed that their expert's prolonged and widespread experience with other "primitives" qualified him for understanding all natives. The expert had no doubts concerning his present duties and saw no need to read anything.

He was convinced that the best approach was to combine firmness and friendliness. To a meeting of the island's population, he declared: "The war is over. Americans and Japanese are now friends. You must work hard to get phosphate to our friends in Japan where millions are starving. I won't stand for any nonsense. If you don't behave, we will throw you off the island." To show good will, abundant supplies of consumer goods were put on sale at a modest cost at a time when supplies were scarce and expensive in the rest of Palau. Congeniality on a personal basis was exhibited in various ways. He acted "informally" in the presence of natives, joking and teasing in the American style, shadow boxing, fondling children, being generous to natives in need. One of his ingratiating gestures to indicate he was a "good Joe" was to put his arm around the shoulders of ranking native men while laughingly tousling the hair on their heads. This is the equivalent in our society of opening a man's fly in public as a joke, for in Palau the head is a sensitive zone.

The islanders were regarded initially by management and the senior officer as friendly "gooks," then with suspicion, following the trouble. In the words of one company official, "You cannot trust the natives: they could get together with the Japanese and really raise hell."[1] Everyone acquired a favorite set of stories about the curious and deceitful ways of the natives and this folklore did little to enhance understanding. At no time was there the callous indifference that the natives were expendable. Rather, there pervaded a patronizing orientation that these primitives were all right as long as they behaved in accordance with the established pattern.

[1] Japanese workers were employed at the mine. They were sent to Angaur following the reopening of the industry.

Fundamentally, no clash of interests existed between the foreigners and the natives. They shared a common desire to gain a profit from the phosphate industry, to contribute services to each other, and to cooperate for peaceful living. There was, in short, no obvious reason in the eyes of the foreigners for conflict. Yet, conflict occurred.

REFERENCES FOR FURTHER STUDY

Embree, John, "American Military Government," in *Social Structure*, edited by M. Fortes. Oxford University Press, New York, 1949.

Oliver, D., editor, *Planning Micronesia's Future*. Harvard University Press, Cambridge, Mass., 1951.

United States Navy Department, Office of Naval Operations, *Civil Affairs Handbook*: West Caroline Islands. Op. Nav. 50 E7, Washington, 1944.

Useem, John, "The American Pattern of Military Government in Micronesia," *American Journal of Sociology*, vol. 51, September, 1945, pp. 93–102.

———, "Americans as Governors of Natives in the Pacific," *Journal of Social Issues*, vol. 2, August, 1946, pp. 39–49.

———, *Power:* A Study in Cross-Cultural Relations. The Dryden Press, New York, 1952.

Answer Questions Presented in the Problem
Before Reading the Rest of the Case.

4. THE OUTCOME

The islanders acquiesced to their rulers' decisions. Those individuals singled out for punishment and reprimand accepted the status of victim as "fate"—an honorable one in Palau culture. Work was resumed at the mine and both management and military administration concluded that the problem had been decisively solved. No alterations were made in the ratings of the workers at the time, for the original charges were never considered by the administration. In the subsequent period the natives worked out compromises among themselves on the distribution of skilled ratings which gradually and unobtrusively were put into effect.

The termination of the quarrel between management and the natives over employment did not remove the sources of dissension between factions. When other occasions arose that were susceptible to manipulation, latent issues became overt controversies. Each conflict was settled by the rulers in terms of the surface issues. As soon as one dispute no longer constituted the focus of the struggles for power, the locus of social contest shifted to other areas of Angaur life.

The "chief" continued in office and sought to devise new tactics in dealing with the new foreigners. One of his clan was encouraged to marry the expert, thereby helping to offset the influence of the G.I. He, in turn, began to discern how he was being used by his wife's clan and, fearful of the consequences, withdrew as much as possible from any active role as mediary between the natives and the Americans. The convicted labor boss served his period of banishment and then returned quietly to Angaur. He was instructed by the chief not to discuss the case with anyone, on the grounds that it might provoke more controversy with the foreigners in an area in which his group was vulnerable. Two years after the end of the incident he still carried in his pocket as a momento of the episode the document citing his offense and penalty—which he showed to friends in private when prompted and reiterated his innocence.

5. ANALYSIS

This case is merely one manifestation of the processes that are intrinsic to transactions between members of two societies who stem from different cultures and are differentiated in power but united in a common enterprise. It is self-evident that good will and mutual interest do not assure unity for achieving shared ends.

A matrix of elements entered into and shaped the responses of the participants. Some of these were unique to the case, whereas others typify the general relationship between the governors and governed.

Representative of the former was the distinctive constellation of social actors among the superordinates at the time. Although the individuals qualified in general for the positions held, they lacked some capabilities necessary to perform some of the functions required of their offices. It is a moot question as to whether formal training would have fully offset the idiosyncratic personality factors; perhaps it might have made for greater sensitivity to the dimensions of the crisis and instilled a mode of approaching the problem. Be that as it may, without this training the individuals displayed no marked capacity for gaining pertinent information and little facility for undertaking the assignment, even though they were intellectually competent. The expert had not learned from his experiences with other ethnic groups the sociological truism that cultures vary and that techniques successful with one group may be failures with another. He was confident of his ability to understand the Angaur people for, in his words, "Natives are all alike."

Other agents of the superordinates in similar circumstances possessed much greater sophistication in their relationships with the subordinates on Palau. Characteristic of the more general relationship between Americans and natives were the sentiments held about the nature of the problem and about primitives. The specific issues which came to the attention of superordinates, such as the disruptions over labor, were viewed in the framework of American images of social problems. One of these images is the personalization of social issues. In the wage controversy there was a "bad" man, who was the source of evil, and innocent natives, who were the victims of his conniving. If the "bad" man is removed, that presumably solves the problem. Superordinates tend to appraise local problems from their own perspective. No realization was exhibited by the administration of the social function of controversy in the native society or of the reasons for conflict. This outlook was reinforced by a belief, commonly found among Americans, that primitives are free of the kind of strains characteristic of modern civilization. The disruption of this projected "utopian" state of life is attributed to abnormal circumstances. The task becomes one of eliminating by direct action the cause and so restoring normalcy. Accompanying the eagerness to get rid of the problem was the resentment of the existence of one in the first place. Through American eyes the important goal was to maintain production and native complaints seemed an intolerable nuisance that should not be allowed to interrupt important operations. Emotions were heightened by the view that the natives, instead of being genuinely appreciative of their benefactors, were trying to take advantage of them. Americans are not inclined to accept with equanimity the prospect of having their good will exploited.

Formal structure and way of life of other societies usually can be readily perceived; the dynamics of power and the subtle interplay between forces in a native society are less likely to be noted. The American stereotype of authority in a primitive society is one in which power is concentrated in a senior-ranking personage vested with the title "chief." Lacking such a figure on Palau, the foreigners created one and acted as though the chief had a "divine right of kings" type of authority. This has produced a precarious position with both opportunities and dilemmas for the occupant. The paradox is apparent in the case under analysis. Angaur's chief was pleased to have the chance to use his intermediary role to gain special advantages for his own in-group, as illustrated in the choice of workers. But he was uneasy over the demands made that he be held responsible for the islanders' conformance to the orders given to avoid any further conflict. Had the warning that he was not to let the matter happen again been followed by renewed conflict over the same issue, the chief probably would have been suspended from office and thereby another series of readjustments would have been set under way. The social processes of power in Palau and the retention within the inner structure of a circular system of authority distributed among many functionaries was overlooked. Though not directly significant in this case, in others it has been a salient one.

An oversimple version of power politics was evinced in the naive accusation that the gang boss had aspirations to become chief himself and so had engineered a plot. Another facet of the same view was the speculation as to what forms treachery might take as a prelude to open attacks on the Americans. This had induced a demand for weapons for defense and generated a state of panic. Had some action of the islanders been misinterpreted in this period, the fears might have evoked aggressions against natives. Such a course of events has occurred in instances of a like nature elsewhere in cross-cultural relations.

The successful end to one conflict served to confirm preexisting viewpoints. The individuals involved cited the episode as practical proof of the efficacy of their opinions on how to handle natives. Oblivious as to why the decisions actually "worked," the experience offered no guidelines for future action at a realistic level. There was no social disaster because the subordinates adjusted to the situation and had sufficient indirect control to prevent any disintegration of the total relationship. The formula of decision used had secondary value in alleviating the anxiety of the superordinates by enabling their self-image as dominants to remain intact and by channelizing their tensions into relatively harmless activities.

From the standpoint of the subordinates, the issue was merely one in a series common to modern life. These contests represent the routine means by which new social arrangements are worked out in human relations. The individuals directly involved were playing ordinary roles called forth by their social positions and the social actors behaved pretty much as they were expected to under the circumstances. There was no personal sense of self-guilt or shame connected with the whole affair, nor any deep feelings of resentment or hostility directed toward the foreigners. The salient questions posed by the native leaders were not ones of justice and blame. The two main foci of interest centered on its implications; namely, was this prognostic as to how the new rulers acted under specified conditions and what tactics might prove more effective in dealing with the foreigners.

Palau is adapted to a status of permanent subordination and its social life is designed to function within this framework. The culture is resilient, yet plastic, and permits its members to adjust their internal dislocations due to external decisions without social disorganization. While areas of friction and divisions of opinion do exist, there remains a hard core of social solidarity. Adjustments required by higher authority are accepted as an inevitable part of life.

The locus of ultimate sanctions has shifted from a supernatural to a superordinate force, but the image of supreme power and the ancestral methods of dealing with it persist. Higher authority is potentially dangerous, yet not inherently malevolent. This conception has been validated by experiences in modern times, as evidenced in the occasionally disruptive yet progressive development of Palau throughout the span of time in which Spanish, Germans, Japanese, and Americans have dominated. Even though these larger forces cannot be totally understood or utilized by most persons, some degree of knowledge and control is possible. The mark of great leadership is demonstrated ability to predict and maneuver these outside powers for local ends. The main preoccupation, therefore, was one of assessing from the experience its implications for future affairs. Those natives who felt they were artisans of the craft of handling foreign rulers were distressed over their apparent failure.

The mistakes of the immediate case, though momentarily upsetting, were not considered serious blunders. It is common knowledge that foreign officials stay in Palau only a brief period and each incoming group knows little about past events. At an appropriate future occasion a fresh approach can be made to elicit a more favorable decision on continuing problems. This took place on Angaur when the company was replaced by the Army. Had the controversy been prolonged, other standard techniques would have been tried; among the most commonly used ones are playing off one official against another, misinterpreting or forgetting orders, work slowdowns and absenteeism, extracting under various guises decisions altering the preexisting one, petitions to more senior officials, winning concessions by capturing the local administrators through sex privileges, flattery, gifts, and so forth. If the established elite groups had failed to find the effective means and the issue had been deemed crucial, they would have faced the threat of dissident factions, who would have capitalized on the crisis to demand changes in the allocation of power on Angaur. These conditions did not develop and the issue was, therefore, relegated to the class of being merely one more adjustment necessary in order that no larger problems be opened with their attendant consequences.

Case 10

THE CREEK "TOWN" AND THE PROBLEM OF CREEK INDIAN POLITICAL REORGANIZATION[1]

by Morris Edward Opler

1. THE PROBLEM

For nearly one hundred years prior to 1937 the United States government tried to establish a central political body among the Creek Indians of Oklahoma. The attempts began because the United States wanted to deal with a government that could speak for all the Creeks and with which treaties could be negotiated. As the Creeks were steadily incorporated politically and territorially into the United States, efforts to remold their political structure into greater conformity with that of the country as a whole were continued.

These efforts met small success. Tension accompanied all business dealings between the Creeks and the United States from the Civil War period until the beginning of this century, when Creek lands in Oklahoma were allotted to individuals. Tension still existed in 1937 between the Indian Service and the Creeks, and it is evident that a century-long effort to introduce new forms of political organization among the Creeks as a means of closer co-operation and better adjustment between Indians and whites has yielded few results. This was true despite the strivings of some Creeks, as well as of Indian Service personnel and other whites, to build the new government.

As a pointed example of the inability of the Creeks to agree upon forms of political organization sponsored by the white man, we may mention a meeting that was held at Okemah, Oklahoma, in 1937 to consider the setting up of a credit association. A number of Indian Bureau representatives were convinced that such

[1] The investigations upon which this case is based were carried out in 1937 when the author was assistant anthropologist in the Office of Indian Affairs, detailed to work on problems of Indian organization growing out of the passage of the Indian Reorganization Act and the Oklahoma Indian Welfare Act. Thanks are due William Stein for assistance in arranging the data and reports in the form presented.

165

an association would fill the needs of the people and probably result in a general raising of the standard of living. In the meeting they encouraged the Creeks to organize along county lines. Much of the discussion was taken up in voluble disagreement between members of two Creek factions. Finally, a representative of one of the communities in the county walked out and the meeting broke up. Thus, it proved difficult in this, as in many other instances, to get the Creeks together even on county lines, to say nothing of organizing the entire Creek Nation.

What factors were responsible for this long-standing resistance to forms of political organization with which many Creek leaders had been quite familiar? What was lacking, if anything, in our government's approach to the problem?

2. THE COURSE OF EVENTS

1. As far as we know, the Creeks originally lived in the territory that is now Georgia and parts of adjacent states. At that time the Creek Nation consisted of a rather loose confederation of communities with economic and ceremonial ties. After early contact with the Spanish, French, and English, in turn, the Creeks moved west to what is now the region of Alabama. After the Revolutionary War, they continued to live in the area as a separate nation having treaty relations with the United States. However, the westward expansion of the white population and the fact that the Creeks were occupying good lands combined to produce friction between the Indians and the settlers. In 1832 they were removed to Oklahoma, where they organized themselves on much the same social and political lines as before.

2. After removal to Oklahoma, the Creeks continued to live for a generation relatively free from interference by white men. Internal strife, while it was not entirely absent, did not break up the people into warring camps. The removal treaty provided that the Creeks were to have their own government, apart from that of the United States or any state.

3. The United States government had experienced some difficulty in the removal of the Creeks. The signatures of all the Creek Town representatives could not always be obtained on treaties.

With subsequent treaties reaffirming that of 1832, the government began to exert pressure on the Indians to form some sort of national body which could vote on treaties and could conduct business with the United States. In 1860 a national government was organized and a constitution adopted. The latter provided that the Creeks be known as the Muskogee Nation, that there be a Principal and a Second Chief and general council, and that the nation be divided into four districts with one judge for each.

4. However, before this constitution could become effective, the country was plunged into Civil War and the Creeks were divided into two opposed groups. They had no recognized government from 1861 to 1866. By the latter date a decided change in Creek-United States government relations was taking place. Because some of the Indians had sided with the South, the whole nation was treated as a belligerent, and a harsh treaty was forced upon them. They ceded one-half of their lands to the government and had to allow right-of-way to a railroad which was to pass through their territory. The treaty also provided that the Creeks were to take steps toward the formation of a territorial government and an intertribal council.

5. In 1867 another attempt was made to form a national government. Most of the provisions of the new constitution reflected the United States Constitution. A council of two houses, the House of Kings and the House of Warriors, was established. Each town was entitled to one representative in the House of Kings and one representative for each two hundred people in the House of Warriors. The Principal Chief was to be elected by a majority of male voters for a four-year term.

The new government did not convene without opposition. Some of the Creeks refused to attend the councils. Although the United States recognized the Creek government and paid all money to it, most of the Indians were hostile to it. In 1871 a group of insurgents marched upon the Creek capitol and broke up the meeting of the Creek council. The United States intervened and civil strife was averted.

6. Meanwhile, the railroad was built and white settlers began to move into Creek territory. The United States Congress passed

a bill to destroy the treaty-making rights of Indians. More land was given up by the Creeks.

Centralization of power was not proceeding smoothly. In 1875 the Creek legislature impeached the newly elected chief, and much bitterness was generated as a result. Many Creeks still declined to recognize their government.

7. In 1880 a rival independent government was formed. The constitution of 1867 was denounced and a government was established by Isparhecher, the leader of the new movement. During the next few years clashes occurred between the two factions. Finally, Isparhecher was defeated and fled from the country. United States commissioners were sent to mediate between the groups and a general amnesty was declared. Isparhecher came back to Creek territory, but his request for a separate government was denied. A new election was called for in 1883. In this election Isparhecher won a plurality of votes, but the Secretary of the Interior intervened and recognized another candidate. This interference was bitterly resented by the Creeks.

8. After the Isparhecher revolt, one incident after another pointed to the final extinction of the Creek national government. In 1886, at an intertribal council, the Indians of Oklahoma agreed to reject all offers from the United States for the purchase of land for white settlers. The Creeks were restless; they were afraid that they were going to be further dispossessed. They resisted strongly the government land survey and the consolidation of the Oklahoma Indian agencies. The presence of so many white men in a region governed by Indian authority raised many serious questions of peace and order. In 1889 a United States Court was established at Muskogee, and, a year later, the laws of Arkansas were extended over Indian territory. In 1893 a commission was appointed to negotiate with the tribes for the extinguishment of the national title to the land and its allotment in severalty.

9. In 1895 a general election to select a Principal Chief of the Creek Nation was held. The opposing candidates were Isparhecher and General Pleasant Porter, a Creek of part white extraction, who had broken Isparhecher's revolt and collaborated with the United States government in the attempt to get the

Indians to give up their lands. Isparhecher won the election. The support for him indicated the position of the Creeks toward the allotment of their lands and the extinguishment of their tribal government.

10. In 1897 a committee headed by Porter reached an agreement with the government. Each Creek citizen and freedman was to receive a patent to 160 acres of land in lieu of common ownership. United States courts were to have jurisdiction over allotment controversies and trials of Indians and whites alike. This agreement was not to be effective until ratified by both Congress and the Creek Nation; Congress stipulated that the Creeks would have to accept it by 1898 by a majority vote. The Creeks were reluctant to bring the matter to a vote. The government consequently resumed the right of protection and control, and, in 1898, an act was passed which provided for the termination of tribal jurisdiction and made allotments compulsory. Isparhecher called an election and the action of the United States was voted down. Nevertheless, the government commission opened a land office in 1899 and began to allot the use and occupancy of the land. Isparhecher lost some of his following, for opportunists and the faint-hearted moved to get the best lands. General Porter was elected Principal Chief. Porter convinced many people that resistance was ill-advised. A delegation of Creeks entered into a new agreement with the commission: the tribal government was to be dissolved by 1906. The tribal government was still maintained during the meantime, but it had few functions.

11. Many of the Creeks still resisted these developments. By 1900 unrest was so prevalent that Chief Porter appealed to the United States government for protection. In 1901 there occurred a movement, known, because of the name of its leader, as the "Crazy Snake" uprising. Government forces had to be sent into the area to put it down. The followers of Crazy Snake nevertheless persisted; they refused to accept the allotments assigned to them.

12. Since the allotment had not been completed by 1906, the existence of the Creek tribal government was continued. However, its functions were little more than a matter of form. It could not be in session more than thirty days in the year, and it

could not act without the approval of the President of the United States. The collection of tribal revenue and the disbursement of tribal funds were placed in the hands of the Secretary of the Interior. All tribal records were turned over to the United States government.

3. RELEVANT FACTORS

At the first white contact, the Creeks were a sedentary, agricultural people who lived in relatively large "Towns" along the rivers of Georgia and Alabama. The basis of their economy was maize. The settlements, about 40 to 50 in number, were true towns in the literal and physical sense of the word. The houses were grouped in a definite pattern around a civic square.

The Creeks were not and, strictly speaking, are not now a tribe. The Creek Nation was a loose confederation of a number of tribes. As a political phenomenon, it stands as the most significant development of its kind in aboriginal America north of Mexico, with the possible exception of the Iroquois Confederacy. The evidence is that most of the tribes which became members of the Confederacy entered the Southeast from the West and that as they settled down to agricultural pursuits and were conquered by the dominant Muskogee, or sought membership for purposes of military safety, they assumed the characteristics of the Creek Town. All the towns of the Confederacy formed a cultural unit when compared as a whole to neighboring tribes; and this greater ethnic similarity was felt by the towns themselves.

The Creek Town is a much more significant political unit than its English name would indicate. There is no exact equivalent in our language for the Creek word *Idalwa*, which is commonly translated "town." The Creeks do not use the term to denote a city or settlement of the white man. For such a center they use the word *Talofa*.

Idalwa refers to a body of people who are connected by heredity and traditions. Every Creek belongs to the *Idalwa* of his mother, and, therefore, membership is a matter of birthright and not of residence alone. The exact meaning of the word comes much closer to the English term "tribe" than to the usual conception of a town. Since each *Idalwa* has its own political organization and leadership, it may be considered a band of a tribe if the Creek Confederacy is thought of as a tribe.

As has been indicated, many of these towns were originally separate tribes, which, for purposes of defense and alliance, became drawn into a loose confederacy; these tribes and their offshoots are now collectively known as the Creek Nation. All were influenced by the stable agricultural life of the Southeast and their settlements became established on one basic pattern. On the other hand, dialectical differences persisted, and each town retained its autonomy, internal government, and individuality.

The many towns of the Creeks were considered by them to be the offshoots of four principal "Mother" Towns. These four (Tugabatse, Kawida, Kisita, and Abika) have been transplanted to Oklahoma and exist today. As their population grew, they are said to have split up. Those who left a Mother Town to found a new settlement carried with them embers with which to kindle their fires at the new site. Therefore, all those towns that are supposedly descended from one of the four Mother Towns are said to "use the same fire."

There is also a moiety or dual division of the Creek Nation to be considered. Two of the Mother Towns are known as the Red or War Towns. They and all the towns that stem from them formed one side of the dual division of the Nation and had particular functions in time of strife. The other two Mother Towns and their associates comprised the second moiety and had functions in the Confederacy appropriate to peace. They are known as the White Towns. When a group joined the Confederacy, it had to become affiliated with one of the two divisions.

Towns belonging to the same moiety had close relations; friendly and cooperative patterns existed among them, particularly in the case of a Mother Town and her offshoots. Marriages would be encouraged between unrelated members of such towns, and they would often cooperate for attack, defense, and in playing lacrosse, the most important ceremonial game of the Southeast. A Creek referred to a town of the opposite moiety from his own as "my enemy Town," or "my unfriendly Town." Nor was this just a matter of speech. In ancient times a Creek who walked into an unfriendly town without an invitation was likely to get a beating. When towns of opposite moieties held a grudge against each other, one might challenge its opponent to a "match game" of lacrosse.

One of the most important ties which bound the Creek Confederacy of tribes together was the clan organization. The clan, of which more than 20 have been recorded, is based on kinship and not on residence. A person belongs to the clan of his mother and all those bearing the same clan name consider themselves relatives. Many clans may and do exist side by side in the same town, and the same clan may be found in many towns throughout Creek territory. In other words, the maternal clan or extended kinship group crosscuts town boundaries, and a given person finds that he has clansmen or relatives in various towns without regard to "use of the same fire," "drinking of the same medicine," or membership in the same moiety.

The clan name was part of the personal name. Marriage within the clan was strictly forbidden, and this is still the inflexible rule. Each clan of a town had definite functions. From one clan the chief, and from another clan, the assistant chief, would always be selected. The homes of the members of each clan were erected in the same section and the clan was assigned farm land for the use of its members.

The heart of the Town was the Town Square, physically located in the center. It consisted of a flat area surrounded by terraces, a council house on a mound, and various ceremonial poles and other items. Around the square were constructed four arbors for the social groups mainly associated with the ceremonial gatherings in the square: one each for the chiefs, the warriors, the youths, and the ceremonial leaders. In the center of the square was the town hearth.

The use of a common fire is the symbol of unity for the Creeks. In the removal from the Southeast to Oklahoma, the first act performed when a group of townspeople reached their destination, was to reestablish formally this physical characteristic of their town. One of their number would put down ashes from the hearth of the old town square which he had brought from the south, and thus a nucleus of a new square would be established.

Once a year, town unity is reaffirmed in the Busk ceremony. The word "Busk" is a corruption of the Creek *Poskita*, meaning a fast. It was applied to many different kinds of fasts, but its main use was for the great annual ceremonial ushering in of the Creek New Year. The Busk, which occurs in July or August and lasts eight days, is supposed to be a peace ceremonial, "the white day."

At the time of the Busk the people of a town and the people who "use the same fire" reaffirm their loyalties as townsmen and neighbors. When the corn is ripe, and before it may be eaten by anyone, the chief appoints a day for the beginning of the ritual. On that day all the fires in the town must be extinguished. Then, from a newly kindled fire in the village square, each householder relights his own hearth. During the festival, all townsmen partake of the "black drink," a concoction of herbs, which acts as an emetic and is thought to erase the blemishes of the past year. At this ceremony, also, the young receive their names and the pubescent their badge of adulthood. But only those who live in the same town or who have the right to "use the same fire" may take active part in the festival. In other words, purification, forgiveness, naming, and initiation are inseparably connected with the identification of the individual with his town. It is not until this has been done that the first of the new corn can be eaten.

The Creek Confederacy was the loosest kind of organization. Such cooperation as existed was mostly for defense against a common enemy. The independence of each town was based on the following factors. It had its own body of officers and advisers. It had its own land, public buildings, town square, traditions and ceremonies, which were, to some extent, distinctive. Moreover, membership in the town was not a matter of choice, but a circumstance of birth. Then, too, towns could and did act alone in military affairs, and no town accepted as valid treaties or agreements affecting them unless ratified by their own officers, as well as by those who spoke for the Confederacy. By all the rules of social analysis, a Creek Town comes very close to the ordinary

definition of a tribe. In many ways, it is one of the most interesting achievements of the American Indian. It was the hub of all
Creek activities: social, political, military, economic, and ritual.
Strong clans existed, but they were subordinated to the needs and
organization of the town.

The formation of a central government in 1867 did not end the
importance or authority of the towns. Representation in the constitutional government was determined by towns, and the leaders
spoke for their membership in the central body. All negotiations
and important actions were carried on between government
officials and the accredited leaders of towns. Annuity payments
were made through the town, the money being paid to the leaders
or *Mikos* and distributed to the townspeople by them. Up to the
time of allotment, the official census of the Creeks was kept
according to towns.

Although the towns have not been definitely recognized since
the time of allotment, the organization still functions. Despite
their removal to Indian territory and despite the allotment
system, the people of the same town have sought, throughout the
nineteenth century and until now, to live as closely as possible
to one another. They have maintained their civic unity to a
remarkable degree. They now have common meeting houses and
a great many have town squares. They fill much the same offices
that their forefathers recognized in the past, and they engage in
much the same rituals and celebrations.

The Church occupies an important place in the modern Creek
Town. When establishment of Christian churches took place,
they in no way crushed or crowded out the Tribal Town, but
simply displaced the Square as the hub of some of the town
activities. The *Miko* sometimes slipped into the position of
preacher, homes sprang up around the Church instead of the
Town Square, and social work and aid to distressed townspeople
went on under church auspices.

In contrast with the town organization, the central government of the Creeks, although still in operation, functions neither
smoothly nor in accordance with the objectives for which it was
originally introduced. A queer medley of usages obtains in respect
to representation. Some towns send no representatives to the

council because they see no reason for it and are uncertain whether they have any authority for such action. Other towns take great care in selecting representatives and scrupulously fill places that are vacated. A number of towns have permitted those men who represented them at the time of the extension of the life of the government to continue to do so. As the years have gone by, some of these representatives have died, but no step has been taken to replace them. Presumably, when the last one dies, the towns in question will be without representation. There are other towns which, because of their populations, were originally entitled to a certain number of representatives. Although the relative populations have changed considerably, these towns still seat the same number of men as when the legislative body was ossified by congressional edict. There are cases in which a town is practically extinct, but survivors come to represent this non-functioning unit simply because the town was in times past entitled to representation. In other words, in a formal sense the national council is in a sad state of disorganization. The Creeks are conscious of this and have come to look upon its monthly meetings as a general gathering to which anyone may come and at which anyone may voice his opinion.

In 1937, as the foregoing would suggest, no form of centralized organization showed any sign of performing truly political functions among the Creeks. Yet, in that year 44 Creek Towns still retained their identity. Moreover, 20 still maintained a full roster of offices. In other words, the old social organization based on the Town was still functioning, despite the harsh days through which Creek society had passed. On the other hand, a new central political organization had failed to emerge, despite strong outside pressures which had been exercised at one time to encourage it.

As a result of reports and analyses containing material of the kind presented in this case study, permission was granted for the organization of Creek Towns, and a number of them were organized. They have been in existence for fourteen years, have engaged in various economic activities, and have a splendid record of achievement.

Answer Questions Presented in the Problem
Before Reading the Rest of the Case.

4. ANALYSIS

In the modern period the Creeks have never developed a central political body. Yet, other tribes in the area have developed central government organizations; for example, the Cheyennes and Arapahoes of Oklahoma, although they live dispersed among white farmers in parts of seven counties. The situation of the Creeks can be explained, for the most part, by the influence of the Creek Town.

The history of white contact with the Creeks is a continuous record of the attempt to break down the autonomy and independence of the component towns. At first, the invaders were satisfied to recognize the existing towns and make treaties with their leaders. The white men soon realized, however, that the lands inhabited by the Creeks would be needed for settlement, and that removal or elimination of the Indians was inevitable. Accordingly, every attempt was made to centralize authority among the Creeks so that the towns would not have to be dealt with separately.

It is plain that through the centralization of power, first sponsored and encouraged by the government, the Creek central body and officers were used as instruments in the whittling away of the rights and lands which they were theoretically supposed to administer. This was immediately sensed by the Indians, and a large section of the Creek people were hostile to the central government and would have upset it on more than one occasion had not the moral support and even the military aid of the United States been forthcoming.

The attack upon the political autonomy and social independence of the Tribal Town was a long and aggressive one. It ended in allotment, when, as far as the United States government's scheme of things went, the towns ceased to be of significance. As the government's "progressive" and repressive steps were taken, it became more and more difficult for the towns to discharge the social and ceremonial functions of the past. But though government of the ancient order was discouraged and ridiculed, churches were, of course, regarded with approval by white administrators. A section of the Creek population took the path of least resistance. Under the aegis of the Church they carried on meetings of townspeople and distribution of goods among them which would have been frowned upon under any other auspices. At the town squares in times past an all-night dance, the *Saiyakida*, used to take place. Today the Creeks employ this same word to designate an all-night singing and prayer meeting which often occurs at a church.

Some officials have assumed that because there exist Christian churches with religious functions and also separate town squares where ancient Creek ceremonies are performed, the two elements are irreconcilable and indicate a sharp division of sentiment among the Creeks. This view rests on the assumption that the average Creek thinks of the Town and the Church as two rival religious organizations and pledges loyalty to one to the exclusion of the other. In the eyes of the Creek, however, the Town has many legitimate functions beside those of a ritual character. In the first place, he recognizes it as a social body to which he belongs by birth, and he further accepts that it should have political, social, and economic as well as religious functions. Therefore, whether he goes to the Christian Church or participates in the rites of the Town Square, the Creek is likely to acknowledge the Town as a suitable instrument for political organization.

As a matter of fact, the distinction between those who attend the Christian Church connected with their tribal towns and those who go to the Town Square at the time of the annual Busk is not nearly so sharp as some have thought. The great majority of Creeks manage to participate in the activities of both Church and Busk without conflict. It should be remembered that all members of the same town recognize themselves as such whether or not they believe in native rites or take part in the annual Busk.

White men have been waiting for the disappearance of the Creek Towns, but they have not disappeared. Government representatives felt that they would drop out as soon as they had lost their functions, but they did not lose their functions. Meanwhile, the government made various attempts, based on the assumption that the towns were no longer important, to organize the Creeks without regard to them.

Until 1895 it was customary for the government to take cognizance of the Creek Towns and their members. Unfortunately, however, the true nature of the Creek Town—the fact that it has tribal and band characteristics in addition to geographic characteristics—was not completely understood. Since, after allotment, the maintenance of the Town as a contiguous group of buildings was made impossible, it was mistakenly thought that the Town was completely destroyed, and that it would not be necessary longer to classify Creeks according to such affiliation. It was evidently considered that, henceforth, Creeks could be thought of as separate individuals living on land of their own, individuals without close political or social ties to any organization other than the Creek Nation as a whole.

As we have seen, however, the Creek's attachment to his town was a matter of birth and tradition, as well as of residence. In spite of allotments, identification with the Town and interest in it did not cease. Since most of the members took allotments in the same general vicinity, physically the Town became a rural community instead of a cluster of adjoining homes. Somewhere within this general concentration of town population, some land was set aside for a Town Square, comparable to the actual Town Squares in the center of the house clusters in times past. As already noted, a large number of the Creek Towns have these squares and meet there to conduct business and for rituals connected with the town organization. The political organization of the Town has likewise been maintained; the same offices are still in existence.

Thus, the picture of contemporary town organization is not unlike the situation in aboriginal times in respect to major characteristics. The towns are divided into two major divisions or moieties. The member towns are closely related and are expected to help one another in ceremonial and practical contexts. Therefore, the people who work best together today are those who belong to towns of the same moiety. Within each moiety there are clusters of towns, which, since the towns composing them were derived from a common source or are in some way historically or traditionally related, cooperate in work, on social occasions, and in religious functions. Twenty of these towns still have town squares. Naturally, the towns are not precisely as they were in 1895 in number, individual importance, and alignment, for social change is continuous.

That the Creeks have transplanted and retained their towns in the face of removal and allotment is not due to some inconsiderate stubbornness or ingrained conservatism, but rather to the fact that the town was so carefully wrought a social instrument, so involved with the life of the individual and the maintenance of other institutions, that it could not be easily surrendered.

Because they are farmers and are one of the "Five Civilized Tribes," the white man has assumed that the Creeks are thoroughly acculturated and at ease in ordinary American society. This, however, is far from true. Only a very small percentage of the population is in any position to compete on equal terms with the white man in professional and business activity. Moreover, the white men of the region in which the Creeks live have not been eager to accept the Indians into the main stream of their social and political life. Therefore, the Creeks have continued to depend on the towns for social and economic support.

All new internal developments in Creek life have been related to the towns. Towns have organized their own land acquisition programs quite apart from government programs. The major social service activities inaugurated by the Creeks themselves are carried on by the towns.

The reason for the failure to form the proposed Okemah credit association is now obvious. While the Creeks were dividing along moiety and town lines, those white men who were present and were urging organization, were thinking solely in terms of a county organization. If the question of organization by towns had not been raised, despite the factional dispute and the divergent towns involved, enough signatures might have been secured to make possible the formation of a credit association on a county basis. But this would only have meant one of two things: a constant struggle for control by factions representing different towns or moieties, or the nonparticipation and lack of interest on the part of a large section of the population.

Thus, in this case, and in others, too, it was found that Creek Towns were hostile to county organization because their members lived in more than one county. They did not want policies introduced which would in any way separate their memberships. They wanted their towns to be the central consideration in obtaining credit and acquiring land.

As an attempt to work out a solution was made, the possibility of organizing as towns under the Indian Reorganization Act rather than along county lines began to be considered. To this there were several obstacles. One was the skeptical and even hostile attitude of individuals within the government. For a long time aid to Indians had moved along on an individual merit basis. The government employee advised, taught, and demonstrated. When he found an Indian who listened to him, learned, and followed instructions, that Indian was encouraged and rewarded. Today, there is a growing understanding of the futility of dealing with each Indian as an individual case. We see the necessity for evoking native leadership, for freeing social forces, for organizing cultural values which are stronger than any words of a coldly regarded white man. But in 1937 concern over Creek Towns seemed particularly useless and provoking to those who had been accustomed to working with the Indian on an individual basis.

There was also the feeling on the part of some officials that since the Creek Town was a very old, and, in fact, an aboriginal socio-economic unit, it would be "turning the clock back" and retreating from the task of "civilizing" and bringing modern American culture to the Indian to make the Town the center of a new venture.

Another obstacle to organizing by towns was the suspicion among the Indians that it would do them no good to permit governmental interference with their towns. From long experience the Indian has learned that often when the government takes a native institution under its wing, the Indian is afterward rarely able to recognize what is left of it.

Yet, despite these difficulties, town-based organization was carried out with good results.

PART III
TYPES OF HUMAN PROBLEMS

SUGGESTIONS FOR STUDY: Finding Common Elements

The cases that follow are somewhat fuller and more challenging, we believe, because of the broad scope of the problems involved. Role identification, role-playing, and interviewing techniques may be practiced further with these cases. It is suggested, however, that an addition be made to the approach already developed.

Efforts to formulate questions and make use of a master checklist will by now have led to building some kind of general framework for analyzing a wide variety of situations, regardless of the specific form of the technological or social change. This may be carried further by comparing the problems to follow with those that have already been studied. Do the new problems have anything in common with the earlier ones? Even though the new situations may be somewhat more complicated and involve different subject matter, are the fundamental questions facing the administrator or technician wholly different in these instances? Is it possible to make any useful generalizations as to the kinds of problems that appear in situations of directed cross-cultural change?

SHEEPMEN AND TECHNICIANS: A Program of Soil Conservation on the Navajo Indian Reservation
by E. H. Spicer with comment by John Collier

1. THE PROBLEM

Between 1910 and 1933 various surveys indicated a condition of extreme erosion over most of the Navajo Indian Reservation in Arizona, Utah, and New Mexico. By 1933 more than 2,000,000 acres of the most productive land had been denuded and was rapidly eroding. It was calculated that the Navajo[1] Reservation alone was contributing 37½ per cent of the silt carried by the Colorado River into Lake Mead above Boulder Dam. This constituted a serious threat to the future well-being of the whole Navaho tribe, as well as to the newly developed water resources of surrounding people. Almost all experts agreed that the situation was critical and that prompt action ought to be taken, if Navaho range and agricultural lands were to be saved.

The United States Bureau of Indian Affairs took action promptly by putting into effect an extensive program of soil conservation. The program was immensely successful. Within fifteen years erosion on millions of acres was checked; hundreds of square miles of eroded land were restored; and a range management program to guarantee the future of the Reservation was instituted.

This technological success in the preservation of land resources has not, however, been recognized or appreciated by the people for whom it was designed. Generally speaking, the Navahos today harbor hatred for all persons connected, or even supposedly connected, with the program. Soil conservation measures have been carried out not only in an atmosphere of bitter opposition from Navahos, but also in the face of attacks by traders and missionaries on the Reservation, many of whom have

[1] As indicated in Case 6, we are following common practice in the spelling of this name except when employing governmental titles.

implacably condemned the Indian Bureau from the beginning of the program in 1934. Moreover, the Indian Bureau program became the subject of periodic waves of adverse newspaper articles all over the United States.

Why did a technologically successful program for saving the land resources of an Indian tribe meet such vigorous opposition? Would it have been possible to have carried it out in a way that would not have aroused the hostility of its beneficiaries, the Navahos, or others interested in Indian welfare? In 1939, after the program was well under way, Indian Bureau administrators were much concerned with these questions, for by that time Navaho and non-Navaho opposition had already strongly crystallized.

2. THE COURSE OF EVENTS

1. In 1933 the Secretary of the Interior, in response to the recommendations of his Soil Conservation Advisory Committee, set up a Soil Erosion Service. Part of its duties, working with Public Works Administration funds earmarked for erosion control, consisted in organizing a program on the Navajo Indian Reservation, based on the Advisory Committee's report.

2. Experts of the Soil Erosion Service in 1934 prepared "A Unified Program for the Navajo Indian Reservation." A major feature of this plan was the adjustment of Navaho stock to the carrying capacity of the range. It called for reduction of livestock to about one-half the number carried in 1933, that is, from over 1,000,000 to about 500,000 sheep units.[1] The Navaho Tribal Council agreed to set aside 50,000 acres for soil conservation experimentation. This included a tract at Mexican Springs, New Mexico (since known as "the birthplace of the Soil Conservation Service") to serve as a demonstration area for the whole Navajo Reservation.

3. In 1934, using specially appropriated PWA funds, the Indian Bureau began the program of stock reduction. In three

[1] That is, the total stock on the Reservation were to be reduced to a number which would consume only as much forage as would 500,000 sheep.

successive purchases they bought nearly 400,000 sheep and goats from the Navahos. Some of the stock so purchased was destroyed where it was bought. Some of the usable meat was turned over to needy Navahos.

4. Simultaneously with stock reduction, the Indian Service instituted a large number of Works Progress Administration and Civilian Conservation Corps projects on the Navajo Reservation. These consisted of soil conservation projects, such as the building of dams and water-spreaders and the reseeding of land, and the construction of roads and new buildings, including 43 day schools, 2 new hospitals, and a million dollar agency plant at Window Rock, Arizona. About $2,000,000 a year was spent on such projects, much of this going to Navahos as wages.

5. In 1935 the administration of the Navahos was centralized. This involved the establishment of one agency at Window Rock in place of the six agencies which had previously existed. Following this the Reservation, including that of the Hopi Indians, was divided into 18 land management districts with a supervisor, responsible directly to the general superintendent, as administrator of each.

6. Congress passed the Soil Conservation Act in 1935. This resulted in the creation of the Soil Conservation Service as a permanent agency of the Department of Agriculture. The Soil Conservation Service and the Navaho agency began cooperation (as the Navajo Service) on a series of intensive surveys of the whole Navajo Reservation. These surveys, extending through 1937 and later, dealt with a great variety of factors involved in Navaho economy—climate, vegetation, soil, water supply, erosion rates, population and livestock distribution, income and subsistence patterns. Beginning in 1937 the Human Surveys Branch went deeply into such matters as Navaho social and political organization.

7. In 1937 the Navajo Service required every stock-owner on the Reservation to register the total amount of stock owned at the time of the summer sheep-dipping. This registration served as the basis for the issuance of permits to graze stock in accordance with the estimated carrying capacity of the range in each district.

8. At a meeting in 1937 the Navaho Tribal Council appointed a committee to draft a set of grazing regulations designed to meet the special Navaho conditions. These regulations were approved by the Tribal Council in 1938, after review by the Secretary of the Interior, and at the same meeting the Council passed a resolution favoring the elimination of nonproductive stock.

9. In 1939 the Arizona courts affirmed the right of the Secretary of the Interior to promulgate rules and regulations for the protection of the Navaho range. The Navaho Tribal Council had previously approved a Code of Tribal Offenses, which defined infractions of the grazing regulations and established penalties.

10. In the same year the Tribal Council approved a program for the reduction of horses, and the Navajo Service proceeded to carry this out in the face of localized opposition from Navahos in various parts of the Reservation.

3. RELEVANT FACTORS

The burst of activity by the Indian Bureau in 1933–1934 did not represent a new and sudden realization of Navaho problems. For more than twenty years persons familiar with the Reservation had been pointing out the increasing erosion, as well as the portentous growth in population. The decision to do something about these matters was a result of (1) personnel in higher government circles after 1932 who were convinced of the need for conservation and (2) the availability of funds through the new relief sources. The program which was formulated cannot be said to have been hasty, so far as the technical aspects went. It was based on numerous studies made prior to 1933 and especially on the careful report of the Soil Conservation Advisory Committee.

The hard facts which the new Commissioner of Indian Affairs faced were these. In the sixty-five years since the Navaho defeat and return from captivity, their population had more than doubled. In 1868 when they agreed by treaty to settle peacefully on 3,500,000 acres surrounding Fort Defiance, they numbered possibly 15,000. By 1933 there were some 40,000 Navahos living mostly on the Reservation. During the period it had been increased to about 11,500,000 acres (exclusive of the Hopi Land), but the greater part of this land was capable of supporting only very small numbers of people. It was apparent, moreover, that the rate of population increase was accelerating, so that by 1940 it was predicted that the Navahos would number over 50,000. (This prediction was borne out. In 1940 the Navaho population was about 55,000, and by 1950 it had increased to about 65,000.) The Navahos were outstripping the natural resources on which they depended.

The livestock population had also increased with great strides since 1900. The government issued 34,000 sheep and goats to the Navahos when it returned them from Fort Sumner in 1868. By 1933 there were 576,000 sheep, 173,600 goats, 44,000 horses, and 21,000 cattle. This was the equivalent of 1,053,500 sheep on a range which careful surveys showed could carry, without permanent injury to the forage and soil, only 560,000 sheep. The surveys showed that this excessive overgrazing had already resulted in great and, perhaps, irretrievable damage to the range.

No possibility existed for enlarging the Reservation. If resources were to be saved, it was urgent that steps be taken to check the erosion and correct the destructive use of land. This was the basis for the decision to carry out stock reduction promptly and to push a large-scale soil conservation program.

At the time the decision was made, there were on the Reservation or available to the Department of the Interior a considerable number of trained and competent specialists in the various fields of soil conservation and range management. Given authority and funds after 1933, they organized their activities quickly. Within a year they had formulated "A Unified Program for the Navajo Indian Reservation," which included proposals for stock reduction, plans for range management, projected surveys, and the setting up of experiment and demonstration areas such as the one at Mexican Springs. They proceeded, according to the highest standards of their professions, to gather data carefully and to demonstrate the conditions under which damaged range could be brought back to productivity. As they continued, they were guided in their work by a principle enunciated by the Commis-

sioner of Indian Affairs that the work would have to be adjusted
to the greatly varying local conditions on the Reservation, "area
by area."

The technical experts coordinated their activities not only with
one another, but also with the Indian Service administrators'
program for solving the current human problems. They were
ready with outlines of projects for erosion control as soon as PWA
and CCC funds became available. They turned over to the super-
visors of work projects plans for check dams, water-spreading
structures, and reseeding jobs, which were promptly put into
effect. They often felt that they had to work too quickly, but coordination of their work with that of the administrators was regarded as an important principle of their activities. They were
not able until 1941 to put together the results of their intensive
surveys into one integrated statement that would serve as a basis
for the continuing program. Nevertheless, their findings during
1934 through 1939 were coordinated point by point with the
over-all Navajo Service program.

By 1933 sheep had become the primary basis of Navaho liveli-
hood. No one knew precisely at that time to what extent this was
true, but the "Human Dependency Surveys" initiated in 1937
began to furnish precise data. There were really three different
Navaho economies. (1) A very few Navahos lived as farmers, in
the newer irrigated tracts in the vicinity of Shiprock, Chinle,
Ganado, Tuba City, plus some here and there elsewhere. (2) A
considerable number of Navahos, in the western and northern
portions of the Reservation, subsisted wholly from their flocks.
(3) The majority of Navahos combined some agriculture with
herding. It was calculated that in 1936 from 60 to 75 per cent of
the total cash income of Navahos came from the flocks of sheep
and goats and their products. About 65 per cent of all Navahos
possessed some sheep. Most of these families—85 per cent—
possessed flocks of fewer than 150. Usually Navahos who farmed
also relied heavily, especially for the purchase of food and other
goods which they did not produce, on the income from their
sheep. It was true, therefore, that the depletion of the range
threatened the basic structure of Navaho economy.

Navaho herding had developed as a mainstay of their existence over a period much longer than the two generations since their return from Fort Sumner. They had taken over sheep-herding from the Spanish during the eighteenth and early nineteenth centuries and along with it had adopted weaving and rug-making. After 1868, with raiding eliminated, herding had assumed the central place in their lives, although subsistence farming was also of great importance. Everywhere on the Reservation families had settled down to peaceful herding activities, living on mutton, the sale of wool, and, in the case of the larger owners, the sale of lambs. In addition, the wool was used for rug-weaving, which had become for a considerable number of families in every part of the Reservation an important source of income.

The pastoral life had led also to the maintenance of strings of horses as well as sheep. One estimate (possibly exaggerated) for the period preceding 1933 is that the average herding family held about 150 sheep, 60 goats, and 10 horses. Families with more than that amount were regarded as wealthy. Wealth was stored in the flocks and in the strings of horses; large flocks and many horses were a source of prestige in any Navaho community. The animals were integrated into Navaho life in many ways—in the prestige system, into recreational activities such as horse racing, into gift exchange in connection with marriage, and into ceremonial life.

For many years the Indian Bureau had encouraged the Navahos to raise sheep. The first issue of 34,000 sheep and goats had been followed by numerous recommendations from various Indian agents for the development of herding among the Navahos. In the 1920's when wool prices were high and the demand for Navaho rugs was growing, administrators in charge of Navaho affairs made efforts to help them increase and improve their wool production. It appeared to the agents, as well as to the Navahos, to be the resource best adapted to the nature of the land.

In the first phase of the stock reduction program, when funds were available for buying animals, an across-the-board reduction was carried out; that is, the government bought a certain percentage of sheep and goats from each stock-owner, regardless of the size of flocks. A large owner was thus often enabled to sell off his cull animals and improve his flock, while smaller owners were forced to bite into the good as well as cull stock. This method of reduction was quickly seen to be inequitable by the Bureau administrators, and therefore a different basis was worked out.

The formula for reduction after 1937 was as follows. The Reservation area was divided into 18 land management districts. Districts were open for the running of stock only to residents. The range management technicians calculated the carrying capacity of each district, that is, the number of "sheep units" which an area could maintain without permanent damage to the range. A sheep and a goat were regarded as equivalent in their consumption of forage. A horse was considered the equivalent of five sheep, a cow of four. Maximum sizes of flocks and herds were defined for each district, based on the carrying capacity and on the count of stock for 1937. The maxima for flocks differed in different districts, ranging from about 70 to over 200 because of variation in carrying capacities. Navahos gradually became aware of these differences in flock size and they were a source of dissatisfaction.

The maximum size of flock was set by dividing the carrying capacity of the district by the number of 1937 owners. Those who had more than the maximum were told to reduce their flock to that number of sheep units. Those who had fewer were issued permits for the amount they had. The regulations did not allow the buying of permits until after 1942, so that a man could not at first build up his holdings to the maximum by acquiring other men's permits. It was the large holders ultimately, the Indian Service claimed, who bore the brunt of reduction. But in the process there was constant misunderstanding and confusion.

The concepts of "sheep-unit," of "grazing district," of "carrying-capacity," of "maximum holding," of "nonproductive stock," and of "base preference" became part of the Indian Service administrator's daily vocabulary during the program. They were simple enough to grasp, once the experts had defined them and after one had lived with them for a few months in staff meetings and in written regulations and reports. But even Navahos who wanted to cooperate, such as many members of the Tribal Council, found difficulty in translating them and in giving meaning to them when they talked with the people back in their districts.

The confusion and feeling of helplessness in the face of the newly imposed regulations is indicated in the following statements made by Navahos in various parts of the Reservation in 1939.

> That's what the Indians don't understand: these district lines. They say maybe so it's a Communistic plan. This is communities. They want us to do our shopping in one district maybe.

> I will go to jail if I can not go where grandma and grandpa went. I born over on the other side of the line. I go over there on that mountain in summer times. I stay over on this flat in winter times. They say, "Now you can not go over on that mountain in summer times."

> I don't like that Window Rock. I don't go over there. [The superintendent] he try to put war on us three years ago. I sure don't understand why he want us to be poor. They reduce all the sheep. They say they only goin' to let Indians have five sheep, three goats, one cattle, and one horse.

> Before, in the six jurisdictions, you could go to your Agent. Now you got to go to Window Rock and you go to every department and never find out anything. I myself went to Window Rock many times to find out different things, and the longer I stayed the less I knew— just passing the buck. I ask [the superintendent]—he sends me to office so-and-so. I go there and they send me some where else.

In the earlier phase of the program, prior to 1939, there was lack of understanding of regulations and objectives not only on the part of the Navahos, but also on the part of Indian Service personnel. Thus, although the Commissioner had written that the reduction was to be carried out "on a sliding scale, the largest reduction to fall on the larger herds, with reduced proportions on the smaller herds and a minimum size of herds on which no reduction at all will be made," in some parts of the Reservation (notably in the northeast) the uniform percentage reduction was applied. Moreover, coercion was employed in various ways, which was not a part of the policy. The following statements by Navahos in 1939 indicate what happened and the state of mind to which it gave rise.

> We were so scared. Everybody was bossin'. It was hard to tell who it was. May be it was a common Indian tellin' us we had to do a certain thing. And we did it. We were so scared of everything.
>
> No Washington people came here to reduce the goats. But policemen told us those were orders from Washington and we had to get rid of the goats. The poorest people were scared and they just reduced the goats and sheep. The ones who had 'bout a thousand sheep didn't do a thing. The policemen made the little people go first and reduce.

From the beginning the Navajo Service sought to work with the Navaho people on the whole problem. It was seriously handicapped in these efforts because of a lack of tribal organization. The Navahos had never had an over-all government. Even at the time of making the Treaty of 1868, no tribal body existed which was recognized by all Navahos. No organization even purporting to represent all Navahos existed until 1923. Then a group of Navahos set themselves up, at the suggestion of the Indian Bureau, to deal with oil companies interested in the Shiprock region. It consisted of some prominent and public-spirited Navahos and some who had learned white men's ways through association with Indian Service personnel and others.

At the time the stock reduction program began this body, after years of irregular and rather informal existence, was called in for meetings with Navajo Service administrators. In 1934 the Navahos rejected an opportunity to set up a more formal representative body under the Indian Reorganization Act. The old "handpicked" group, as many Navahos referred to it, continued in operation. It approved the assignment of land for experimental and demonstration purposes and various subsequent proposals by the administration, including the special Navaho and Hopi Grazing Regulations, the making of a Code of Offenses which set punishments for breaking the Grazing Regulations, and the reduction of nonproductive stock. In 1938 the Navajo Service formalized the Tribal Council with regulations for the election of its delegates by districts.

The Council members rather consistently approved the various parts of the Navajo Service program as they were put before the Council. Often, as in the 1938 meeting with the Commissioner of Indian Affairs when the Council approved the special Grazing Regulations, no real alternative was offered and both Washington and Window Rock personnel skillfully applied strong pressure. However, frequently the approval of the measures presented by the administrators was a result of understanding and acceptance by the Council of the need for them. Some Tribal Council members were undergoing, in their association with agency staff, intensive education. They were for the most part the more acculturated men from their districts, and in contact with people (at the top of the agency staff) who were well versed in, and generally enthusiastic for, the whole conservation program. These contacts had strong influence on some of each incoming set of councilmen. The turnover of personnel in the Council was heavy and no chairman was elected to more than one term of office.

The Navajo Service officials showed in other ways their awareness of the human aspects of the problems with which they were dealing. The technical surveys were extended, beginning in 1936, to cover the human aspects of the problem, as well as the physical. The "Human Surveys" resulted in the accumulation of a great deal of data on the income of the Navahos and its sources. They resulted in the definition of basic units in the Navaho social organization, not only the family and clan, but also the "consumption group" and the "land-use unit." With these studies, the Navajo Service was discovering the link between the technical and the human aspects of land management on the Reservation. The studies were pushed further to make clear the patterns of leadership that obtained in these basic socio-economic units in Navaho social life. These data were incorporated as an integral part of the "General Statement of Conditions in the Navajo Area," which was prepared by the Division of Planning in 1941 as a general basis for administration.

Such efforts to understand clearly the nature of Navaho social structure were in progress as the Navaho opposition intensified in 1939 and as outside groups carried out and completed their investigations of what was taking place on the Reservation. Were the reorganization of the Tribal Council and the studies of Navaho social organization to herald a new and more successful phase of the stock reduction program?

REFERENCES FOR FURTHER STUDY

Fryer, E. R., "Navajo Social Organization and Land Use Adjustment," *Scientific Monthly*, vol. 55, November, 1942, pp. 408–422.

Kimball, Solon T., and John H. Provinse, "Navajo Social Organization in Land Use Planning," *Applied Anthropology*, vol. 1, July–August–September, 1942, pp. 18–25.

Kluckhohn, Clyde, and Dorothea Leighton, *The Navaho*. Harvard University Press, Cambridge, Mass., 1946.

Navajo Agency, E. R. Fryer, General Superintendent, *General Statement of Conditions in the Navajo Area*. Window Rock, Arizona, 1941.

Answer Questions Presented in the Problem
Before Reading the Rest of the Case.

4. THE OUTCOME

From 1939 on, the Indian Service put added emphasis on three approaches that had been conceived earlier. This newer phase contrasted sharply with the first direct attack.

In the first place, efforts were increased to improve the quality of Navaho sheep in order to offset losses through reduction. A laboratory was established at Fort Wingate in cooperation with the Department of Agriculture, where experiments in cross-breeding were carried out in order to develop a type of sheep suitable to Reservation conditions and more productive in pounds of wool. By 1950 the breeding station was producing over 100 rams a year of the improved type, which were available to the Navahos. Much skepticism existed among the Navahos in regard to the ability of these sheep to withstand drought conditions, but Indian Service claims were that the improved type, together with the introduction of Rambouillet rams and ram pastures, had resulted in greatly improved yields.

The Navajo Service placed increasingly heavy emphasis on "education" of the Navahos to understand the reduction program. This took many forms. Charts were prepared, showing in pictures the reasons for the grazing regulations, explaining carrying capacity and other concepts, and indicating the progress of the program. Moving pictures on soil and range conservation were secured. These and other visual education materials were taken about the Reservation and shown to the Navahos, even in remote communities. Adult education in the Navaho language was also undertaken. Reading materials were prepared and a Navaho language newspaper was issued in which items appeared dealing with the stock reduction and other administrative programs. In addition, teaching materials for use in the schools were written, also with chart illustrations. The basis for these was a volume entitled *Dineh and Government in Kaibeto District*, which was a summary in simple English of all that had been found out about one district through the various surveys. Later simplified into *A Primer of Navajo Economic Problems* in 1942, this was designed for use in the upper grades of the Navaho schools. It explained in the simplest sort of English the economic life of the Navahos and its relation to the physical environment and to the outside economic life. It also described the whole conservation and reduction program and the reasons for its institution.

A third approach consisted in emphasizing the reduction of what the Navajo Service defined as "non-productive stock" rather than all stock, regardless of productivity. This approach began in 1938, when the idea was made acceptable to the Tribal Council, and was followed up with the program for horse reduction which was accepted by the Council in 1939. The procedure was to get owners to agree to sell their horses, down to the number of about ten, to outside buyers who were then called to the Reservation by the Indian Service administrators. Confusion and misunderstanding and vigorous opposition followed on this program; nevertheless, many horses were sold.

It is not possible to evaluate the specific effects of each of these attacks on the problem, particularly since in 1939 a severe drought resulted in large-scale sale of sheep by Navahos who preferred to sell rather than lose them by starvation. Whatever the influence of the various parts of the program, the Navajo Service announced in 1947 that carrying capacities had been attained in 15 out of the 18 districts. The total sheep units on the Reservation had been reduced to about 644,000—about 100,000 above the quota set in 1933. In the previous year the Navaho Tribal Council had recommended a five-year rest on stock reduction, in view of the near attainment of carrying capacity. No action was taken by the Indian Bureau until 1949, when it was proposed to the Tribal Council that it make a complete revision of the grazing regulations by April 1, 1950.

The Indian Bureau stated also that the Navaho livestock industry had been improved in a number of important ways during the fifteen years of the stock reduction program. In the first place, income from the livestock had increased:

| 1933-35 | Total average income | $ 953,619 |
| 1945-47 | "   "   " | 2,429,149 |

Expressed in 1935 dollars, the 1945–1947 income from sheep was about $1,518,210, or an increase of 60 per cent.

As a result of the stock improvement program . . . and the soil conservation work, the total wool production remained approximately stable (despite stock reduction):

1933–35	Total pounds	2,089,121
1945–47	" "	2,046,597

During the same 15-year period, the average weight of wool per sheep increased 50 per cent . . . the weight per lamb increased [about ten pounds].

The total reduction carried out in the fifteen-year period was as follows:

Goats	from	173,000	to about	56,000
Horses	"	44,000	" "	35,000
Cattle	"	21,000	" "	11,000
Sheep	"	570,000	" "	358,600

The program of stock reduction could be summarized as having largely attained the ends originally set, without reducing the Navaho income from livestock. The experts held that erosion had been successfully checked and that the range had begun to recover. No predictions had been made in 1933 as to the effects of the program on the human beings who would undergo it. Those effects cannot be put into figures, but they can be indicated in a variety of ways.

An Assistant Commissioner of Indian Affairs in February, 1947, came to Window Rock to discuss with the Tribal Council a proposed program for Navaho schools. When he had finished an outline of his proposal, a tribal delegate from District 14 made a long speech from which the following excerpts have been selected:

> . . . Some twelve years back we have been hearing about the special program for the benefit of the Navahos and to our knowledge these programs as set forth by the Government have been detrimental to the Navahos. Before this program of getting the Navahos educated, getting the Navahos what they need, they were well off. I am particularly referring to Mexican Springs. Previous to those

twelve years the Navahos were well-fixed, had good homes and had plenty; but since that they have been listening to programs to help them and they have given up rights they have previously enjoyed and they are staring want in the face now. . . . They have given up their land, their hogans, and other things that meant well-being to them by listening and accepting Government programs. By watching the drawings on the walls [referring to the historical murals on the walls of the Navaho Tribal Council House] of the Navahos and their activities we see when they were returned from captivity they were given a way to make a living. You see on the walls where the women are occupied in weaving and spinning to support themselves. That was given to them as a means of support. They were doing well when they were again given help, so-called, by the Government, to dispose of the things from which they had been deriving a living, the live-stock and wool which meant their living. Now they are without these things. That "help" has taken these away. I blame this help of the Government for the Navahos for dispossessing the Navahos of their livestock, taking away the work of our women folks, making of rugs, spinning, and so on. . . . The particular place I mentioned, Mexican Springs, the people do not know which way they are headed for. They are like a beetle that just wanders around. They are so poor they do not know whether they are going or coming. . . . After listening to [the Assistant Commissioner] about the program for the benefit of the Navaho Indians, I am wondering if this help he has in mind will further deprive the Navaho Indians; up to twelve years ago we had plenty. . . .

The speaker went on to recommend the increase of the maximum flock size in his district. His speech, touched off by a presentation of plans for schools, was characteristic of Tribal Council sessions throughout the 1940's, as it had been during the 1930's. Education plans, medical programs, agricultural development, all that the Indian Service was attempting to do was intertwined for Navahos with stock reduction. Many hours of time and many thousands of dollars of tribal and government money were spent in the council house and out, giving vent to the deep grievances that Navahos felt as a result of the stock reduction program. It was very far from being a closed issue in this year when the Indian Bureau announced the virtual attainment of the program goals.

In this same year, the Indian Bureau proposed to reappoint as general superintendent of the Navajo Reservation the man who had so vigorously prosecuted the conservation program there in the 1930's. During the war he had been called to various other posts. His appointment was opposed immediately from many quarters, and one of the most insistent protests came from the Navaho Tribal Council and its chairman. They opposed the re-appointment on the basis of the efficiency with which he had carried out the stock reduction. Because resistance to him was so strong, his appointment was withdrawn. Success in the Indian Service program as conceived in the 1930's had become a real disqualification for office.

In District 12 in the northeastern part of the Reservation in 1944, the district supervisor, his wife, and a range rider were kidnapped and held for a few days by Navahos. The complaint against the administrator was enforcement of stock reduction. Navahos were still not reconciled to the program, and its enforcement had to be handled gingerly in the face of latent opposition and hostility.

In 1948 individual Navahos in that part of the Reservation looked back at the program. Said a farmer's wife:

> I was here in 1937. It sure was hard for us. They took away our sheep. That old . . . [Commissioner of Indian Affairs]. We had about one hundred goats, but they killed them all, and gave us one dollar apiece for them.

A community leader, who had been a tribal delegate during the stock reduction period, said:

> Long time ago we had 20,000 to 30,000 sheep around here, but now they cut us down to 30 or 40 heads, and some of the people are in pretty bad shape. They got no piece of meat, and no way to get it.

Everywhere over the Reservation, the Indian Commissioner who had instituted stock reduction had become a sort of symbol of responsibility for all the ills of the Navahos. Past troubles and present poverty were blamed on him or Washington or "the government" and traced to stock reduction.

By 1950 the situation had changed little on the Reservation as a whole. Antagonism to government workers, regardless of what they were trying to do, focused around stock reduction and came up in connection with almost anything. When a government livestock agent went to remote communities to show a carefully prepared color film in the Navaho language on the best-paying ways of handling wool, he was met repeatedly with angry harangues. The speeches had nothing to do with the film (which the Navahos generally liked); they dealt with stock reduction. Much time in Tribal Council meetings continued to be spent discussing stock reduction, and frequent orations were delivered on the subject.

5. ANALYSIS

The range conservation and management program of the Navajo Service appears to have been extremely successful by any technical standards which may be applied to it. It has been successful in that it has saved from destruction and brought back to productivity a range which, if measures had not been taken, would by 1950 have had only a fraction of the productive value which it now has. The fact that the program has been so successful demonstrates the great power of coordinated government organization and technical skills in the modern world. It shows how, in a relatively short time, such a combination may move to rebuild the foundations of a people's economy, even against the people's will. But it also demonstrates how effective action in this manner may foment hostility and hatred, which hinder and block the development of cooperative working relations.

Stock reduction, in aiming at the reconstruction of Navaho economic life, also struck directly at the foundations of Navaho economic security. Sheep were pivotal in the adjustment which man and nature had made over a period of two centuries in the Navaho country. Taking away sheep constituted, for individual Navahos whose horizons were bounded by a few square miles, a threat to existence. As such, the plan required a more careful presentation and a slower beginning than it was given. The direct attack on flocks starting in 1934 was felt inevitably by Navahos, as many said, as "a war" against them. It threatened their existence and, as it continued, attitudes were engendered which obviously were the same as those which accompanied Kit Carson's campaign and the captivity at Fort Sumner. Within a few years, possibly months, stock reduction attained the same sort of symbolic meaning for Navahos that the "Long Walk" had attained in the 1860's. And, like the latter, once so formulated it has not died out as a symbol, but has become more meaningful as a focus of Navaho solidarity against whites and "the government," as well as a renewal of the symbol of the superior coercive power of the government. There is no reason to expect it to disappear any more quickly than has the memory of the "Long Walk."

It cannot be questioned that there were many good reasons for acting quickly. Erosion conditions were extreme and funds could not wait to be used. In these circumstances, it is clear that the viewpoint of technical experts was allowed to prevail over the view of persons more experienced in human relations. There was an abundance of technical experts on the Reservation. Their plans were accepted and trusted as the basis for work projects. The participation of Navahos in this phase of "rehabilitation" was virtually limited to wage-workers. With few exceptions, Navaho communities were not asked how they thought money could be spent to best advantage in their areas. Presumably, this was regarded as a waste of time: Navahos would not know enough and would spend too much time in discussion.

However, we may compare what happened on the Papago Indian Reservation in Arizona when CCC funds suddenly became available.[1] No abundance of technical experts existed; but there were similar conditions of illiteracy and lack of acculturation. Nevertheless, work projects were set up on the basis of recommendations by the village councils. The Indian Service administrators later felt that they had saved time by relying on the knowledge and needs of the local people. Incidentally, but most important, they had begun a tradition of participation by Papagos in the application of technological aids to their problems, and this tradition was followed with marked success later when the Papago Tribal Council itself planned and carried out a program of stock reduction. In the initial phases of the Navaho

[1] See Case 12, p. 214.

program such opportunities for participation were only rarely allowed. And it was in the beginning that the attitudes of the Navahos were crystallized.

Where the Navajo Service did try to get participation was at the top of the social structure, or at what they regarded as the top. They knew that the Tribal Council was not really representative and tried, after a few years, to make it more so. It was a place to begin, unsatisfactory though they felt it to be. What they did there demonstrated the feasibility of getting Navahos to understand the program. Some members of the Council repeatedly showed their capacity for understanding the need for conservation and even for understanding the technicalities of the regulations. Education went on continuously at Window Rock. Participation developed there to a certain degree, but it was never extended through the councilmen to the general population. The real problems of participation, namely, the pushing of local responsibility and conferring on local leaders the right *to make mistakes* were tackled only in the later phase of the program through bringing Navahos into consulting relations.

There was even a tendency to nip the development of local responsibility in the bud. The Chapter groups which had existed since the 1920's here and there on the Reservation became frequently in the 1930's centers of opposition to stock reduction. This was inevitable in view of the sudden attack on economic security in 1934. It meant that the Chapters were beginning to have a real function as political organizations. However, this was not accepted by the administrators as the beginning of political responsibility. Such Chapter functioning was opposed and undermined by the administration and, as a result, there continued to be nothing to work with in the way of organization at the local level. The contacts of local leaders continued to be chiefly with enforcement officers and only occasionally with those who explained the program, such as the top Navajo Service personnel who dealt with the Tribal Council members at Window Rock.

The damage to cooperative working relations had probably been done by 1938. From then on, with no program for concentrated effort at building the local leadership, it was a matter of pulling and hauling until the livestock statistics read in accordance with the administrative plan. The administration focused on education and undoubtedly had some success in spreading knowledge of the program, but the teaching through Navajo Service personnel struck Navahos, in the context of the attitudes which had already been engendered, more as propaganda than as education. Reduction went on in an atmosphere of coercion, however mild the means, rather than of cooperation.

COMMENT

John Collier, who was Commissioner of Indian Affairs during the years of the stock reduction program, was invited to criticize the reporting and analysis of this case. He very kindly responded with the following observations:

"I think the case record is accurate and its analysis valid *as far as it goes*, but it does not go far enough.

"1. The effect of haste—short-run programs with 'crisis' psychology—did more than dis-affect the Navahos. It prevented the consecutive and really experimental development of administration programs. (2) Navaho administration 'centralization' was intended and announced as a step toward effective turning over of responsibility to local areas, but that correlative step was never taken. Integration of services at (even) the soil conservation district level *was never seriously pursued*. Still less, the integration of services with the effective local societies of the Navahos. (3) Commencing some six or seven years ago, Indian Service 'alibied' its partial failure through blaming Congress for the nonsupply of great sums of money, thus still more effectively diverting its own and the Navahos' attention from the need and practicability of locally and sociologically oriented programs and practices. In 1943 there was an effort to persuade or drive the Navajo Service *and the Washington bureaus* toward the institution of real, controlled, indigenized and noncostly-oriented *local* experiments, an effort made in vain.

"Many factors, including numerous ones not directly related to the conservation program, entered into the above-sketched complex. (Frozen-appropriations, civil service, the classification system, the World War, etc., etc.) It was the business of Indian Service to find ways to circumvent such factors. Instead, they accumulated like barnacles and weeds on an old schooner never hauled out and cleaned.

"Here are some that I consider to be universal Point IV propositions:

"1. Conservation is technology but much more—95 per cent of the whole—is psychology and human organization. This is the case in the U.S.A., Sweden, and other countries, and how much more necessarily and properly so in Navaholand, Africa, and so on.

"2. The relationship between 'modern-occidental' administration, leadership, education, and so forth, and the 'non-modern-occidental' peoples is something different from a mere agglomeration or drift of particulars. Rather, it tends to have an idiosyncrasy and individuality which is detectable in the 'reactions' at both ends.

"Now, when, as on the Navaho, the white superiority and the omnipotence of technology are tacitly or openly declared all over the place, and are represented by an administrative set—of an *ethos* essentially managerial (sometimes authoritarian)—then decidedly there will be found 'idiosyncrasy' and 'individuality' in the reactions of the group being pressured or missionized. Any detail is likely to be absorbed into this total reaction, the more entirely so, in the measure that the detail is painful or obnoxious to the pressured group.

"I leave the proposition thus very general; but it may explain why I feel that the *whole* of the administration and *spiritual* situation on Navaho (and anywhere in Asia or Africa!) has to be considered, in interpreting any part of it.

"Let me conclude by saying again that while the case is good, the analysis does not go far enough. Except in its reference to failure to consult Navaho local groups as to projects, it seems to leave the impression that the psycho- and sociopathological eventuality was inevitable. And this, I suspect because the chapter implies (or more) that (a) the knowledge as to the nature and physical dimensions of the Navaho community was put into effect; and (b) the conservation enterprise and the rest of the Indian Service enterprises were integrated. Both implications are misleading.

"Now, it might be that a sustained effort to identify the effective social units, to genuinely counsel with them, to develop placement for their leadership, would have been in vain. As it was, however, the sustained effort never was made (and I refer to the whole identification of Navaho problems and the whole flow of Government-Indian effort at solutions). By 'made' I mean not merely conceived, proposed, preached, and even ordered to personnel, but wrought out in administrative practice.

"The fundamental Point IV hypothesis is, I take it, that success depends on managing somehow to bring about what was not brought about on the Navaho, but is implied immediately above."

Case 12

EXPERIMENT IN CONSERVATION: Erosion Control and Forage Production on the Papago Indian Reservations in Arizona

by Henry F. Dobyns

1. THE PROBLEM

In 1945 the soil conservationist of the Papago Indian Agency returned to duty, after serving in the United States Navy, filled with determination to make the world a little better place in which to live. Eager to reverse deterioration of Papago lands, he faced serious local erosional problems.

At Gu Achi village, for example, the Papago school-bus driver complained that the big arroyo by the village constantly cut back its banks, threatening school buildings. People wanted something done to protect not only the school, but also their own houses and fields where one flood could make six-inch gullies or bury bean plants under silt.

The Indians lacked both capital and knowledge to undertake corrective measures. Unable to raise a crop since 1941, they depended on wage work outside their reservations. Grazing lands were virtually grassless after two droughts in a decade, which wiped out most small ranchers. Surviving herds had insufficient forage, especially during the hot summers. The Papagos watched helplessly.

The conservationist lacked funds to do more than survey and advise. In 1946 for the 2,855,021 acres he had only the assistance of a clerk and one irregularly employed Indian helper, and $9,557 for salaries and expenses. The Papago reservations had already lost three inches of topsoil from 50 per cent of their area, nine inches or practically all the topsoil from another quarter of a million acres. (Connecticut, about the same size, had, in 1949, 28 Soil Conservation Service employees, costing $101,277 plus $22,368 for expenses, and yet only 6 per cent of the land had lost one-fourth to three-fourths of its topsoil.) What could the conservationist do with his minute facilities?

2. THE COURSE OF EVENTS

1. During 1946 the soil conservationist and extension agent got erosion control work carried out on 527,842 acres of grazing land in Schuk Toak District. A community pasture was built, a truck trail constructed, a *charco* (an artificial basin to catch flood waters) deepened, 15 miles of fence repaired or built, 5 corrals repaired, a new *charco* built, brush cleared from a Johnson grass meadow, and several brush dams put in gullies on the Tribal Herd Ranch. Papagos living in Schuk Toak did all this work (except the *charco*, which was constructed by a private contractor) without capital investment. Since 1946 further work has been done there on a small scale by local initiative, but not under Agency supervision.

2. After his Schuk Toak experience, the conservationist felt he could act on the critical situation in Gu Achi District. Five huge earthen water-spreading dikes were constructed in 1947 by private contractors at no investment cost to Papagos, and with only survey work being done through Indian Bureau funds. Dikes were thrown across a large arroyo draining about 100 square miles. The staggered series forced flood waters over an area of some 2,000 acres. In 1947 and 1948 all runoff was absorbed, indicating the watershed had been removed from the flood-producing class and rendered practically harmless. A heavy crop of annual grasses grew on the formerly totally unproductive area flooded, and water was held by the dikes for stock grazing on the new forage.

3. In 1948 three more large dikes were constructed in Gu Achi District. In 1949 sleek, fat cattle grazed on a very heavy crop of grasses seeded over the spreader area. Construction began on a flood-control dam upstream from the village on the arroyo threatening the school and houses. By the end of that year one dike had been washed out by an unusually heavy flood because of faulty location, but was an insignificant loss to the total program. During that year 1,952 structures were built, costing $62,250. None of the conservationist's $28,000 appropriation went for this work.

4. The conservationist had increased his effectiveness by well over 200 per cent merely in terms of money devoted to erosion control. Actually, his increased effectiveness was far greater, since he was getting work accomplished when he could do next to nothing with his own appropriation. And his work was bearing rich fruit in Papago interest and effort toward erosion control, range management, and forage production.

5. How had he been able to accomplish so much with so little? How could Papagos without capital hire so much heavy earth moving? How had he persuaded them to undertake so ambitious a program, these Indians who blame whites for lack of rain? Why had he accomplished so much more in Gu Achi than in Schuk Toak District?

The answer to such questions is a sketch of the actions of an able administrator.

3. RELEVANT FACTORS

The Papagos live in southern Arizona. Papagueria, as their country is called, is the southern end of the Basin and Range physiographic province. Steep fault-block mountains separate nearly level deep-fill valleys. Intermittent streams cut the surface, but no rain falling on Papagueria ever reaches the sea.

This is arid country. Rainfall is highest—about 18 inches—on Baboquivari Peak, decreasing westward to about 5 inches at Tinajas Altas. It is concentrated in late summer, usually falling in brief, intense storms, which fill dry stream channels with angry, muddy waters, frequently reaching cloudburst proportions. Little rainfall stays where it falls except on flat valleys, since sheet erosion removes soil not held by plant roots. Therefore, vegetation is spotty and xerophytic-thorny and wax protected.

Stock is kept out of fields by barbed wire on mesquite posts, so that pliers and wire-stretchers are familiar Papago tools. Corn, beans, pumpkins, tobacco, and cotton were grown before white men appeared; Spanish missionaries added wheat, peas, lentils, barley, melons, and chili, along with Catholicism. Papagos domesticated *eohuk* (*Martynia louisiana*), the pod bark being their black material for basket designs.

Frost danger ends in mid-February but sowing cannot begin till July rains enable plowing, and start the luxuriant weeds that must be hoed out. Late rains, insufficient rain locally, too much flooding, early frost can all result in failure. Papago farming walks a swaying wire to success across disaster. People show constant concern over lack of rain, many insisting it has not rained so much since the whites came.

Missionaries introduced domestic animals: horses, cattle, sheep, goats, and swine to enrich the food supply and complicate range use. Sheep and goats were not adapted to hot country and soon were dropped. Few swine are raised, since there is little feed. Papagos long hunted cattle as deer, when large wild herds roamed. Practical Papagos learned to manage them, but handling still is rough (animals are feared because of illnesses they are believed to cause). Mexican political unrest and a United States cattle depression, ending the long post-Civil War boom, dissolved many non-Papago ranches in and near Papagueria, leaving numbers of cattle to the Indians around the turn of the century. Enterprising men built large herds; perhaps a third of the men became ranchers.

Flash floods flow with nearly every summer storm. Absorption being low, most runoff is in sheets, gathering into dry channels cut by previous storms. Steep mountains give floods tremendous velocity, and cutting power is great because of a maximum silt load; rapid erosion results.

Social Organization

The family is the basic social unit among Papagos as with every other people. While the eldest man usually heads a household, descent is reckoned through both parents. Although subordinate to men, women are not downtrodden, each sex having definite responsibilities. Ridicule, gossip, and praise keep people in line and stimulate them to act. No one is forced, merely persuaded, since spoken words achieve all things.

A typical Papago settlement is a *rancheria*—a group of houses scattered through the brush barely within sight of one another.

Real villages have grown up in the past forty years around drilled wells which furnish a permanent water supply—something the Papagos previously lacked.

With its officers and activities, each village functions as a political entity. A headman acts for the villagers in outside contacts, especially with non-Papagos. He may inherit office or be elected by the village council, but holds office only by common consent. He may be replaced any time his work becomes unsatisfactory. Seldom ahead of village opinion, he is spokesman rather than leader, expressing village attitudes rather than forming them. The more accurately he reflects his village, the better he is at his job. No good Papago makes himself "big."

Yet, a headman may be powerful. Remarkably foresighted, concerned with his people's welfare, he is responsible for them and expected to feel his responsibility. Villagers look to him for ideas. Therefore, although he may not formulate opinion, he guides and helps it along. He calls meetings of the village council —the adult men—to talk over decisions of any importance.

Said one headman:

> When we're going to have a meeting I go around and tell everybody what time we're going to have it. Meetings are held here at my house.
>
> If somebody from the Agency is coming, they send word so I can go round and tell the people to come. I tell the people there will be someone coming, and if I know his name, I call it. At the meetings sometimes I tell the man's name, and tell why he came over, and what he's going to talk about. I tell them to go ahead and say what they want to.
>
> We have to use interpreters because some of these old people don't understand English.

A headman does not act on important matters until his council agrees on the course. Unanimity is a strong Papago idea—one they usually achieve at the cost of speedy action. It may take weeks or months. Some issues, never agreed upon, are never acted upon. When outsiders demand fast action, not allowing time to achieve unanimity, Papagos are disturbed.

Subsistence

At mountain edges where gradients level off, streams flowing after rains spread and slow down. Here Papagos clear the brush with axe, hoe, and rake, digging ditches to bring water from an arroyo, building low dikes to spread it uniformly. A horse or mule team breaks ground with a steel plow for hand seeding.

To bartering people who had no banks, horses became wealth; surpluses went into half-wild herds. A tired mount was released and another roped. With an inexhaustible supply, Papagos little minded the quality of their stock. Carrying capacity of the range is rated around 12,000 cattle units today. By the mid-1930's 50,000 animal units and more abused the range— cattle were estimated at 30,000 head, horses probably equaled that figure.

Effects of astronomical overstocking on range, poor to begin with, defy imagination. Grass was eradicated in many areas, and replaced by mesquite. Drought came during the 1930's and hundreds of animals died from want of water. Then came dourine, an infectious and incurable horse disease; it was eradicated by destroying infected animals. Permits issued under the Tribal Council's ten-horse maximum are usually for fewer horses, so that each man feels he needs more than his permit allows, although all agree permits are needed. All look longingly back to the good old days when thousands of cattle ranged, and blame the lack of feed on diminished rain.

Stock has natural water only after rains. When rain-pools dry, animals must go to *charcos* or wells. There were no wells until 1912 and fewer than 30 by 1934. Then the Civilian Conservation Corps (CCC) built stock wells that opened large areas to grazing, but most of the range still has *charcos*. Few are permanent where evaporation from an open water surface is nine feet annually and where silting is rapid.

Through the CCC many Papagos made their first close contact with Anglo-American technology and cash economy, though numbers had worked for wages in kind. When young men went to work, economic domination by patriarchs ended. The war caused even heavier demand for Papago labor at much higher wages. Barter and gift-exchange are gone, and Papagos operate within the wider American cash economy.

Administration

Federal. Papagos live on three United States reservations— lands held in trust for them by the government. These are administered and certain services rendered the people by the Papago Indian Agency, in the Bureau of Indian Affairs of the Department of the Interior.

Under a superintendent, Agency divisions carry out specialties. *Education* operates seven schools. Domestic and stock wells are drilled by *Irrigation*, which also operates two small irrigation projects. *Roads* builds and maintains roads and trails. *Medical* operates one inadequate hospital and a token field program. *Forestry* devotes most of its attention to the range. *Extension* supposedly does for Papagos what county agricultural agents do for non-Indian stockmen and farmers. *Soil and Moisture Conservation* does for Indians what Soil Conservation Service does for non-Indians.

Every administrator is theoretically accessible to any Indian who wants to talk to him. Most Papagos find the Agency so forbidding that they stay away unless summoned or are in serious difficulty. Conversely, some Indians are well acquainted with administrators, using this connection for their own ends.

Tribal. No tribal organization existed until 1937, when Papagos organized under a written constitution, authorized by the Indian Reorganization Act of 1934. The tribe elected twenty men to write its constitution in an election in which only three western reservation villages voted, leaving that section almost unrepresented. Like the Agency, the organized tribe came into being because of the growing contact between Papagos and whites. Their primary task is adjustment between Papago and Anglo-American cultures.

During the 1930's the Agency fenced the reservations into eleven districts, roughly following territorial divisions among the Papagos but intended as economic units. These became political districts for the tribe, two delegates from each composing the Tribal Council.

According to the constitution each district elects a council of no fewer than five. In 1937 this practice was followed and councils functioned with village headman members. After causing serious local Papago opposition for two years by doing work where and as they thought of it, CCC planners decided to try to adapt their program to local wants. In 1936 they had begun attending meetings in each village to ask for suggestions. Gratified at being consulted, the people put in requests for everything they would like to have the government provide. The CCC men recorded all, fulfilled what they could, and referred the rest to the Agency. They were in closer touch with the people than the Agency, which lacked comparable funds or personnel. When district councils were elected, CCC men found they could save much time planning programs on a district rather than village basis. Councilmen then held the village meetings that had taken so much CCC time, and relayed requests at district council meetings. Councilmen in this way came to handle considerable patronage—they could get things done, and people realized it.

War ended CCC programs and practically ended the usefulness of district councils, which gradually ceased to meet.

The over-all tribal organization fared better. The council elected a chairman and settled down to a routine of monthly meetings at the Agency town. It strengthened by surviving crises and surmounting obstacles: eradicating dourine, reducing horses on the range, taxing traders, insuring its budget with a cattle sales tax, paying its own officers, and so forth.

State. Papago reservations occupy parts of Pima, Pinal, and Maricopa counties, Arizona. Problems of state jurisdiction over reservations is a point at issue between Arizona and the federal government.

Only recently has the state, under federal pressure, begun to include Indians in its welfare program, since federal grants-in-aid to the program are based on total state population, including Indians.

In other aspects of work, there is less friction. Pima County Agricultural Conservation Association distributes federal funds to farmers and ranchers who carry out conservation practices on their land. From 1943 to 1945 the Papago Tribal Herd Ranch (operated under supervision of the Agency Extension Division) received benefit payments for conservation practices—mesquite control and piping water to even the grazing load. Schuk Toak District, where the Ranch is located, was the only district eligible for benefits. Under regulations of the Production and Marketing Administration (United States Department of Agriculture) all the other districts had livestock populations too far above their rated carrying capacity to qualify.

Arizona's State Livestock Sanitary Board exercises as much authority over the reservations as it can. It pays half the salary of a joint State-Papago Tribe Livestock Inspector to enforce branding and cattle sales inspection regulations.

The state and counties build roads across the reservations to gain access to non-Indian towns. The tribe grants rights-of-way willingly, viewing improved communication as one of its greatest needs. Papago officials occasionally confer with school and health officials off their reservations in connection with work for Indians during agricultural harvests.

REFERENCES FOR FURTHER STUDY

Castetter, E. F., and W. H. Bell, *Pima and Papago Indian Agriculture.* University of New Mexico Press, Albuquerque, 1942.

Hoover, F. W., "The Indian Country of Southern Arizona," *Geographic Review*, vol. 19, January, 1929, pp. 38–60.

Joseph, Alice, Rosamond B. Spicer, and Jane Chesky, *The Desert People: A Study of the Papago Indians of Southern Arizona.* University of Chicago Press, 1949.

Secretary of the Interior, *Papago Development Program:* Report of the Papago Tribal Council. Washington, 1949.

Answer Question Presented in the Problem
Before Reading the Rest of the Case.

4. THE OUTCOME

The Papago Indian Agency's conservationist faced a nearly impossible problem, but tackled it courageously. Having inadequate funds, he decided that a reservation-wide program would merely dissipate his energies without significant accomplishment. He chose to concentrate on a limited area. If he succeeded, he would have an example to follow. If he failed, he would not be irrevocably committed everywhere, but could start over somewhere else. As an administrator, he reduced his problem to proportions with which he could reasonably expect to cope.

The conservationist also limited his goals. His small appropriation would not pay for expensive work. Neither could the Papagos afford it, but they could perform jobs that required no more tools than the shovels, hammer, and so forth, they all owned and used. Work should be such that little direction would be needed—work Papagos were used to doing. It had to fit the current sociocultural situation of Papago tool ownership and mastery, habits, capital, and attitudes toward range land.

The conservationist thought there was an opportunity to get Papagos to perform erosional control work which would qualify them for benefit payments by the Production and Marketing Administration (Agricultural Conservation Programs Branch). He therefore decided to concentrate first on Schuk Toak District, because it was eligible for benefits.

Less damaged by overgrazing than other regions, it seemed to present a chance to show impressive results. The county Agricultural Conservation Association designated the district as one project, which meant obtaining consent of the district as a whole —bringing to life again a moribund district council.

The conservationist and extension agent decided to try to persuade the Schuk Toak people to undertake erosion control works. They drove to nine villages and talked to headmen, asking them to call meetings. They attended five village meetings, some lasting from 2 p.m. till midnight. They tried to explain to villagers types

of practices for which PMA (Production and Marketing Administration) paid benefits. Looking back, they said:

> We tried to give people at the meetings the general idea of PMA.
> We gave them the different types of practices, such as fence con-
> struction, well development, *charco* development, erosion control and
> water-spreading, and range management.

This was all presented through interpreters, and they found it
paid to use interpreters liked by each village. "The villagers do
not make any bones of their dislike; they say 'Don't bring that
man back here again.' At X . . . . the chief was very indignant
and told me that." Accurate interpretation was sometimes sacri-
ficed to good relationships.

Meeting the villagers, the Indian Bureau representatives found
everywhere a barrage of requests for specific improvements.
Casting back in their previous experience with white men, people
at once thought of the CCC planners of a decade before. Trying
to classify new administrators, they drew a parallel to meetings
held by CCC men, and equated PMA with CCC. This made it
difficult to explain that PMA would pay benefits a year after
work was done. People expected PMA to hire them, paying for
work as it was done. They lacked experience from their wage-
work careers to prepare them for a concept of delayed payment.
Patiently explaining over and over at each gathering, the Agency
men clarified the situation.

After seeing villagers on their home ground, the officials succeeded in having a district meeting called. Some fifty people
came. "The District organization was very fluid, and it was hard
to know who were the representatives and who were the spec-
tators," said the conservationist. The extension agent admitted
he "may have resorted to flag-waving to get them to understand
that the U. S. government, of which they were a part, was aware
of them and wanted to help them conserve their resources, so that
the government was willing to help by paying them money if the
people were interested and would provide the work." The two
administrators went back over ground covered in villages. Suspicious of a gift, the people went home without a decision, still
confused.

So the officials went back to headmen, asked for more meetings, talked points over again. People discussed the issue among themselves. When the Agency was able to have another district meeting called, a decision had been reached. "We told them that if they signed these papers the government would give them some money. The explanation was on that scale. They were only confused otherwise. We didn't want them to reject it; we had to sell them." (There was a time limit on applications set by the county Association.) The district council signed agreements with Pima County Agricultural Conservation Association.

The program was left to the Papagos. The conservationist surveyed, advised, set up minimum work standards so that improvements would qualify for benefits. Papagos did the rest. Except for work on the Tribal Herd Ranch, projects were selected by villagers. Headmen assigned men to work, either under their own direction or that of a range foreman. Fencing, corral repairing, brush dam construction, and clearing were familiar tasks. But *charcos* were another matter, silting having increased beyond the scope of horse equipment. The conservationist found a contractor with earth-moving equipment who was willing to perform the job for the amount of the benefit payment and to wait to be paid until the people received their benefits. The district approved and a *charco* was constructed and another deepened.

The district council received $7,918 in payments for work approved. The contractor was paid. Unable to agree on a district program after the first year under the conservationist's plan, the council allotted benefit money to villages. They used it to purchase groceries for men working on further improvements and for hay for their horses. Work continued with the conservationist advising the people, but the amount of work done was not what he had hoped for, despite his having worked through Papago political organizations.

The conservationist remembered that Gu Achi villagers felt a need for erosion control work which the Schuk Toak people lacked. They already were asking for aid to protect their village. The conservationist conferred with the Gu Achi headman, who called a meeting. Through the local bus driver, the official explained erosion control methods. With an extension employee whose home was in Gu Achi, he explored the vicinity for two weeks, assessing erosion. At another meeting he explained that Gu Achi could get work done by assigning contractors their benefit payments.

Returning to headquarters, the conservationist left the burden of persuasion on the bus driver and local extension man. The latter held a long meeting, during which people hurled questions at these men which they hesitated to ask the headquarters official. The program fitted Gu Achi's sociocultural situation well. The villagers realized their need of assistance and wanted it. They chose earthen spreader dikes to control some of the worst flooding.

The conservationist called in an engineer from the Bureau's Area Office to survey, since his own funds were inadequate. The engineer surveyed a good technical layout, but when the village leaders went over the ground they objected. The conservationist recovered his fumble. He resurveyed according to the wishes of the villagers, who had been ignored by the Area man. He turned planning back to them, restoring the feeling that the project was theirs. "We started to try to go more and more with what the people wanted wherever feasible." Technical advice was not allowed to become planning; over-professionalism was avoided.

The headman and bus driver led in securing necessary signatures on agreements with the County Association and contractor. After surveying and bringing contractor and people together, the administrator left execution of the project to the people.

When completed dikes functioned as predicted late that summer (1947), growing hundreds of acres of forage, Gu Achi was convinced. Changed regulations designed to equalize benefit payments (which tended to go too much to large corporate farms) held up work in 1948, but a solution was worked out. In 1949, twelve Gu Achi men signed two pooling agreements for $4,500, and four from neighboring Akchin signed a $3,000 agreement.

5. ANALYSIS

How did the conservationist achieve greater success in erosion control and forage production in Gu Achi District than in Schuk Toak? In most respects his activities in both areas were the same. His programs answered immediate economic needs, meant more income from more productive ranges, could be carried out by the people without capital. He dealt through Papago political organizations, through the headmen and village meetings. He allowed full discussion as long as possible. Once decisions were made, he left villagers to execute plans on their responsibility, not interfering even when he thought he could do the job better.

Apparently the Schuk Toak program suffered from being a first attempt, somewhat experimental. The conservationist wisely had not committed himself throughout the reservations to this type of program. Being committed in only one district, he could proceed elsewhere unhandicapped. In Gu Achi District he knew much better where he was headed and how to get there.

A fundamental difference was the "felt need" in Gu Achi and its lack in Schuk Toak District. The administrator showed Gu Achi how to satisfy its need. However, he had to sell Schuk Toak people not only a bill of goods, but also on their need for the goods. This largely explains Schuk Toak District's failure to carry on for more benefits—they lacked the urge which in Gu Achi was constantly moving people to act.

Joined to this factor was planning. The administrators sold Schuk Toak people a plan, somewhat cynically as far as the extension agent was concerned. Though consulted, the Indians felt pressed because of the application deadline; they did not have time to discuss, understand, and adopt the plans as theirs. The program remained the property of the Agency, accepted for the money it would bring. Cash, not improvement, was motivation. The amount was insufficient to produce continuation of the work once pressure relaxed.

In Gu Achi District Papagos planned every step of the way. The administrator presented alternative solutions to their felt needs. They chose, although the conservationist influenced their choice by selecting solutions to present. He almost erred, as in Schuk Toak, by calling in the engineer from the Bureau's Area Office, who did not consult the people's wishes and superior knowledge of local terrain. The conservationist got back on the right track by ignoring this unilateral plan, laying the project out where the people said it should go. Furnishing only technical knowledge, he left planning to them.

The conservationist faced a complication in Schuk Toak in bringing to life again the impotent district council. Since it had no other function, it quickly lapsed into ineffectiveness. PMA regulations forced this on the conservationist. Changed regulations simplified his problem in Gu Achi District.

Another factor differentiating Gu Achi from Schuk Toak District was residence in the village of a member of the administrative group who was accepted by the people as a part of the local group. He was included within the in-group feeling. Therefore, his position on erosion control was ultimately more significant than that of the headquarters official. The brunt of selling the program fell on him as the administrator on the spot. Although he was not employed by the conservationist, he sold the program. This illustrates the necessity for field personnel in close contact with administered peoples to be as flexible as possible, and to have the background, ability, and willingness to represent almost any aspect of the culture the administration seeks to present to the people. For he *is* the administration to the people.

PEOPLE OF THE HINTERLAND: Community
Interrelations in a Maritime Province of Canada [1]
by Allister Macmillan and Alexander H. Leighton

1. THE PROBLEM

The subject of this case is a cluster of 118 people living in 29 houses scattered along 2 miles of road in one of the Maritime Provinces of Canada. We shall refer to it as "The Road" and the rural county of approximately 20,000 in which it exists will be called "Stirling." These, together with all other proper names in this study, are fictitious.

The community is an economically depressed hinterland of the immediate coastal region. Its outstanding characteristic is the reputation of its inhabitants in the neighboring communities and, to a large extent, throughout Stirling County. Although variously expressed, it may be summed up by saying that these people are alleged to have an exceedingly high rate of (1) feeblemindedness, (2) insanity, (3) promiscuity, (4) inbreeding (including incest), (5) crime and delinquency (particularly theft), (6) laziness and unreliability as employees, and (7) alcoholism.

It is also said that the people of The Road "won't pay their taxes" and cost Stirling County large sums of money annually in relief, institutional care, and similar items. The attitudes of the neighboring communities are condensed into the nickname "Monkeytown," and it is often said, "Once a monkey, always a monkey—they are just no damn good."

The central problem of this case presentation is why these people have such a reputation. Are they actually as they are represented? If not, what is the nature of the community and what in it has inspired the reputation? If it has particular defects, what is their origin and are they being perpetuated? If so, how and why?

[1] The authors wish to express their indebtedness to Professor W. H. D. Vernon of Acadia University, Wolfville, Nova Scotia, for his suggestions and guidance and to the Canadian National Research Council and the Department of Sociology and Anthropology of Cornell University for financial assistance.

We are, unfortunately, not able to offer self-evident and clear-cut answers to these questions, but it is hoped that a review of data that have been obtained in a study of The Road will be informative and provocative of insight. Some of the dynamic factors do stand out and it should be possible for the reader to lay out and evaluate sets of alternative explanations. We think that many aspects of The Road problem are common in rural areas, even if in milder form, and are consequently important in any program aimed at raising living, health, and educational standards.

2. THE COURSE OF EVENTS

In the summer of 1949, one of the writers (A. M.) undertook the giving of intelligence tests to all the children of The Road in order to see if there were not some who were normal enough to be salvaged by special educational efforts. Preliminary contacts with the community threw considerable doubt on the accuracy of popular opinion regarding their mentality and behavior. As a consequence, the scope of the study was broadened to include data regarding all the alleged characteristics of The Road. This, in turn, led to exploring the economic, social, and cultural makeup of the community and its history from its origin in the mid-nineteenth century down to the present time.

1. In the 1850's the shore of Stirling County near what is now The Road contained a village of about 50 families which we shall call Port Harmony. It was predominantly an English settlement with a very active economic life centered in building wooden sailing ships and in exporting timber cut in forests lying inland beyond The Road. The leaders of Port Harmony were merchant-ship builders and the next in status were the ships' officers and skilled tradesmen, such as carpenters and smiths. The work of Port Harmony also required a good deal of labor, and much of this was supplied by young men from predominantly French-speaking settlements that lay farther westward along the shore and in a valley of the interior. These men were usually surplus labor in their community of origin; that is, they had not inherited

their fathers' farms, or other means of subsistence and were consequently attracted by the work available at Port Harmony. By
1860 a few of these men had settled along The Road because it
was adjacent to their work. In those days it was as it is now—
barren, rocky, and of little use for farming or even lumbering.

2. In the succeeding decades, The Road grew to be increasingly convenient as a spot to live, especially when it became very
profitable to haul timber with ox-teams from the interior to the
shore. This wood was largely cut by the members of a French
farm-lumbering community, which we shall refer to as Beau Pré
and which lay inland about eight miles from Port Harmony.

The men on The Road, therefore, lived from wages and occupied a place between English-Protestant-commercial-and-pros-
perous Port Harmony from which they got their income and
French-Catholic-farming-woodcutting-stable Beau Pré, to which
they were tied by kinship, tradition, and value systems.

3. Although there were economic fluctuations, and a world-
wide depression beginning in 1873, the people of The Road
continued relatively prosperous because shipbuilding and the
exploitation of forest products remained active in this region.
Oldtimers tell of a life that was full of parties and "frolics," a
society evidently adequately equipped with recreation and social
organization. Emigration to the United States absorbed every-
body desiring work beyond what was available locally.

4. However, as a result of the passage of time and their socio-
geographic position, the people of The Road became somewhat
detached from their cultural and actual kin in the French communities, without achieving integration into English-dominated
Port Harmony. Although tied to the latter by vital economic
bonds, they occupied the lowest rungs of a society which, unlike
the French communities, had very marked class structure. Cultural heterogeneity, or confusion, on The Road was further pro-
moted by intermarriage with Protestant families of Scotch-Irish,
English, and German origin.

5. Perhaps the most significant single cultural factor was the
establishment in 1870 of a Baptist Mission at the inland extremity
of The Road, with the stated purpose of converting Roman

Catholics to that faith. The Mission lasted until 1890, when it
was abandoned because "it did not succeed in making a permanent impression on the stubborn environment in which it had
attempted to establish itself."[1] This statement is probably true as
far as making Baptists is concerned, but it fails to note the effect
the Mission had in weakening the previous faith and in dividing
families on religious issues. The failure of the Mission, which had
received considerable support from the merchants of Port Harmony, also served to mobilize hostility against all the French in
the area, particularly the people of The Road.

6. Early in the twentieth century, both lumber exportation
and the building of wooden ships began to decline. The former
because large timber was becoming exhausted and because a
formerly brisk New England market for wharf pilings was closing;
the latter occurred as a result of steam and steel hulls replacing
the schooner. There was a temporary boom during World War I
and a complete collapse afterward. Port Harmony as a shipbuilding and exporting center vanished, leaving only a few rot-
ting remains of wharfs to give any hint that this was once a port.

7. Descendants of the original inhabitants, however, continue
to live in the vicinity. Compared to the "old days," they have
come on hard times, but, being on the shore, on the main highway, on good land and having had considerable property, capital,
and prestige with which to make the adjustment to new socio-
economic conditions, they have managed much better than the
people of The Road. The latter have come to be defined more
and more as "monkeys."

This name appears to have been given by a storekeeper in one
of the English-speaking communities on the coast near The Road
in the latter part of the nineteenth century. In the winter the men
from The Road used to crowd into the store and hang about the
stove all evening. At that time they spoke English with a very
strong French accent mixed with many French words. The "jab-
bering" plus the crowding habits finally got on the storekeeper's
nerves and he roared out one night, "You damn bunch of jabber-

---

[1] Levy, George E. *The Baptists of the Maritime Provinces.* Barnes-Hopkins Ltd.,
Saint John, New Brunswick, 1946, p. 346.

ing monkeys, get out of here and don't come back." The people on the main road had a great laugh about the incident and "monkey" (or, more accurately, a similar kind of name) became a permanent label.

8. The study carried out in 1949 went into each of the counts on which the people of The Road are believed to be different from others in the region. The conclusions reached may be briefly summarized as follows. The people of The Road have normal intelligence, are not particularly psychotic, are not inbred, lazy, criminal, alcoholic, or highly expensive to the county.[1] It was found, however, that they differ from the surrounding society in being at a lower economic level, in sometimes being casual and informal about marital arrangements, and in being weak in regard to normative values concerning reliability (particularly as employees), provision for the future, and the practice of religion.

Against this historical background and in the light of the study results the problem may be posed again: Why do these people have a reputation for deficiency or excess in so many matters in which the evidence shows them to be otherwise? In order to answer the question, it will be necessary to consider factors operating in their present social and economic condition.

3. RELEVANT FACTORS

Inhabitants of The Road number 118 men, women, and children, living in 29 houses scattered along a little less than 2 miles of gravel road. Of the 118, there are 66 who are under the age of twenty-one. When comparison is made with average figures for the Province, The Road is seen to have two striking features: a complete lack of elderly females and a very small percentage of both sexes in their twenties. The latter is explained by the residents as due to young people moving away in search of work. No explanation is available for the former.

Of the 19 married couples, 17 live in separate establishments and 2 live together. Of these unions, about 8 or 9 are past the age

[1] A fuller study giving details in regard to these findings is now in preparation.

of producing children. Six single males live in separate homes and range in age from 22 to over 60. One bachelor of 90 boards in one of the married households and 3 bachelors who are "still eligible" live in their fathers' homes. Three elderly widowers and 3 men whose wives have left them maintain separate domiciles. There are no widows at present on The Road, and only two single females, both under 30 and both living with their families. One of these spinsters is blind.

Among the 66 children (infants to 20 years inclusive), there are about 20 per cent more males than females (we say "about" because uncertain of the sex of one or two infants). This preponderance of males is an exaggeration of a general characteristic of unknown origin in Stirling County.

Most of the adults on The Road do not have any skilled trade and there does not appear to be much chance in the vicinity for acquiring such education. About half the male adults (around 20) depend on clam-digging for their main source of income. Numbers of these also take other jobs if available, such as cutting pulpwood or day labor for a farmer or a construction company. In most cases such laboring work is preferred and clamming is something one falls back on when nothing else can be had. This is not hard to understand since, while relatively lucrative, it is extremely arduous, exposes one to all kinds of weather, varies with the tides, and necessitates traveling 20 miles to reach the clam beds.

A young man, single and in good health, may enjoy it for a time, but once he marries, clamming as an occupation presents a number of serious difficulties. It takes the father away from home, income varies capriciously with weather, season, and the luck of finding clams. A steady job, even if paying less per working day, begins to look attractive, though very difficult for a Roadite to find locally. Yet, for those who have married it is virtually impossible to amass the necessary capital to move to another part of the county in the hope (and it could only be hope) of finding steady work.

About half as many as those who go clamming work primarily for lumber companies, either in the woods or at sawmills. This is a little higher order of skill than clamming and most of those who do it have had the opportunity to learn the methods in their families.

Other kinds of occupation in which one or more people engage, at least part time, include driving mail from railroad to post office, trucking, working on the railroad, and trapping. Several people draw old-age pensions and one draws a war pension for service during World War I.

On the whole, the people on The Road feel they are discriminated against in the matter of jobs, being the last hired and the first fired.

One of the main sources of secondary income on The Road is from the work of wives in clam-shucking plants in the town of Bristol. Of the 19 wives on The Road, 12 do some shucking and 6 of these are fairly regular in attendance. The importance of this work goes beyond the immediate wages because the shuckers are eligible for unemployment insurance while the clam diggers are not. Thus the wives' summer jobs frequently help also in winter when weather shuts down clam work for both husband and wife.

This opportunity and the strong economic pressures for wife as well as husband to work affect family life. Care of younger children falls to older ones or to neighbors during the entire day and instances were noted where the result seemed to be neglect of the youngsters in terms of meals, as well as in love and attention.

Like most of the other residents of Stirling County, the people of The Road own the land on which they live, but, having said this, one must add that it is poor land, being good neither for farming nor for wood as a source of cash. Not only is the land poor for crops, but no one resident owns enough of it to do modern farming—even if he had the necessary knowledge and capital. Such lumber as existed was cut long ago and the residents keep the new growth pretty well cleaned off for their fuel.

Out of the 29 establishments on The Road, 16 have some kind of garden from which vegetables are obtained for home use. Few of these produce enough for winter storage and at least 7 families with children at home have no garden at all.

Fishing from wharfs on the shore and an occasional rabbit, partridge, or deer from the woods completes the sources of non-cash income.

The Family Allowance Act of 1944 was introduced for the purpose of equalizing opportunity for the children of Canada. The amount is paid monthly at so much per child, though it varies with the total number of children in a family. All children are eligible, regardless of socio-economic status. On The Road this source of income is very important to those families having children of school age.

Aside from drinking, hunting, and the movies in Bristol, recreation is extremely limited. Neither social patterns nor physical facilities seem to exist. The drinking is largely confined to the men and must make serious inroads on the money they earn.

The family units on The Road are organized according to the usual western cultural pattern, the father being the nominal head and the mother being responsible for the home and most of the care of the children. The daily round of routine chores about the place is divided among the members of the family and children are expected to begin doing their share fairly early in life. If the family has any cows and chickens and the husband is working, while the wife is not, she and the children look after feeding, pasturing, and milking. In the evening after the father returns from work, he takes care of repairs that are needed to windows, shoes, spades, saws, axes, and so forth.

Four definite kinship groups, or extended families, are evident, each of which looks back three or four generations to a male ancestor who settled on or near The Road. Three additional family groups trace themselves to more recently arrived predecessors and there is one individual who is unconnected with any of the preceding.

Of these eight family lines, seven are French and one Scottish in origin. However, in the course of the hundred years of the community's existence many have brought in English, Scotch-Irish, and German mates. English is now the prevailing language and only a few of the population, mostly old people, are able to speak or understand French to any significant degree.

Many of the communities adjacent to The Road contain both French and English families, but so far as we are able to estimate, they do not have nearly the same amount of intermarriage.

In one respect family organization in some groups on The Road has a characteristic that is unusual—employing the maternal rather than paternal name for purposes of identification. Like many other regions in both French and Scottish Canada, the surname for identification has little value because a majority of the people, whether related or not, have the same one. In such cases it is the custom to use paternal given-names as a means of identifying the children.

On The Road maternal names are used in this manner for a number of people. Thus, one not only finds individuals known as Frank-Tom and Bill-Tom (sons of Tom) but one also finds Henry-Mary and Charlie-Mary (sons of Mary). It appears that on The Road families may be oriented toward and known by either parent. This flexibility seems to us to be another indication of rather loose social organization and weak norms and it fits with what has been previously said about a certain casualness in marital relationships. We have here, it appears, biological and individual determinants taking precedence over social patterns.

Most houses on The Road are small frame "one-and-a-half" story buildings, frequently shingled on the side as well as the roof. There are no full basements with furnace-heating plants. A small summer "cool storage" space is provided in some houses under the ground floor, but there are no refrigerators or ice houses. The average number of rooms on the ground floor is three. All upstairs space is of the garret variety and is usually reached by means of a ladder, though a few have stairs. Lighting was by oil lamps until the year of the study, when a power line was established and several houses were wired for electricity.

Water is obtained by bucket from shallow wells or natural springs in pastureland behind the houses. None is protected from the contamination of surface drainage. Toilet facilities consist of the outside privy.

Fuel for heating and cooking is chiefly wood obtained from the pasture.

Only five individuals keep cows, chickens, or pigs. The total number of dogs seen was three and no cats were in evidence.

On the whole, the houses give the impression of having seen better days, even when they are actually of recent construction. No attempts are made to cultivate flowers. Although the yards are not piled with trash, they do, with three exceptions, give a feeling of untidiness.

The interiors of the houses are all very similar. Stove cleanliness and brightness seems to be a status symbol. The floors have linoleum laid over soft-wood boards. Family photographs are displayed in pasteboard frames on the walls together with calendars, a few pictures of the Royal Family, and still fewer crucifixes or other religious symbols. Only one house has a genuine living room, with woven wicker settee and matching chairs.

Privacy is practically nonexistent as the rooms are small and not fully separated from one another.

Although for convenience we have frequently referred to The Road as a "community," it fails to qualify as such on a number of counts. It has no store or other service and is not held together by any definable social organization. Two school districts are straddled, with the children at one end of The Road going to the inland school, while four or five at the opposite end attend a school at the shore. The Road has identity partly from geographic relationships, but primarily because the people are disowned by the adjacent communities and because they themselves recognize that they have in common this rejected lot. As one informant said with lowered eyes, "They call us monkeys."

In the communities near The Road and even in others many miles away, one hears very strong expressions of opinion against the people of The Road moving in among them. "They have to keep their place" and "We don't want them here" are general attitudes found equally in French and English groups. This must serve as an important source of deterrence for residents of The Road who try to get established in better opportunities elsewhere in the county.

For the same reason it is difficult for a Roadite to find a mate unless he travels a long distance and even then he is likely only to obtain someone who is also, even if for other reasons, a social rejectee.

There are no formal associations of any kind on The Road. The only outside organization to which any of the members belong is the Catholic Church of the parish in which The Road happens to lie. Even here, none of The Road women belongs to the church associations, so far as could be determined. This lack of membership in formal organizations is very unusual and is, perhaps, one of the most distinctive features of The Road. It deprives the inhabitants of the opportunity for gaining feelings of worth, belonging, and accomplishment; and it reinforces the differences between The Road and neighboring areas.

As has been mentioned earlier, the schools which the children attend lie outside The Road. These are partially controlled by local school boards, but the Roadites are not represented.

Informal association on The Road seems largely confined to patterns of visiting, of which three could be discerned: (1) within kinship groups; (2) among women who have married into the community and have no kin there; (3) among the four common-law wives.

Leadership on The Road is very limited and what there is seems primarily oriented toward economic activities. One man leads a wood-cutting team for a nearby lumber operator and one woman musters other women for shucking in a clam factory in Bristol.

So far as could be determined, the adults' education seems to be the equivalent of Grades IV and V, with none having had even junior high-school training. There were at least eight adults, however, who could not read or who did so only with great difficulty.

The fact that the Province has a system of grading teachers according to qualifications made it possible to review conditions for the previous fifteen years in the schools attended by Road children. It became immediately evident that they had been exposed to a series of "pinch-hitters," that is, unqualified teachers (some lacking even high-school training) who had been allowed to function only because no one better could be obtained. Thus, the majority of the children on The Road at the time of our study had never had the benefit or stimulation of a real teacher.

The only way a Road child can receive a high-school education is to board in the town of Bristol about ten miles away. Given the economic condition of the inhabitants of The Road, this is impossible.

It was interesting to note that mothers seemed aware of the advantages of education and that daughters tended to stay in school longer than boys. Fathers, on the other hand, were inclined to be contemptuous and opposed to giving "free board and lodging" to children old enough to earn a living. This facilitates the tendency of the boys to identify themselves as men as soon as possible by getting away from school, going out to work, and having money of their own with which to buy such items as a .22 rifle. Thus, a longer view of the future is eclipsed and the young man who leaves The Road is likely to find too late that his lack of education tends to bar him from any but the lowest paid and least stable kinds of work.

Only one person on The Road reads the daily paper. Books aside from school books are almost unknown. An occasional magazine such as *Life* is seen, but there are no magazine subscribers except the blind girl who receives a monthly periodical in Braille.

There are half-a-dozen battery radios which operate when the batteries are not dead. Those who listen do occasionally pass on items of news to others.

Movies are perhaps the steadiest medium of communication from the outside world and most of the older teenagers seem to manage to get to Bristol on Saturday night to see them.

It is likely that the bulk of information about the world comes in through those who go out to work in various jobs such as clamming, shucking, and lumbering and who pick up bits in conversations with others. The quality, under these circumstances, is probably not high.

Our information is not sufficiently quantitative to permit accurate statements regarding beliefs and attitudes on The Road, but some impressions have been obtained. Money is certainly considered one of the most important things in life. People often say that "in the good old days" it was easier to make a living. Toward the present and the future there is an attitude of hopelessness and helplessness. There seems to be no thought of attempting to initiate any business or industry, but rather a feeling of dependency on outsiders for opportunity and leadership. This is scarcely surprising when one considers their lack of education, lack of capital, and lack of exploitable raw materials on their poor houseplots, woodlots, and pastures.

Even though in their own and everyone else's eyes, the people of The Road occupy one of the lowest status levels of the county, status distinctions exist among them and are the source of considerable intragroup hostility and jealousy. Prestige items like the ability to read or the owning of a radio are conspicuously displayed and a number of individuals were heard to condemn other members of the group in almost the same terms as those employed by outsiders. It was as if each were saying to the interviewer, "I may live here, but I am not as low as the rest of these monkeys."

Steady jobs like working on the railroad as a section laborer have top occupational status. A close second is a job filled by one individual who does hauling with his own truck. Work in the woods is probably next, giving, as it does, a measure of independence and having more or less steadiness. Clamming is a last resort for older men, but doing day labor at odd jobs seems actually the bottom of the hierarchy.[1]

Beliefs and attitudes in regard to religion were also of interest on The Road. Although there are both Catholics and Protestants in the group, often in the same families, few individuals are strong adherents. On the other hand, a number were extremely hostile to one or the other of the denominations and it was clear that here again was a source of considerable intragroup tension.

Between job competition, status jealousies, and religious antagonisms, it seems to us that there is a currently high level of intra-

[1] As noted on page 230, day labor, although of lower occupational status, is preferred to clamming for economic and other reasons. It may be added here that the status of labor is raised if the work is for a "big organization" or an influential man.

group hostility and "self-hate" on The Road. Informants indicated that this had developed noticeably during the past twenty years.

What has been said about the people of The Road being at the bottom of the socio-economic scale of the county and having a sense of inferiority must not be construed to mean they lacked all self-respect and pride. Despite rough manners and crude eating habits, they do try to "keep up appearances" in their homes to the limit of their meager resources and the limitations imposed by having numerous children.

One may summarize their whole structure of beliefs and attitudes by saying that virtually all the values found in both Protestant English-speaking and French Catholic rural communities are present, but confused and in pale pastel shades rather than in vigorous color, except for the sense of shame and inferiority.

Answer Questions Presented in the Problem
Before Reading the Rest of the Case.

4. ANALYSIS

If we turn back to the original questions raised in "The Problem," it is clear that the people of The Road are not as they are pictured by the residents of surrounding communities, but it is also clear that they have a number of characteristics which mark them as distinct and at a disadvantage. These include low income, apathy, pale values (including unreliability), and lack of social organization. Discussion may therefore deal, first, with why the reputation of The Road is so different from its actuality and, second, with the reasons for the defects which the community does display.

Since no study was made of individuals or communities outside The Road in order to discover the reasons for their beliefs and attitudes, our remarks must be speculative. We may suppose, however, that, as a result of the friction of living in almost any society at any time, there is a certain latent hostility that is likely to discharge on whatever target comes into focus. In consequence, an individual or group that is distinctive may readily attract attention and become the customary object upon which aggression arising from many sources is discharged.

If we add to this situation the special conditions of a society that is frequently or continuously subject to strong anxiety, then the tendency to find a scapegoat might be increased. The brief résumé of the history of Port Harmony that has been given is enough to show that the communities near The Road have been subject to marked economic stress and threats to status for more than fifty years. The region as a whole has had numerous ups and downs, but the dominant trend has been toward greater and greater subsistence anxieties as raw materials from farm and woods have become difficult to produce and as world markets have shifted. In addition to this, there is considerable indication that the whole society is undergoing marked alteration in its structure and value systems with progressive dependence on employment and wages and progressive loss of independence, both economic and political. There has also been a breaking up of the large, mutually supporting family units. In such a changing scene, numerous anxieties are generated by uncertainty, by threats to security, and by conflicting loyalties.

In the particular case of the shore communities near The Road, one final factor may be added. The Roadites were formerly dependent economically on the people of the shore and tied by family connections to the people of the French communities. When hard times came, their plight and their needs were an implied demand on both former employers and kin to do something for them. These two groups, however, were also in straitened circumstances and faced with either increasing the threat to themselves by attempts at sharing or with rejecting the claim. To facilitate rejection, The Road had to be defined as objectionable and as being in its deplorable condition as a result of its own folly.

Having taken this position, guilt became added to the emotions of the rejectors and the stage was set for even stronger expressions of hostility as a means of suppressing uneasy feelings.

There is much in the situation that recalls what happened to the farmers of Oklahoma and Arkansas who were caught in the dust bowl and in the general economic depression of the 1930's.

Turning now to the people of The Road, the history of the community suggests that two main sets of factors were at work for many years in producing the picture we see today. The first of these might be called a kind of "acculturation" in which the people of The Road became confused between French and English values and customs. Separation from French communities, contact with English speakers, the Baptist Mission, and intermarriage all tended to weaken their orientation and security in their own cultural system. On the other hand, geographic position, lack of real acceptance in the English group, low status in that system, lack of education, language difficulty, and the hold that the French way of life still maintained, all prevented effective absorption of the new culture. The result was a loosened and confused system of values and practices. The people of The Road lived in a world in which there were two answers to most questions, often contradictory.

It is possible that the conflicts of acculturation were supportable for most of the group as long as they were economically well off. In any event, the present picture appears to have begun to emerge clearly at the time the community lost its economic base with the collapse of Port Harmony. One is tempted to believe that the disorientation and cultural weakening that preceded the loss of subsistence strongly predisposed to the kind of situation seen today in which apathy and lack of social organization and lack of norms are such prominent features.

As a result of the nature of the defects, and the reactions of other communities, many almost automatic systems have appeared for perpetuating the situation. Because of their lack of strong values and lack of leadership, the people are unable to make full use of the few resources and opportunities they do have. Being low in education, they do not know how to improve opportunity for learning and so their children remain at the same level or grow worse. Because they have no skills and are tagged as undesirable, they have difficulty getting work, which, in turn, means they have little opportunity to learn good work habits and acquire skills. Because of the poor land, they can do little to improve their lot on The Road and they meet resistance when they try to move elsewhere.

Because of their reputation, they have to travel far to find mates and, when they do, these are likely to be defective in one way or another and so add to the deterioration of the community.

Home life is disturbed and the children grow up with even less opportunity for training and personality development than their parents, owing to the amount of time necessary to make a living and the distances that have to be traveled to jobs.

These cycles could be described at greater length, but enough has been said to point to some of the factors concerned in perpetuation. The people of The Road have had many experiences which give them little reason to feel they owe loyalty or consistency as employees, while, on the other hand, those who have employed them have also had experiences that justify the charges of "unreliability and shiftlessness."

Both The Road and Stirling County are caught in a web of interdependent forces. The question is where could counter measures be applied to set social dynamics moving in healthful rather than pathological directions. The greatest obstacle is the widespread conviction of the constitutional inferiority of the people of The Road—and the most fatal aspect of this belief is that they themselves share it. They resent it and they regret it, but they believe it.

Nevertheless, some things could be done and in concluding this case a few of them will be briefly sketched.

The outstanding needs of The Road may be summed up under three general headings: (1) social organization and social values with emphasis on leadership, (2) education, and (3) economic development. Enough has been given in the case presentation to enable the reader to visualize in a general way what is meant by each of these headings, even if details are missing.

If one begins looking for resources with which to meet the needs, he soon discovers that there are a number of possibilities. On The Road itself there are several families which, despite their lack of knowledge and skills, do have incipient leadership qualities. Furthermore, among the families of the surrounding communities, there are a number who could be counted upon to participate in a program aimed at helping the people of The Road, and who are at the same time influential in their own groups. There are, in short, both on The Road and in the communities near it, some opportunities in the social system.

If one looks further afield, he finds that there are a surprisingly large number of agencies both public and private which might be brought to bear on the problems of The Road. A partial list is as follows:

1. Through the Guidance Division of the Provincial Department of Education, it is possible to place selected individuals in Canadian Vocational Training Courses and in the Provincial Apprenticeship Training, with maintenance provided.

2. Night School classes are regularly held in Bristol during the school year. Bus transportation for rural areas is available.

3. The Adult Education Division of the Provincial Department of Education is equipped to provide local study groups in subjects ranging from elementary education to training programs for rural leaders.

4. Books and educational films (including projector) can be had through facilities available in the Province.

5. The Department of Lands and Forests is a potential source of programs including employment aimed at reforesting areas not suitable for agriculture and for promoting Christmas tree raising industry in poor pasture land.

6. The Department of Agriculture has facilities for analyzing the soil and a number of other services which could be utilized in developing appropriate crops in those fields that are worth cultivating.

7. The Department of Industry and Publicity endeavors to establish new industries wherever a suitable labor force and raw materials are available, and in all regions it is ready to assist in the promotion of handcrafts.

8. The Department of Health and Welfare now maintains a public health nurse who gives considerable of her time to The Road. There are, however, other resources in the Department that might be mobilized, such as various types of examinations and programs of health education.

9. Both Roman Catholic and Protestant churches have organizations that might be interested in the problems of The Road.

The list could be extended much further, but enough has been said to indicate that a thorough investigation of agencies and facilities could bring to light a number of opportunities for aiding in the development of leadership, education, and standard of living. The problem is a matter of initiation and of coordination, including the finding of someone willing and capable of fulfilling these functions. It is our view that the best starting point is in the field of education and that the teachers in the schools could well perform the double role of educating children and promoting local improvement projects in which The Road would participate. Such teachers would, of course, have to be chosen by the Department of Education on the basis of special qualifications and motivation for this kind of work.

Case 14

RESISTANCE TO FREEDOM: Resettlement from the Japanese Relocation Centers During World War II

by E. H. Spicer

1. THE PROBLEM

Within a year after persons of Japanese ancestry were evacuated from the West Coast at the beginning of World War II, the government agency administering them—the War Relocation Authority—established a definite policy of resettling the more than 110,000 evacuees outside the "Relocation Centers" in which they had been placed. Resettlement was voluntary and could be to any part of the United States except the West Coast.

Despite deep dissatisfaction with the physical discomfort and government supervision in the centers and despite steady depletion of financial resources while resident there, evacuees responded to job offers and opportunities to resettle in only small numbers. Even after two years of the resettlement program, nearly two-thirds still remained in the centers.

Was their resistance to resettlement a result simply of the war and fear of American hostility? Was it due to a desire to hinder the United States war effort? Was it due to the security which had been provided in the relocation centers? Or was it due to other factors?

2. THE COURSE OF EVENTS

1. Some two months after the creation of the War Relocation Authority, a change in directorship was made—in June, 1942. Within a few months the new chief conceived a policy that had not been clearly established earlier. This consisted in arranging for the resettlement of as many as possible of the evacuees out of the centers, even while the war was still in progress. The policy and some of the means for its execution were developed between August, 1942, and the spring of 1943. Evacuees and the adminis-

trators at the local level in the relocation centers did not understand the policy very clearly until February, 1943.

2. The administrative mechanism for carrying out resettlement was established in its first form by March, 1943, a year after creation of the centers. It consisted of an Employment Division, with personnel in each of the ten centers, and small regional offices in various areas of the United States where resettlement opportunities existed. Later in 1943 each center was equipped with a "relocation officer" and staff, whose function was to inform evacuees of job offers and arrange for their transportation.

3. The pushing of resettlement was delayed while the War Relocation Authority (having foreseen pressure from Congress in this direction) worked out a program for segregation of loyal and disloyal evacuees. The segregation program was not completed until December, 1943.

4. The Washington office of the War Relocation Authority moved vigorously toward a strong resettlement program in the winter of 1943–1944. "Relocation Teams" visited each center. The teams consisted of War Relocation Authority employees armed with information about jobs and living conditions throughout the United States. They showed motion pictures of housing and working conditions. They addressed evacuee meetings and gave advice to individuals and families who had plans for resettlement.

5. The response to the resettlement program came as a surprise to the policy-makers in Washington. During the spring of 1943, when it first went into operation, fewer than 7,000 of the 110,000 evacuees in the relocation centers went out to stay permanently. The administrators spoke of this as "resistance to freedom" and began to discuss the causes of the meager response. The advisability of a "tough" policy, that is, making the centers definitely unpleasant places to stay in, was considered and rejected. "Forced relocation" was not to be official policy so long as the West Coast home area remained closed to evacuees.

6. During 1944 administrators at the local level in the centers, with few exceptions, seemed to believe that no techniques could be devised to get more than a thin trickle of evacuees to resettle.

Jobs of numerous kinds had been uncovered in many parts of the United States. Numbers of resettled people were well established in good jobs under good living conditions. Antagonism to persons of Japanese ancestry had been largely overcome. Yet, the outward flow of evacuees was very small. By the end of 1944, after two years of effort at resettlement, only about 35,000 had left the centers.

What were the factors involved in this resistance to resettlement? What means could be devised for persuading more evacuees to leave the relocation centers?

3. RELEVANT FACTORS

The original evacuation decision had been reached in the emergency of military mobilization and in the midst of pressures by genuinely fearful people and by conniving self-interest groups. The policy of resettlement, coming in the wake of evacuation, was formulated by men who spoke of it sincerely as a program of "human conservation." They were moved by the following considerations: No real need existed for confining evacuees who were not classified as dangerous. It would be easier to integrate them into American life during the war period of industrial and economic expansion than during a postwar period of retrenchment. Living under conditions of direct supervision by a federal agency would create attitudes of dependence, and the evacuees should therefore be given a chance to get out of the centers as quickly as possible. The development of relocation centers as productive units in American economy was fraught with insurmountable difficulties since they would be government-subsidized projects in competition with private enterprise. These were the stated working assumptions of the War Relocation Authority administrators who formulated the resettlement program.

Their plan, while not without basis in the original Executive Order establishing the War Relocation Authority, constituted a change of policy over that stated to evacuees during the period when they were moving into the relocation centers. They, as well as the administrators in charge of operations, had been led to believe that the centers would exist for at least the duration of the war. Centers were organized during their first months on that basis. At best, some center administrators had expressed hopes to evacuees that some kind of resettlement would be a possibility. The announcement of the new policy in the fall of 1942 was received, therefore, as in some degree a reversal.

The government's statements in regard to resettlement came at a time when there were strong indications throughout the United States that great hostility existed toward the Japanese Americans. Two months earlier Selective Service had classified the Nisei (second generation Japanese Americans) as ineligible for the armed services. About the same time the national officers of the American Legion had advocated imprisonment of the evacuees in the centers for the duration of the war and pushed this plan as far as the United States Senate, which began an investigation. The House Committee on Un-American Activities was giving wide publicity to charges of subversive activities in the relocation centers. State legislatures in Iowa and Arkansas voted against Nisei being allowed to go to school or settle in their states. The War Department had begun to put up watch-towers and fences around all centers that did not already have them. In the vicinity of most centers evacuees had been threatened and even shot at by local people. Under these circumstances, the centers were rife with rumors about attacks on Japanese Americans, and evacuees were generally fearful of what they had already come to call "The Outside."

Immediately on the heels of the announcement of the resettlement policy came two other programs. One of these was Army registration, which took place in February, 1943, and which from the point of view of the War Relocation Authority administration was a step toward furthering resettlement. The Army, considering reopening Selective Service to Japanese Americans, registered all adult citizens of military age in each center. Simultaneously the War Relocation Authority conducted a registration (officially titled "Registration for Leave Clearance") of all other adults.

The registration forms contained questions—later known as the "loyalty questions"—which required the Nisei to declare themselves loyal or not loyal to the United States, and Issei (first generation Japanese Americans who had never been permitted by our laws to become citizens of the United States) to declare their willingness to abide peacefully by United States laws. The whole program of registration touched on explosive issues for the evacuees. Tule Lake Center in California was turbulent for days as young men refused to register. At Heart Mountain a group of Nisei, invoking Jefferson and other heroes of the American Republic, agitated for nonregistration. Other centers suffered greater or lesser degrees of conflict. The basic issue to them was not loyalty to the United States, but rather the injustice of evacuation to American citizens.

A few months after registration the War Relocation Authority began to put into operation its plan for the segregation of the "loyal" and "disloyal," or "nonloyal." This involved new upsets in all the centers as the disloyal were moved to Tule Lake Center and the other nine were declared "relocation centers" from which anyone could resettle. There was much turmoil during the classification and moving of evacuees, turmoil which uncovered the great complexity of motives among the evacuee population.

During the autumn of 1943 a special division of the War Relocation Authority came into existence, replacing the old Employment Division. It was called the Relocation Division and maintained offices in each center with the relocation officer in charge. Through these channels a sort of employment and housing agency began to operate for the evacuees, with arms reaching out all over the United States. From this point on, the director announced, resettlement (or "relocation" as the War Relocation Authority administrators continued to call it) would be the central focus of all administrative action.

The resettlement which had taken place was chiefly a movement of young people. The 15,000 who had gone out by the beginning of 1944 were isolated individuals, young couples, or a young son or daughter in a family of several children. These were primarily from families who were the most thoroughly Americanized—in speech, in dress, in food habits, in occupational background. They constituted a fringe of the basic Japanese community, not members of its core. Resettlement was up to this point a sort of thinning of the most Americanized families.

The War Relocation Authority administrators foresaw that success in resettlement would depend not only on digging up jobs but also on devising ways of communicating the nature of the opportunities to evacuees. During the early stages such communication was poorly developed. In the centers it was chiefly the young Americanized Nisei working most closely with the administrators who learned what the War Relocation Authority was doing. Everywhere in the office buildings they were faced with posters, lists of job offers, and figures on the number of "relocatees." Out in the blocks, on the other hand, people could go for weeks without hearing the word "relocation," except occasionally at a meeting and even then only in the sense of an evil which the government was trying to impose.

Each center had by the end of 1943 a definite community structure. The Japanese family system, with male dominance, was strong, and Nisei were largely controlled by their Issei parents. The families were organized into blocks, the neighborhood groups which the physical makeup of the centers had imposed on the people. Over-all community organization varied among the centers, because War Relocation Authority regulations had not worked out identically in all ten. In the main, however, it followed the same basic pattern: a Community Council of elected representatives from each of the blocks and an organization of Block Managers consisting of administration-appointed individuals from each of the blocks. By the beginning of 1944 the effective communitywide organizations in all centers were dominated by Issei.

As the framework of the relocation center communities became steadily more definite, a public opinion took form which was remarkably similar in all the centers. Block Managers or Councilmen usually did not dare to speak favorably of resettlement or to push it in the block, even if privately they had decided that it was the best course. Block leaders who themselves were planning resettlement frequently created the impression to War Relocation Authority staff that they were "anti-relocation," often up to the day of their departure. Block opinion was such that almost everywhere persons in positions of leadership had to maintain the appearance of being opposed to resettlement.

When the staff in any of the centers tried aggressive moves toward resettlement, they were usually frustrated by encounters with this well-meshed sentiment system. Some administrators understood a little of its origins and felt sympathy and respect for it. Others believed that they were working against something sinister, perhaps a subversive organization in the center which sought to interfere in whatever way it could with the efforts of the United States to win the war.

When Relocation Teams came to the centers they found that the staff were able to arrange meetings for them; they found that Block Managers were generally cooperative and helpful in getting appointments with evacuees. They usually discovered that people came in considerable numbers to see the pictures and movies.

Block Managers could help the teams make contacts; they could post notices in the blocks; they could even get a few men in the block to clean up a recreation hall for a relocation meeting. They could cooperate to this extent, because the people recognized that such activities were part of their job as Block Managers, as liaison men with the administrators. Moreover, people were increasingly eager for any breaks in the routine of center life; movies about cherry-picking in Ohio, for example, might be very refreshing.

But the response to the Relocation Teams was not resettlement. Even when the teams were supplemented with men who spoke Japanese and who had known Issei for years before evacuation (in order to make sure that the older people were reached), the response was still not resettlement.

Relocation officers or members of the teams might be very popular with evacuees and make real friends among them. Nevertheless, the evacuee feeling remained that such persons were paid to carry out a policy which they distrusted or even regarded as a vicious threat. As hirelings of the War Relocation Authority, even though they were interesting and pleasant men, they could not be wholly trusted when they spoke about "The

Outside." They did not seem to be aware of vital issues, such as the relation of the outcome of the war to the future of the Japanese and the significance of the Issei stake on the West Coast, and, hence, how could their judgment be trusted on such a crucial matter as resettlement?

In a sense the policy of the evacuee leaders in regard to resettlement was a façade. Behind the façade of opposition the feeling was widespread that staying in the centers was no real solution to Japanese-American problems. Notwithstanding the fact that the old men repeated again and again that one could not plan until the war was over, men and women went to bed at night worrying about where and when and how the new start would be made. It was part of the family pattern that such things not be discussed while the children could hear; such issues were smiled away in the daytime. But after the children were in bed, the matters were talked over gravely, or in some families, almost hysterically.

"The Outside" changed rapidly in the year following segregation. The War Department lived up to promises—and went beyond. Selective Service was reopened. Speakers in uniform were telling the people of the United States about the great record of the 100th Battalion and the 442nd Combat Team— all-Nisei units. The wordy blasts of some witnesses before the House Un-American Activities Committee against the Japanese Americans had turned out to have no real basis. Evacuees who had gone out had encountered no serious antagonism or persecution. Such things were definitely on the decline. The best measure of this was the world of rumors in the isolation of the relocation centers. Here the difference from 1942 was very great. Tales of violence and shooting had given way to stories of Americans failing to identify Nisei as Japanese in various situations and mild rumors of refusals of service in barber shops or bars. "The Outside," in other words, even in the centers of anxiety from which rumors arose, was regarded as comparatively safe. Nevertheless, the curves posted on the walls of relocation offices were not rising sharply upward. Instead, in the fall of 1944, they fell sharply.

Real resistance in the face of an all-out administrative effort could not be denied. What could be done about it?

REFERENCES FOR FURTHER STUDY

Embree, John F., "Resistance to Freedom: An Administrative Problem," *Applied Anthropology*, vol. 2, September, 1943, pp. 10–14.

United States Department of the Interior, War Relocation Authority, *WRA: A Story of Human Conservation*; *The Evacuated People: A Quantitative Description*; *Impounded People: Japanese Americans in the Relocation Centers*, Washington, 1947.

Answer Questions Presented in the Problem
Before Reading the Rest of the Case.

4. THE OUTCOME

In the spring of 1943 the War Relocation Authority staff in Washington had considered the advisability of "tough" policy, that is, making the centers places the evacuees would want to leave quickly. At the same time certain other proposals were made for bringing about a better response to the resettlement program but were set aside for approaches which seemed to promise quicker results, such as the Relocation Teams.

Now, during 1944, the earlier proposals were increasingly emphasized by the administration, who labeled them "evacuee participation" and "family counseling." The former meant to administrators the bringing of evacuee leadership into the channels of communication which the Relocation Division was setting up. Specifically it took the shape of either evacuee or joint staff-evacuee committees in each center. The relocation officers maintained close relations with such committees, giving them information in regard to resettlement opportunities and discussing with them ideas for stimulating evacuees to resettle. The committees were thus designed to be channels of communication and catalytic agents in the communities.

"Evacuee participation," as it worked out in the centers, took many different forms and developed wide ramifications. In some centers, the Relocation Committee was a standing committee of the Community Council. In others, it was a group of evacuees who had close administration contacts, but were not necessarily members of any other over-all body. In still others, it was a group of staff members and evacuee leaders with various connections. Some sort of Relocation Committee was brought into existence in every center but the amount and kind of activity varied greatly. At one place, it did diffuse information more widely than the administration could. At another, the members never met except under pressure from the staff.

A few relocation committees took up the idea of evacuee participation and pushed it vigorously. This resulted in groups of evacuee leaders being financed by the War Relocation Authority to inspect relocation opportunities and come back to the centers to report in their own words on what they had seen. The principle of participation also led the staff to do intensive work with recognized community leaders, such as Buddhist and Christian ministers, believing that they might persuade their flocks to resettle more or less as units and thus give the security of the group in the initial adjustments. War Relocation Authority increasingly paid the expenses of any Japanese who would return to the centers and urge relocation. In the summer of 1944, for example, it helped one Issei come to a center and give a series of talks on his belief that Japan was shortly to be thoroughly defeated by the Allies. Evacuee participation was thus a policy which more and more brought Japanese into the communication channels of the agency.

The other important aspect of the increasingly many-sided War Relocation Authority approach to resettlement was what, in administrative circulars, went by the name "family counseling." This also had been recommended in a general form in the spring of 1943, but it was not under way as an "implemented" program until the summer of 1944 (and then only partially). Placed under the joint supervision of the Welfare Section and the Relocation Division of the agency, family counseling was conceived as an organized attempt to reach directly every family in every center. Interviewing schedules were set up and the centers were, according to the plan, to be systematically covered block by block. The first interview was merely an effort to collect basic data about the composition of the family and plans for the future. The family was not urged to resettle. Whenever definite or tentative plans to resettle came to light, however, follow-up contacts were made either through visits to the family in their quarters or by invitation to come to the relocation office. The plan called for successive contacts with each family, spaced a month or more apart, whether or not there were any plans for resettlement.

Family counseling proceeded according to design in few centers. It was an expensive program, requiring many interviewers. Funds were never quite sufficient, and adequate personnel to meet the needs was never available under the wartime conditions. It was at least begun in each center and in several carried along almost as planned during part of 1944 and 1945. In most centers it is possible that every family was reached at least once, and resistance to family counseling did not develop in active form in any center. In practice the program was held fairly well in line with the original conception—as a counseling service rather than as a forcing technique—and introduced something of value into center life, namely, direct contacts between administration and all family groups.

The specific effects of these additions to the resettlement program cannot be determined with great precision because other factors entered the situation which interfere with evaluation. In December, 1944, the War Department lifted restrictions on the return of evacuees to the West Coast. Simultaneously the War Relocation Authority announced that the relocation centers would all be closed within a year. This, of course, altered the whole situation. Resettlement was no longer on a purely voluntary basis. Ultimately everyone, if he did not move out of his own accord within the year, would be moved out by the Authority.

Nevertheless, for the first nine months of 1945 resettlement was continued on the old basis under the direction of the Relocation Division. A steady acceleration took place, despite the appearance of resistance to the policy of closing the centers. By the time of the Japanese surrender in August, 1945, the number of resettled persons had reached 60,000, more than 20,000 of these having left the centers in the period from December, 1944, to August, 1945. It is probable that evacuee participation and family counseling techniques had some influence on this increased volume of resettlement.

5. ANALYSIS

The War Relocation Authority voluntary resettlement program cannot be called either successful from the viewpoint of the administrators, or satisfactory from the viewpoint of the administered. Furthermore, it cannot be classified, from the general standpoint of good administration, as a sound program in its use of human relations principles or in the desirability of its results.

It did yield some measure of success in carrying out the aims of the administrators and in producing some measure of improvement in the condition of the evacuees. These achievements, however, were at considerable cost in human energies and good will; smooth and effective cooperative working relations were the exception rather than the rule. Our analysis will seek to point out both the reasons for the measure of success and for the costs in human relations incurred.

In the first place, it must be recognized that the whole program operated in a context of resistance. This appeared at the very beginning and cannot be said to have declined. Up to the end evacuee leaders and center administrators dealt with one another gingerly, for confidence between them was at a minimum. Even though thousands of people resettled, they did so with a feeling of having been pushed around and denied humane treatment. These feelings arose, not out of the nature of contacts with specific administrators, but out of the framework of human relations within which the administrators found themselves working.

What were the causes of this continuing resistance and the unsatisfactory working relations? It may be held that the total situation was one in which such attitudes were inevitable. Given the initial situation of evacuation from homes and businesses for reasons never accepted as sufficient by the evacuees, how could any favorable or really cooperative attitudes toward the government agency develop? This basic situation from which the resettlement program proceeded might, however, have conceivably been altered. The resentment and bitterness was due originally to forcible deprivation of almost all bases of security which the Japanese Americans possessed—land, property, income, place in community, full citizenship status, choice of residence, and participation in government. Accepting evacuation and attendant losses as facts to start from, was it necessary to continue the same procedure in barring the Japanese Americans from participating in further decisions about their future? It is clear, for example, in the Poston (Arizona) Relocation Center that bringing evacuees into the planning and management of community affairs reduced tensions and resistance resulting from the initial imposition of a purely administrator-conceived community organization.

The point to be made is that the resettlement program was formulated in Washington without any evacuee participation. However much it was discussed later with evacuee leaders, and modified slightly to fit the conditions which evacuee leaders made known to administrators, the announcement of policy came as a *fait accompli*. Moreover, it came under conditions which made it possible to interpret it as an arbitrary policy change ignoring the interests of evacuees as they perceived them. These two features were basic causes of evacuee resistance. It was frequently said by responsible evacuee leaders in the months following the announcement of the resettlement policy that they could not rely further on what War Relocation Authority administrators told them. First set up as war-duration homes, the centers suddenly and without notice became, as defined by the Authority, "way stations into American life." In short, the resettlement policy seemed a continuation of evacuation policy, as a plan without reference to evacuee interests. It reinforced the distrust of government motives, which was already intense.

Whether or not evacuee participation in the making of the policy could have prevented resistance cannot be surely demonstrated. It seems a reasonable inference, however, that some sort of give-and-take between administrative policy-makers and evacuee leaders would have produced a different set of working relations. Through serious discussion between leaders and War Relocation Authority administrators prior to making policy commitment, some sense of participation in the planning of their future might have been brought about in the evacuees. It could also have acquainted the administrators with practical obstacles to resettlement, for example, evacuee attitudes and beliefs. An understanding of these factors came to the administrators only much later, after the program had been well launched and they had, through various statements, become fully committed to the original formulation. Except at the very end, and then only in connection with minor aspects, evacuees did not take part in the making of this program, which was tied up in such complex ways with their past and future in the United States.

The question of whether or not any such participation was really practical is a very relevant one. It is certain that the director of the Authority believed that evacuee participation in decision-making or planning was wholly impossible in the year 1942. He felt that the actual hostility and potential hostility of Congress and the American public toward the Japanese Americans made such participation in planning with a government agency entirely out of the question. Nevertheless, with hindsight to help, it seems reasonable to hold that, since it turned out to be impossible to push resettlement for two years anyway, the possibility existed for fuller discussion with the evacuee leadership before final announcement of policy.

Probably no more effective way to promote resistance to resettlement could have been devised than that inadvertently chosen by the War Relocation Authority. Sumner has said that the surest way to promote the solidarity of a group is to attack it from without. The announcement of resettlement came as an attack from Washington on the only security which the Japanese Americans had achieved after evacuation. The relocation centers had meaning as places in which to stay in the midst of a generally hostile United States. They were places in which families could be reorganized after the disorganizing experience of evacuation. They were the only places in which lodging, food, and education for children were guaranteed to persons of Japanese ancestry. They were, moreover, regions in which people were beginning to have status as members of communities again. The achievement of these securities had been the focus of evacuee activity during the months following evacuation, and the center administrators had encouraged them.

At the very moment when they seemed within grasp, the War Relocation Authority administrators in Washington announced that they did not think these securities were good for the Japanese Americans.

The deep-going reaction was a crystallization of sentiment around the centers as the only security left. Recognition of this system of sentiments became the only workable basis for real leadership in the center communities. No leader could function unless he accepted, or appeared to accept, the system. The solidarity which grew up in the centers during 1942 was based on it. The resettlement program, as a threat to the new value (security in the centers), became in itself, as a common focus of opposition, one of the most important integrating factors in center life.

Consequently, forays in the direct attack, such as the Relocation Teams, could meet only with general resistance. Whatever was pointed out as benefits derivable from resettlement could have only an individual appeal. As individuals, evacuees might respond to an opportunity to go out and make some money, but as members of relocation center communities they had to interpret all good things said about "The Outside" as lies or merely as advantages from a non-Japanese viewpoint, based on ignorance of what had happened to the Japanese Americans.

In this situation, an approach that could bring about real changes was the one the War Relocation Authority ultimately adopted, namely, family counseling. "Evacuee participation" came too late. The scope for it was limited, but, more important, it consisted in evacuee participation in a non-evacuee program, and, therefore, could not be regarded as real participation. On the other hand, family counseling did avoid head-on attack, going, as it were, behind the leadership and under the sentiment system. It probed the individual anxieties and the specific family problems largely responsible for the community organization set up to fend off the administration and its demands.

Family counseling thus was not designed to work through the community, with which the War Relocation Authority had long since reached an impasse. It was designed to ignore the community, and in this way was in line with the Authority administrators' official conviction that the relocation centers were unhealthy. It was justifiable, from that standpoint, to ignore, or to go in through the interstices of, the community and bring the appeal to the families and the individuals. This is the process that was begun as the final step in the voluntary resettlement program. It would have been a process of destroying the communities which the evacuation and the initial War Relocation Authority policy and procedure had built. It was probably the only way of breaking the impasse—short of "forced relocation," which evacuees expected and which ultimately came at the end of the war with the order closing the centers by 1946.

Case 15

DEMOCRACY IN PROCESS: The Development of Democratic Leadership in the Micronesian Islands[1]

by John Useem

1. THE PROBLEM

An attempt is being made to incorporate democratic processes within the native power structure of the Micronesian Islands. With the transfer of the islands from the status of Japanese mandates to American trust territory, the incoming administration hoped to establish a degree of self-government at the local level in accordance with American conceptions of democracy.

The first program was planned not as a total reorganization of the indigenous political institutions, but rather as an introduction of democratic procedures by the election of native officials. This reform was believed to be, in part, a liberation measure that would free the islanders of Japanese-imposed puppet chiefs and, in part, as an American contribution to the advancement of human relations. Elections of "chiefs" were held in an orderly manner.

The initial responses to the introduction of the election system varied from island to island. On Palau, one of the major groups in the trust territory, there was a general readiness to adopt the social rules proposed by the new foreigners. The islanders were impressed with the martial supremacy, superior technology, and wealth of the United States. If democracy, as claimed by the Americans, was one of the forces making for such greatness, Palau was willing to adopt the pattern. Individual reactions ranged from enthusiastic receptivity to indifference and acquiescence.

The natives of Palau had been accustomed to the rule of a hereditary elite class who held a monopoly of power. Yet, the introduction of parts of the American system did not disrupt the

[1] This case is drawn from a larger study by the author, *Power: A Study in Cross-Cultural Relations*, The Dryden Press, New York, 1952.

traditional arrangement. How were the natives able to adjust to the new features of political organization? What were the consequences for the power structure in Palau of choosing local officials by popular vote?

2. THE COURSE OF EVENTS

Palau was an autonomous society prior to the nineteenth century. No outside group had ever tried to conquer it and it had no aspirations to conquer any outside group. The islanders were independent though not totally isolated from the rest of the South Seas. There were intermittent immigrations from surrounding areas and continuous trade with neighboring peoples.

1. During the past century and a half, Palau has experienced both acculturation and subordination. The Spanish exercised formal control for fourteen years, from 1885 to 1899; the Germans for fifteen years, between 1899 and 1914; the Japanese in the thirty-year span, 1914–1944; and the United States since then. The relative brevity of the Spanish and German eras, plus the limited emphasis on the development of the islands, restricted their influence on native institutions. The Japanese, on the other hand, had decisive effects.

2. There are six distinctive features in the history of Palau's relations with the foreigners.

(a) No effort was made by any of the foreign groups to eliminate the inhabitants either as a means of obtaining the islands' resources or to assure the security of occupying forces. The natives have been encouraged to participate in newly introduced programs and to assimilate selected features of the foreigners' ways, rather than shunted off to reservations or isolated from the outside world. The people of Palau have displayed little hostility toward the foreigners and there has been no widespread conspiracy to oust them.

(b) Both the foreign and native groups have shared a favorable outlook on cultural pluralism in which subgroups were more or less free to work out their own ways of life. While the foreigners did reform selected aspects of native life and indirectly influenced others, no systematic attempt has been made to destroy or suppress the native social order. Official policies of every outside government have been to support and preserve Palau's basic patterns. The changes made, in the main, have been in external forms more than in internal processes. The foreigner has replaced the supernatural as the source of ultimate validation of cultural patterns among recent generations and serves as a model of the highly regarded values of power and progress.

(c) Continuing cultural contact with the foreigners has resulted in what natives consider general improvement in the levels and styles of living. Even when there have been temporary setbacks, the expectations of advancement have persisted. Foreign practices have high prestige in Palau and there is relatively little nostalgia for the ancestral culture. Those who preferred the old ways, were, for the most part, permitted to practice them. There is a demand for more rather than fewer foreign introductions. Differences of opinion exist as to what should be altered in a single generation, but there is little disagreement over the ultimate goal.

(d) Changes have modified the social architecture without undermining its foundations. Palau's culture is both durable and plastic. The façade of native institutions is quite different from that of the past, yet the basic principles of ordering human relations remain fairly intact. Though there is not tight integration of the separate parts, and though areas of friction do exist, there is no sense of total bewilderment or total collapse.

(e) The successive foreigners influenced Palau in the same general direction. While there have been interruptions during transitions, there have been no breaks in the pivotal institutions as rule passed from one nation to the next. This does not imply that the foreign governors had the same motives, that they focused on the same aspects of Palau life, or that they acted in identical ways. But it does indicate that the consequences for Palau were changes in the same general direction, and that native techniques developed for dealing with foreigners remained much the same under successive administrators.

(f) Palau has a well-organized set of political institutions capable of being transformed to fit the emergent patterns. The decision-making, legitimizing, and executing aspects of power have continued to function in new media.

3. The German and Japanese administrations in Palau set under way a chain of events which, though they did not precipitate a political upheaval of revolutionary dimensions, did result in a series of changes in political arrangements. The two successive administrations were primarily concerned with questions of how to utilize and supervise effectively the native government. This inevitably required reforms in order to bring traditional institutions in closer accord with the foreigners' habitual modes of political management.

The governors converted Palau from a circular to a linear type of authority and from a dispersed to a centralized structure, for they preferred to deal with a few native leaders rather than with congeries of social subdivisions, each with its own distinct leadership. The symbolic status of senior-ranking position was made into a functional one of "chief," who was assumed to be supreme within his jurisdiction in a manner like that of the sovereign in the homeland of the foreigners. Power was concentrated to a greater degree than before in the elite sections of the population through the reduction of the controls exercised by persons in lower social statuses. The heads of loose confederations, who had limited power, were converted into permanent all-inclusive positions of authority. The political influence of women was virtually broken through the demise of their own organizations and through disqualification to hold high native offices—public affairs in the foreigners' cultures being considered the province of men.

Ultimate power shifted to the foreigners, and native officials who failed to cooperate, or were deemed otherwise unsatisfactory, were removed from office. To shield the native leadership from foreign pressures and, in part, to carry out duties assigned by the foreigners, a dual power structure evolved. One political organization "faced" the foreigners, while the other "faced" the natives. The former consisted of offices which represented the group in negotiations and which assumed the official role of headship whenever foreigners came to a locality. The latter made the decisions in connection with domestic, traditional affairs. Each system contained its own consultative-legislative bodies. The two segments were integrated by a number of different schemes. In a few localities a struggle for dominance developed between the two groups, with one or the other gaining ascendance. In most, however, the dual system evolved a set of divided responsibilities with an elaborate pattern of checks and balances. Thus, the foreign-facing chief might be a member of a clan lower in status than that of the native-facing chief and hence be dependent on him. The foreign-oriented legislative body's procedure was subject to veto by the native body, or confined to only those actions specifically requested by the foreigners. The outward-facing body, in turn, could refuse to follow the dictates of the other group if it seemed likely they would arouse opposition from the foreign rulers.

The prestige of Palau's traditional leaders declined during the period between the two world wars. The younger generations who had attended the foreign schools and all those who had been converted to foreign religions no longer fully accepted the doctrine of the sacredness of their rulers. Native leaders became restricted in their authority, since decisions could be extracted from foreigners to counter the orders of the native officials. By comparison with the foreigners, the old leadership seemed ill equipped to advance Palau in the modern era. New influential groups attracted wide followings even though they held no public offices. A continuing flow of foreign introductions altered established relationships and the old elite was divided in power contests and caught in the changing values of the society.

4. Following the surrender of Japan, the American forces, which heretofore had been confined to the outer islands, occupied the whole area. The initial American military governor for Palau

as a whole asked the first natives he met who was the high chief. He was informed that there were two high chiefs who headed confederations of districts. These two individuals were instructed by him to assume the duties of heads of states. On the premise that ancestral customs were being reestablished, the governor delegated to these two officials more authority than they had ever possessed before, and the confederations were transformed into formal political states. The heads of the confederations were eager to capitalize on this rare opportunity to strengthen their control and proceeded to do so.

5. Soon thereafter, elections of local officials at the district and village levels were held under the joint supervision of the two high chiefs and the Americans. It could now be affirmed that democratically elected officials were universal in Palau. Most of the men chosen were the same persons who had held the offices previously. Those, however, who proved unacceptable to the foreigners for one reason or another were removed from authority and new elections staged. Persons so removed usually continued to exercise power by maintaining control over the native-facing political institutions and by contriving to have elected persons subject to their orders. In a few instances new struggles for dominance ensued between the supporters of the deposed and the new chief. No pronounced change in the power centers took place, yet the leadership was made aware of its dependency on followers for future support at elections. Heretofore individuals eligible for office by inheritance could be passed over by decision of their clan or local legislative body. Previously this effective control had been confined exclusively to the elite class; now the base of potential power was enlarged. In only a few communities has this increased access to power been actualized through usage. However, the class from which the leadership is drawn has become apprehensive and there is a feeling in some circles that in future generations it will be easier to elect leaders from a greater number of candidates within the elite class rather than submit to the choices made by the elite. In this atmosphere political maneuvers are constantly being made by various interest groups within the elite to enhance their strength.

3. RELEVANT FACTORS

The management of Palau affairs has been concentrated in the past almost exclusively in a series of groups made up of the senior-ranking members of leading clans. Their legitimate authority was symbolized in titles (*dui*) of public office. Title-holders (*rubak*) are designated by these titles and never by personal names. Titles are graded within each village and district, although they are not standardized in nomenclature for Palau as a whole. Male and female titles are independent of each other, but at every status position there is one for each sex. Female titles invariably continue in the maternal line, whereas male titles have, in some instances, become patrilineal.

Rubak were superior not only in secular affairs but also in sacred matters. (In the modern era the upper ranks of this class, the *meteet*, are thought of as the real rulers of Palau, the lesser titles having lost most of their power.) In all social relationships they expected to be treated with deference and accorded special privileges: commoners stepped off the pathway and bowed when a titled person approached; half-crouched at a respectful distance, with face averted, in their presence; spoke softly and only if the conversation were initiated by the *rubak;* passed the home and clubhouse of the elite quietly and slowly, and, if possible, avoided coming too close; remained outside the house of a *rubak* until invited to enter; maintained a quiet household if a *rubak* entered; observed precedence in the order of going in and coming out, seating, and eating arrangements; contributed choice portions of the fish catch; obeyed the requests of the elite without debate; and accepted the basic doctrine that only those with titles had the right to lead and decide.

Power was distributed unequally and along hierarchical lines; yet, it was circular rather than linear. Legitimate authority was an attribute of office and not the private property of persons. While the first-ranking title (of a village, district, or confederation of districts) outranked other title-holders, the right to rule was circumscribed. No senior title-holder could act without the approval of other title-holders. In theory, the order of rank was changeless; in reality, there were numerous cases in which it was changed. Inheritance rules set the order of succession to titles but did not guarantee anyone the right to positions of authority. Those in line of succession to titles had to prove their qualifications for office and those in office had to demonstrate a reasonable capacity to govern. There was no automatic inheritance of a *rubak* position; the leading candidate had to be passed on and, failing to qualify, could be passed over. Through actions of a ruling council made up of heads of ruling clans, a *rubak* could lose his title. Assassinations and forced resignations of *rubak* could be engineered legally by members of a title-holder's clan. No rank was beyond social control. Officials who violated the mores were subject to punishment ranging from fines to death. Authority for Palau was not concentrated in a single group of men. Each locality had its own titles and within each locality a division existed between male and female title-holders.

From childhood, individuals were taught to obey and fear the ruling class. By adolescence, those eligible to become *rubak* began to exercise positions of leadership over their contemporaries. Life on Palau was highly organized and through these organizations discipline was maintained over the adult members of society. There were relatively few individuated types of activities, and natives preferred wherever possible to work and associate together. The elite exerted direct control through their headship of societies and indirect control through the interlocking of associations which ultimately were subordinate to the *rubak*. Thus, a *rubak* could issue orders through his own clan and also through the council. The clans were large and contained families or subclans, whose heads held lesser offices in many organizations. The lines of administration left no one in doubt as to the source of authority.

Fines, banishment from the group, confiscation of property, loss of social privileges, and death could be ordered by the *rubak* against those who violated their regulations. An obstinate person might witness the forced withdrawal of his wife and children to their clan. Perhaps the most effective technique of social control was the use of open scolding, which put a person to shame. Nothing is more feared by a common man than having a member of the elite publicly ridicule him and thereafter act as though he does not exist. Palau people are deeply eager to avoid loss of respect. "We swallow our saliva so nothing will happen." The loss in reputation reflects not only on the person involved, but also on his family, clan, and village. The counter pressures exerted by these units to avoid such a disgrace induces the individuals to be most careful not to arouse the disapproval of the elite. Because the individual is so highly dependent on groups and can do so little as an isolated being, he is keen to retain his good standing.

The possibilities of escape have been rather limited. A person could not run away to start all over again among strangers, even if he felt so impelled. To leave Palau required a hazardous sea voyage over many hundreds of miles and was ordinarily inconceivable to a person in trouble. The primary defense open to offenders was a verbal one. Fabrication of the facts, for instance, was a well-developed art. One learned early to appear innocent and tell a story that would sound sufficiently true to avoid censorship. Rationalization of the acts performed to make them seem as though they were motivated for the benefit of the group, plus reiteration of a past replete with instances of self-sacrifice for the larger welfare, also helped. But these were uncertain defenses, for one could not talk back to the elite. An offense against a *rubak* was not a personal injury, but a crime against the state. Criticism of the elite, even in private, was also a grave offense and few dared to be caught engaging in this kind of "agitation." A more common procedure was overtly to acquiesce in any orders given, but to evade their execution. The order might even be enthusiastically applauded and then either "misunderstood" or tackled without ever being accomplished. These negative defenses against the elite never undermined the system of power itself. There is no known instance of commoners seeking to overthrow the ruling class and seize power for themselves.

The mores surrounding the use of authority allowed for some latitude in the behavior of the rulers. There were pronounced differences in tradition between districts in the ways the elite functioned, as well as the expected contrast among the personalities of the chiefs who successively held office. One prominent district was renowned for the use of violence in administration (death penalties were rather frequent), whereas in another equally outstanding district fines were more common.

Two stereotyped figures emerge from the folklore: a chief who ruled "by the torch" and one who ruled by "using bait." The former was alleged to have pushed through those plans which would enhance his own glory; to have constantly proclaimed his right to dominate; to have clumsily administered social activities, resorting to coercion to secure obedience and rushing decisions before people were ready for them; to have failed to assume his share of the burdens; and to have oppressed the people in general. The other type was said to have used his authority to advance the condition of the whole community; to have fully consulted with the members of his council, and yielded when in error; to have accorded the respect due to lesser-ranking chiefs and associated with lower-ranking people without constantly reminding them of their differential status; to have employed flattery and persuasion to motivate others; and to have skillfully worked out social arrangements even to inventing new customs which met the needs of everyone. This polar classification reflects as much the current controversy over the proper behavior of chiefs as it mirrors the past. It is now reiterated in some circles that chiefs in ancient times were more of the latter type, whereas the present ones are more like the former—thus using a selective idealization of the past as an ideological weapon in the present. Upon closer inspection the division into what appears to be desirable and undesirable traits in a ruler is not so sharply drawn. Everyone concedes that an effective leader uses some deception and trickery; and such acts are greatly admired when their clever use results in success. Many rulers maintain that to keep the confidence of the group they must not appear in doubt and go around asking people their opinion. To confide in the common people or to invite open discussion of issues brings agitation, unrest, and confusion—for ordinary people know little about Palau regulations and see issues only in relationship to their immediate personal wishes. Moreover, they point out that the Palau people are quick to enthusiasm for any new idea and this mercurial quality must be checked from completely upsetting the social order.

Hence, it would be proof of weakness rather than of strength of character for an official to fail to issue firm orders or not to be a "real elite" in demeanor. Justification for the self-interest of the official in his own clan is also offered. No greater disgrace could befall a chief than to be responsible for his clan's losing out to another. Ambitious rival clans are alert for any opportunity to grasp the title of those above them. Moreover, the lower-ranking elite can afford to be more concerned with the public interest, for they cannot directly gain as much from issuing orders, whereas the first-ranking position can so profit and it would be foolish, indeed, to pass up the opportunity. No one actually advocates complete equity in the distribution of rewards, and there are no records of anyone openly urging any reform in the power structure—until the coming of the foreigners.

The coming of the foreigners was a challenge to the men of power in Palau to invent new techniques or refashion old ones to fit the changing social scene. They were not a unified group and their personal interests diverged on many issues; hence, they differed among themselves over the means and the urgency of corrective measures. Despite these internal divisions, and without a formal plot, the elite succeeded in retaining the hard core of their authority. The first asset they possessed was the retention in the mind-set of the population that the elite are to be accorded their due respect. Even the most zealous reformers have not openly repudiated this premise. A second strength lay in their continuing dominance. As long as they remained ascendant, they were in a position to guide if not to dictate the actual decisions made and to supervise their execution. The task was to thwart those programs which jeopardized their standing, to administer measures so as to perpetuate their interests, to delay the execution of reforms which could not be rejected, to exert pressures on those segments of the society which threatened their power. These actions were not systematically and calculatingly pursued at a conscious level. Yet, they took place. Several illustrations may serve to make the patterns more explicit.

The foreigners recruited and trained natives to serve as administrative assistants. Because they were close to the seat of ultimate power, they were in a strategic position to influence policies. Interpreters, for example, controlled most of the channels of communication between the foreigners and other natives. They became not merely translators but experts in knowing what to say to the foreigners to elicit favorable responses, arbitrators of which questions were worthy of the attention of the government, and explainers to their compatriots of the foreigners' intentions. Natives expected interpreters not merely to convey precisely what was told them, but to offer advice on what tactics to pursue and to design the right formulas to bring success. The manning of these crucial roles was, therefore, of the utmost importance. The leading clans early perceived the advisability of placing some of their ablest members in such positions. Buttressed by the belief that a low-ranking person could not function easily in roles which required such prominence in Palau, the competent young members of the elite gravitated into the foreign service.

Still, the elite were not fully protected, for some of these young men began to place their allegiance to the "modernization" of Palau even above their own clan interests. Various corrective remedies were attempted. In the German period, for example, one person who proved too informative to the foreigners was killed. But this traditional technique of handling extreme deviants carried with it the threat of counteraction from the foreigners. Other pressures of a more subtle but convincing nature were subsequently applied. These ranged from conferences with the civil servants to exercising indirect influence through negative sanctions affecting the individual's prestige. A civil servant invited to advise a high-ranking district official is performing an honored role according to traditional Palau custom. Yet, lacking the prescribed right to argue with *rubak*, the individual is compromised, for the agreement reached in such conferences is binding. Only the most skilled native politicians have been able to maneuver these situations to enhance their own interests. But since the control which the elite class can exercise is imperfect, they are at times deeply anxious over the hidden motives of the men who work for the government. The civil servants are not a highly cohesive group with a single set of loyalties. This, too, has helped limit their collective power. But, perhaps most important of all, the civil servants contain only a few who would like to change the elite system; the majority lean toward the development of an educated, modern-oriented elite.

A special problem in control appeared with the rise of a new wealthy class of businessmen. While there have been persons of wealth without rank in the past, their numbers were small and their prestige modest. The members of the new business class are more numerous and have some standing because of their close ties with the foreigners (which appeals to the younger generation) and their wealth (which attracts the older). Their economic success has been accompanied by a slight rise in their political fortunes. In many districts they are now invited into the community councils. In these, however, they usually speak only when specifically invited to do so by the elite. The business group has developed some solidarity, but so far it has not been used for political purposes. They tend to accept the existing system; some are endeavoring to use their wealth to acquire titles (which has occurred in the past, although it is not usually admitted). Many have private sympathies for selective reforms; yet, they outwardly submit to the elite and support them in all major affairs.

The introduction of foreign schools has provided an orientation to youth which holds up other cultures as models of life. Spearheaded by the schoolteachers, the educated have increasingly favored changes in Palau—many of which would undermine the ruling classes. The reorganization of the men's societies in the Japanese period also contributed to this state of mind. The young men's societies carrying the foreigners' flag were collectively guided into embracing ethics of the outside world. Yet, despite their criticisms of the *status quo*, these groups of educated men have not yet emerged as a dominant political force. They submit to the pressures of their superiors. Their right to attend or speak at high policy meetings is not recognized and, in most communities, they complain in private and acquiesce in public. The elite are not alarmed, but they are uneasy.

REFERENCES FOR FURTHER STUDY

Keesing, Felix M., editor, *Handbook on the Trust Territory of the Pacific Islands.* United States Navy Department, Washington, 1948.

Oliver, Douglas, *The Pacific Islands.* Harvard University Press, Cambridge, Mass., 1951.

Useem, John, "The Changing Structure of a Micronesian Society," *American Anthropologist,* vol. 47, October–December, 1945, pp. 567–588.

———, *Power:* A Study in Cross-Cultural Relations. The Dryden Press, New York, 1952.

Answer Questions Presented in the Problem
Before Reading the Rest of the Case.

4. THE OUTCOME

Democratic processes and theories, introduced since 1945, have brought a new dimension into Palau politics. The younger generation, for example, stressed the theme of liberty, which was interpreted by them to mean the right to do what they pleased. The elite countered with the argument that this could not be the meaning of liberty, for surely the victorious foreigners in the recent war displayed group discipline. The inauguration of the scheme for the popular election of chiefs made the latter slightly more public-relations-minded in dealing with the rest of the native population but did not cause any immediate shift in power. Most of the hereditary chiefs were elected. However, there has intruded into the thoughts of some circles the possibility of electing someone more competent from the groups supposed to provide the chief—possibly from the male rather than the regular female line or even from another branch of the extended family. A few unusual events of this sort have already happened and may become more common in the future. The elite are not entirely united in their view on the subject, for they see in this development, according to their relative positions, opportunities for climbing or descending the sociopolitical ladder. There is little anxiety that these processes will get out of hand and the common people will try to take over themselves—even the commoners would regard this as inconceivable at present. Though the elite have less formal control in many spheres, they continue to serve as the pivotal power in Palau.

There have been greater changes in the external façade of political institutions than in the inner structure. Those elected officials who were removed by the foreigners and those who inherited official positions but were not elected by the natives continue, in many instances, to retain control over the decision-making and execution of decisions. Still, their total power has been impaired and they must now negotiate with other groups and placate many more in order to maintain control. The foreign-facing officials can invoke the demands of the foreigners

276 HUMAN PROBLEMS IN TECHNOLOGICAL CHANGE

as a means of legitimizing their own decisions and this source of
sanctions often carries more weight than those which can be used
to counter them from traditional sources. It remains to be seen
whether in the future the seat of power will shift from the inner
to the outer circle. Probably, in terms of Palau political practices,
numerous specific compromise arrangements will be worked out
in relation to the constellation of interest groups in each locality.

In the estimation of the governors, the first steps in the direction of establishing democratic patterns have been taken and as
long as the native society appears to function smoothly the induced changes have achieved their desired immediate ends.
Where the local groups are sharply divided and a major persisting
conflict develops and comes to the attention of the governors,
efforts are made to mediate the differences. The native official is
invited to resign and new elections are held.

Several attempts have been made to introduce a democratic
pattern at the higher political levels of Palau. A Palau government has been formed, made up of the two heads of the con-
federacies together with the members of the civil service bureaucracy and an elected assemblage of delegates. The delegates are
individuals without rank or high office in the native structure and
they form the Palau Congress. Its authority has fluctuated between a legislative and a consultative one, with the tendency to
emphasize the latter function. During the initial meetings members of the Congress, in accordance with Palau mores, have
tended to respond to the pressures exerted by the two high chiefs
and the civil servants. Those who dissented from the positions
taken by these powerful influences have seldom dared to speak
out. However, there is a native interest in the potentialities of a
democratic legislative body and considerable discussion of the
possibilities at the "taro-root" level. A democratically elected
executive branch headed by the two "high chiefs" is also a matter
of some speculation. Though no one has publicly favored their
election, many are concerned over the power concentrated in
these two positions. It will be recalled that in the early period of
American administration, these two pivotal figures were made
virtually into a dual headship. More recently their power has

been reduced to some degree by returning to the heads of individual districts semi-autonomous control and by opening direct lines of communication between foreign officials and district chiefs. The heads of the two confederations are now in an unstable state of power. They work together for common interests but are rivals for ascendancy in influence. This patterning of the executive branch of the native government probably will undergo numerous changes with alterations in the policies of the administration and with native pressures.

The extent to which the elected leaders of a subordinate society may exercise the prerogatives of self-government is a complicated problem. Some natives prefer more active, direct foreign administration, on the grounds that their own leadership is largely Japanese in outlook rather than American and that desired reforms cannot be instituted as long as the present vested interests monopolize the posts of authority. Though opinions are divided, the consensus probably would be today that the democratic patterning of elected leadership thus far has done no great damage to Palau, that it can be fitted into the social system without undermining the political structure, and that it may in the end have some advantages. The major change has been in the social rites preceding assumption of office rather than in the conduct of those in authority. It would be an error, however, to presume that there is no real democracy in Palau's traditional patterns. As has already been noted, its ancestral forms were such that while autocracy could be practiced, extensive controls over the ruler were in effect and the risks attendant on an unsuccessful autocratic ruler were far greater than those for another type of ruler.

5. ANALYSIS

One of the main goals of American foreign policy is the introduction of democracy into areas now apparently without it. The tactics and strategies for achieving this end in cultures markedly different from those of the western world have seldom been examined. Studies of acculturation reveal that social forms diffuse more easily and rapidly than their meanings. The democratic type of social organization may be introduced with comparative ease into any plastic social system that is fairly intact and receptive to alien introductions. The form, however, may become a manipulative means for achieving ends not inherent in the democratic ideology or may become a symbolic pattern to placate the foreigners. The instilling of democratic spirit into various types of social arrangements calls for sophisticated comprehension of the democratic way of life itself. Cultural agents of the western world are not always conversant with the nature of democracy in their own societies. Some tend to project an idealized version, ignoring the way decisions are influenced and the actual roles played by political pressure groups. Such persons view native politics with scorn and contempt, and the inability to gain the prescribed ends is taken as proof that the natives are not yet ready for responsible self-government. Others accept the realities of power in human relations and seek to work within the given system to achieve the avowed goals.

It is essential to comprehend the means used in relation to the ends desired when introducing democracy. Otherwise, there is the very real prospect of *eliminating* existing democratic patterns while trying to *introduce* democratic forms in accordance with western institutional structures. Thus, in the case of the Sioux Indians, the indigenous organization was a fairly democratic one. There were no power monopolies in which authority was vested in a closed group, and individuals were elected to most offices. The first foreign governors of the Sioux were eager to civilize the "savages" and considered one means to be the suppression of pre-existing organizations. The established groups were broken up and their members scattered to different reservations. War chiefs were assumed to be the only chiefs and no effort was made to work with other types of leadership. The traditional means of legitimizing individual qualifications for office were abolished. As a result no social system survived to make decisions or to execute them. An extended bureaucracy of whites was required to supervise the population. Only in the past few years has there been any recognition of the need to develop democratic political arrangements which are meaningful and effective within Sioux society.

Democratic forms may be designed to enhance the control of foreign rulers rather than to strengthen the native society. In many colonial areas of the world and in satellite nations, a façade of democratic organizations has been created. Natives have not been deceived into believing that their rulers view the established systems as more than a convenient device to further their own interests. The election of native officials who serve thereafter as the agents of authority by receiving support not from below but from above do not become local leaders in a movement to expand the concept of democracy. Such elected leaders may become the objects against which revolutionary movements are organized.

An immediate problem that confronts any administration of a society with a hereditary system of authority is that of determining the extent to which inheritance precludes democratic processes. It cannot be premised that inheritance implies autocracy in primitive societies. The traditional lines of leadership may actually, as in the case of Palau, provide for a regular line of succession to office but permit a change in office-holder when the individual is deemed unsuitable. The establishment of a parallel set of offices apart from the hereditary ones has been tried, especially in colonial areas in which the established leadership could not be controlled by the administration. In these cases two power centers developed and, in turn, provide the foundations for struggles for dominance. The tasks involved in creating new power patterns need to be viewed in terms of the cultural contexts, taking into account the skills and resources of the foreign governors and native governed. Otherwise democracy may result in a manipulative symbol without substance rather than a human value of worth.

In this particular case the election of leaders was an effective starting point for a gradual introduction of democratic processes. The change had consequences but was not disruptive. In other cases there may be different focal points of entrance. Whatever the crucial zone of power, the foreign administrators may, if so desiring, bring into being democratic values of varying types.

Thus, increased recognition of the dignity of the individual is a vital democratic pattern and the absence of any racial distinction between "civilized" Americans and "primitive gooks" is another. For the native, appraisal of foreign introductions is inextricably linked with native experiences with the foreigners themselves. In Palau the experience has been on the whole a democratic one, given the structure of the rulers and the ruled in a cross-cultural situation.

SUGGESTIONS FOR STUDY: Recurrent Groups of Problems

The effort to look for similarities in the problems facing administrators and technicians should have led to something like a classification. We offer the following for comparison as an attempt that may be useful in identifying situations and as a basis for developing principles for solving human problems.

1. Problems of Cultural Linkage

   These arise because of failure to understand the connection between certain beliefs and customs, as in Case 2, Case 5, Case 6, and Case 10.

2. Problems of Social Structure

   These arise from failure to work through existing social organizations or from miscalculation as to what the functioning social units are, as in Case 3, Case 6, Case 7, Case 8, Case 10, and Case 11.

3. Problems of the Role of the Innovator

   These arise from poor relations between the people of the different cultures involved, or from misunderstanding, or poor definition of the role of the innovator, as in Case 4, Case 7, Case 9, Case 11, and Case 14.

4. Problems of Cultural Bias

   These arise from interpreting behavior in one culture in terms of another culture, as in Case 9, Case 12, Case 13, Case 14, and Case 15.

5. Problems of Participation

   These arise from failure to bring people into the planning and carrying out of a program of change, as in Case 7, Case 8, Case 11, and Case 14.

6. Problems of Buffer Organization

   These may develop from any of the above problems and result in the organization of resistance to change, as in Case 14 and Case 15.

Once such recurring types of problems have been recognized, it becomes possible to size up a particular situation rapidly and to begin the solution of the problem involved, guided by one or another of the general principles of human behavior which have so far been worked out by social scientists. Some of the attempts to formulate such principles which will prove useful are the following:

Experience with Human Factors in Agricultural Areas of the World. By M. L. Wilson and others. United States Department of Agriculture, Washington, 1949.

The Governing of Men: General Principles and Recommendations Based on Experience at a Japanese Relocation Camp. By Alexander H. Leighton. Princeton University Press, Princeton, N. J., 1945.

Human Relations in a Changing World: Observations on the Use of Social Sciences. By Alexander H. Leighton. E. P. Dutton and Co., New York, 1949.

Techniques and Cultures: A Manual of Applied Social Science for Point IV Technicians. By Conrad M. Arensberg. Department of State, Washington. Forthcoming.

Technological Change and Mental Health: A Manual. Prepared for United Nations Educational, Scientific and Cultural Organization by the World Federation for Mental Health, 1951.

As a final exercise, it is suggested that the student prepare, on a basis of experience which he himself has had if possible, a case modeled on the cases that have been presented.

PART IV

CONCEPTUAL TOOLS FOR SOLVING
HUMAN PROBLEMS

PART IV. CONCEPTUAL TOOLS FOR SOLVING HUMAN PROBLEMS

The aim of this book is to provide a number of cases which may be used in a variety of ways for a variety of teaching purposes. In consequence, suggestions for study and the delineation of principles have been held to a minimum. It has been our feeling that the volume would be most useful if teacher and student were free to employ their own interpretations in the light of their experience and of existing literature, unhampered by detailed formulations from the editor.

A second consideration is the fact that any adequate formulation which took into account all the cultural, sociological, and psychological aspects of these cases would be exceedingly lengthy. It seemed best, therefore, to think of such an effort as an additional volume which would endeavor to state relevant social science principles in a form that would be useful for administrators, educators, and technologists. Such a work is now in preparation.

These considerations do not remove the need for a concluding statement that endeavors to pull together some of the ideas that are evident in the body of the book. The complexity of the problems forces an arbitrary limitation and we have chosen to take a few points within the fields of anthropology and sociology that are fairly well in line with the analyses provided by the authors of the cases. A number of important principles, especially in psychology, are thus left for further treatment.

Like the concepts of physiology and genetics, the concepts of social science are ways of summarizing phenomena for the purpose of thinking out experiments or observations, and understanding the results. With the guidance that physiological theory has given us, we have been able to develop new forms of medical treatment; with the guidance of genetic theory we have been able to develop varieties of plants and animals for human use. Similarly with the existing theory of human behavior we are moving toward understanding of human relations and perhaps toward their intelligent control.

The cases of the introduction of the wagon, the axe, and hybrid corn illustrate the nature of human custom. They show how customs are linked with one another, how a change in one may affect many others, or how one well-established custom may prevent or retard change in another. When the nature of customs and the fact of their linkage is grasped, one has a primary frame of reference for planning and directing a program of change. This frame of reference is spoken of by social scientists as the concept of culture.

It is simply the understanding that all people everywhere behave in accordance with patterns which they have learned in the process of growing up in society and which make sense to them as an over-all design for living.[1] Whatever a person brought up in one tradition may think or feel about the efficiency or sensibleness of another people's customs, to those who practice them they are the right and good ways of behavior. They are so because they have been held up as proper by parents and other respected persons from childhood. They are so because they have been learned slowly and sometimes painfully through the years.

The fact that a long learning process lies behind every established custom for each individual has several important implications. On the one hand, when we view the wide variety of foods which different people have chosen to eat or the various ways of organizing village life or the differences in any other set of customs, we become aware of the almost infinite possibilities for human adaptation. It is apparent that individuals of whatever racial background can adapt to a vast variety of situations, that they can learn to behave in a tremendous number of different ways. On the other hand, an understanding of customs as learned behavior makes us aware that change involves some degree of unlearning and of new learning. Once this is realized, it is apparent that we can find help in guiding change through using

[1] See especially items 2, 9, 11, 12, 16, 19 of the references for further reading listed at the end of this section.

what is known of the psychological processes of suggestion and of learning.[1]

However, it is not merely with individuals and their learning processes that we are dealing in changing customs. We are working also with the meaningful design which the whole set of customs makes for the people of a culture. Any given custom has meaning not only in itself as satisfying a particular need, but also as part of a larger whole which constitutes the way of life of a people. The texture and the taste of "Indian corn" in New Mexico were qualities which had been given high value through customary usage over two centuries. They were linked with the procedures of preparing food and the satisfactions of family eating. They were knitted widely into the women's way of life and only somewhat less thoroughly into the men's. Navaho sheep- and horse-raising (once they were borrowed from the Spanish) had also been linked with prestige values and the social life of the Indians. In all societies the existing customs have meaning for the people in relation to one another. They have learned to practice them as a part of a pattern of living, and the continuance of that way of life is in itself the source of feelings of security. A large part of the activity of each individual as he grows up has been devoted to achieving such a sense of security and well-being through behaving like others and through obtaining their acceptance as a result. A change of apparently small magnitude in one aspect of the culture may, therefore, seem to threaten the whole system, or at least require the learning of a new viewpoint toward a whole series of customs.[2]

However, it is apparent that there are different degrees of interrelatedness among customs. The introduction of the wagon to the Papago set off a number of changes in the division of labor, in pottery-making, and other aspects of the technology, and even in the form of village organization, but there is no indication that there were any direct effects on the religious life of the Papagos. Later developments, such as the introduction of modern medical practices, did affect Papago religion because

[1] See references 4, 6, 7, 15, 21, 27, 28 at end of section.

[2] See especially references 8, 13, 17, 18, 20, 22, 23, 34 at end of section.

much of Papago supernatural belief was linked with concepts of disease and curing technique. It is apparent from the Papago case, as well as from others in the book, that a knowledge of how a given people's culture is integrated, how the different customs and beliefs are related to one another, gives a basis for predicting what the effects of a proposed change will be.

The first two cases are designed to make clear these few fundamentals as to the nature of culture and to show how the concept may be employed in understanding and guiding a specific instance of cross-cultural change. Awareness of the nature of culture is, of course, merely a first step toward the solution of human problems. Nevertheless, it appears to be a necessary fundamental on which the successful use of the other concepts of social science heavily depends.

The case of the cotton-picking incident in the Japanese relocation center illustrates another important characteristic of human behavior. It shows how people act as members of groups rather than merely as individuals pursuing purely individual gains.[1] This was true even in the relocation center where evacuation had brought about the breakdown of many previously established groupings. Many Japanese leaders and some of the administrators were convinced that it required the incentive of individual wages to get the people picking cotton. Possibly that would have worked, but the key to understanding what actually did happen is a knowledge of the social grouping that had taken place in the centers. The block had taken form as a functioning social unit, and that group's interests, forms of cooperation, and public opinion began to work in the new situation, once they had been focused on cotton-picking. The center whole had not yet taken form as a social unit and, hence, could not be employed effectively for carrying out the program of the community leaders and administrators.

A social organization, that is, a set of customs in terms of which people cooperate, is a part of every culture. The social organization consists of recognized groups of individuals who are accustomed to act together for certain purposes and who abide by

[1] See especially references 4, 7, 10, 14, 15, 19, 27, 28 at end of section.

certain codes of behavior, however unconscious of these codes they may be. The codes consist of rights and duties which the group expects its members to abide by and which are the basis of their cooperation.

Some groupings are formal, recognized by name. Thus, every people recognizes a family unit in some form, and some societies have many other groups based on kinship, such as the joint families of India, or the clans of China. Almost all societies have groups based on contiguous residence with formal organization, such as the rural villages of most modern nations and our own cities, counties, and states. Most, except the simplest, societies also have formal groups set up to pursue some limited interest, such as our social clubs or political parties or the political associations of the West Africans. In addition, the kinship groups or associations may be ranked into organized classes or castes or minority groups, so that a formal organization in terms of social stratification may exist.

There are, however, informal as well as the formal organizations in every society.[1] Cliques of like-minded people and the temporary following of influential men are examples of such informal grouping. The informal organization of factory workers has been found to be of fundamental importance in connection with industrial management. Such groupings may be of very great significance in introducing new ways.

The social organization of any people, like the culture of which it is a part, constitutes an interrelated whole, and changes in one section will have greater or less repercussion on others. The important consideration for our purposes is that all peoples have such organizations, however difficult to define or different in form they may be as compared with groupings to which we are accustomed. It is important in any program of cross-cultural change that they be recognized, since the existing channels of communication and cooperation constitute a beginning point for the introduction of anything new. They represent generations of effort in the establishment of working relations and consequently a means for the enlistment of human energies in new directions.

[1] See references 5, 7, 24, 25, 29, 32, 33 at end of section.

If we begin with the concept of social organization in mind and attempt to find out its nature, we have a basis for establishing communication concerning a proposed change and for channeling energies toward furthering it. On the other hand, if we ignore social organization we fail to use the most vital of available resources.

The application of the concepts of culture and social organization provides us, as it were, with maps of the terrain in which we are working. The first three cases are designed to show how these two concepts may be employed in defining situations. Every case of directed change, however, involves by definition something new. Spelling out the cultural linkages and mapping the social organization is merely the groundwork for solving the given problem. The nature of the new element in the situation sets the problem. It is never merely the proposed new technique or form of organization; the new technique is always introduced by someone—extension agent, technician, administrator, or native leader. The innovator is, thus, also a part of the situation and his role as a factor must be assessed.

Whatever the case, foreigner or native carrying out the innovation, the actions of the innovator must be evaluated with reference to the culture and social organization of the people. They may be, like those of the labor expert in Palau, in conflict with the customs of the people with whom the innovator is working or they may be, like those of the village workers in India, adapted to the native behavior in some way. The history of the relations of the innovator's ethnic group with the people among whom he is working may be an important basis of favorable or unfavorable attitudes toward him, regardless of his own individual characteristics. His attitudes toward local customs, not only the techniques that he is trying to change but also other customs not closely related, will be observed and will influence his relations with the people. His success or failure may be very largely a result of the perception of him held by the people he is trying to influence.

To assume that, simply because natives have been induced to accept the role of innovators, success will be achieved, is also dangerous. Native innovators may be such because of aberrant qualities not generally approved and may therefore hinder acceptance. On the other hand, native innovators with prestige in the existing social system may be especially effective.[1] Although few widely applicable generalizations can be made, it is apparent that the role of the innovator as a factor in change is susceptible of analysis and that such analysis must be employed for the understanding of any given situation. The fourth case is designed as an introduction to dealing with this factor.

The three concepts which have been discussed ought to be always used in conjunction with a fourth. This is the concept of cultural bias. The case of the labor dispute on Palau gives one of the simplest illustrations. The labor relations adviser rather consistently interpreted the behavior of the islanders in terms of his own experience in American culture. The result was thoroughgoing misunderstanding of what was taking place. Like all of us, the adviser tended to see behavior in another society as having the same significance that similar behavior would have in his own. The fact is, however, that identical behaviors in two different societies may have quite different meanings.

Thus, vigorous, aggressive acts among the Pueblo Indians of the southwestern United States are disapproved under all circumstances, while among us they are highly approved in business or in seeking political office. An established set of values in Pueblo culture conditions those who grow up in that society to behave in nonaggressive ways. An administrator who encourages a Pueblo to exercise the same sort of aggressiveness in political behavior that is regarded as desirable in our culture is likely to isolate the individual from his people rather than to encourage his development as a leader.

It should be constantly borne in mind in cross-cultural situations that the cultures in which we grow up predispose us to certain views and values.[2] We come to another culture with preconceptions about what is good and what is rational or sensible which do not hold good universally and these preconceptions may result in great misunderstanding. Setting aside those preconcep-

[1] See references 1, 4, 7, and items listed in footnote [2] on p. 287.
[2] See reference 7 at end of section.

tions, especially in the highly developed fields of technical specialism and administrative management in our culture, is one of the most difficult, as well as most necessary, disciplines in any work that goes on across cultural boundaries.

The four concepts which have been discussed appear to be primary for use in guiding cultural change. They constitute the means for appraising a situation, for planning steps in initiating change, and for getting at causes of success or failure. Needless to say, the systematic asking of questions and interviewing which is discussed in the "Suggestions for Study" in the body of the casebook should be guided by these concepts of culture, social organization, and role of the innovator; and the results of such procedures should be constantly corrected for cultural bias. The question remains: given a body of information which clearly reveals cultural and social factors, are there any principles which are well established for inducing acceptance or for dispelling resistance to change?

It is not our aim to go here into the evidence for and against various generalizations that are made concerning the nature and causes of cultural change. There are, however, two or three principles which may be presented as having much evidence in their favor. How they should be stated may be questioned, but we shall nevertheless attempt to give them here as simply as possible.

The first proposition is that people do not vary their customary behavior unless they feel some need which existing ways do not satisfy. The response to feeling such a need is to invent or to borrow from some other people a technique or form of organization or belief which is felt to satisfy that need. This in essence is the basic process of cultural change.

Needs cannot be established by fiat. Ordering people to adopt a new custom may focus them on resisting the command rather than on the advantages of the required change. Since people often behave in this way in response to commands, it is clear that resistance may be forestalled by finding ways to establish a sense of need before proceeding with the change. One technique widely used by agricultural extension agents is securing participation by the people in all phases of the innovation process. Real participation involves taking part in the planning and discussion of advantages to be gained, in the devising of methods for introduction, and in the execution of the innovation. Participation through their own social organization not only gives people a chance to develop a feeling of need for the change, but also enables them to work out in their own way adjustments of the new to the pattern of the existing customs.

Devising means for participation in the light of knowledge of culture and social organization would seem to be a fundamental procedure in the process of directing cultural change. However effective imposed changes may appear to be at the level of overt behavior, as in the Navaho conservation case, the accompanying effects of imposition in the form of antagonism to the innovator and all that he represents may raise serious obstacles to further progress. The principle of participation can be regarded as a working tool for action, the employment of which depends on knowledge of the culture, the social system, and the role of the innovator. It is one of the better-tested means for preventing resistance which is unrelated to the inherent nature of the innovation itself and for establishing conditions for orderly and constructive change.[1] The Navaho and Papago conservation cases illustrate respectively the negative effects of nonparticipation and the positive effects of participation.

It is shown in the cases of the Navahos and of the Japanese Americans that resistance to programs of improvement may be centered not on the specific innovations but on the way in which the programs are administered. When such resistance is allowed to develop it may become organized, so that people's energies are channeled into opposition to the innovators, while the innovations themselves become symbols of that opposition. The two cases illustrate the end products of failure to make use of the concepts and principles which have been discussed. Every situation should be considered with reference to whether any resistance that arises is toward the specific innovation or whether it is toward the innovators and the methods they have used. In the former case, the whole scheme needs to be reexamined. In the

[1] See references 3, 7, 24, 27, 28 at end of section.

latter, analysis can be made guided by the ideas which have been discussed. Such an analysis would give answers to the following questions:

1. Have the cultural linkages been discovered and utilized in the procedure?
2. Has work been carried on through the existing social organization or have social organizations been set up which conflict with those previously in existence?
3. How are the innovators' purposes and ways of behavior regarded?
4. Have the innovators misinterpreted the responses of the people through cultural bias?
5. Has the maximum possible participation been encouraged and allowed to develop?
6. Have the needs that are felt been obscured by opposition to methods of introduction?

The answers to such questions as these will at least provide a diagnosis which may then be a basis for action in ways determined by the specific situation.

Finally, it must be emphasized that the concepts presented are not to be thought of as applicable only in situations where there are wide differences between the cultural backgrounds of the innovator and the people among whom he is working. The differences between the islanders of Palau and the Americans who worked there are marked and easy to see. But the differences between the backgrounds of a trained technician in the United States and the people of an ordinary rural community in the same country are of the same kind.[1] The technician is deeply immersed in one subculture that exists among Americans, while the rural people are in another. If the view is adopted that almost all changes proposed as a result of the extensive knowledge of modern science and technology originate in one subculture and, to be accepted, must be made intelligible and given value in terms of another subculture, then it will be seen that the concepts and principles outlined here are applicable and can be used in guiding change.

[1] See reference 33 at end of section.

REFERENCES FOR FURTHER STUDY

1. Barnett, Homer G., "Personal Conflicts and Cultural Change," *Social Forces*, vol. 20, December, 1941, pp. 160–171.

2. Benedict, Ruth, *Patterns of Culture*. Houghton Mifflin Co., Boston, 1934.

3. Brunner, Edmund deS., and Douglas Ensminger, *Farmers of the World*. Columbia University Press, New York, 1945.

4. Cottrell, Leonard S., Jr., "Analysis of Situational Fields in Social Psychology," *American Sociological Review*, vol. 7, June, 1942, pp. 370–382.

5. Gardner, Burleigh B., *Human Relations in Industry*. Richard D. Irwin, Chicago, 1945.

6. Gillin, John, *The Ways of Men:* An Introduction to Anthropology. Appleton-Century Co., New York, 1948.

7. Hartley, Eugene L., and Ruth E. Hartley, *Fundamentals of Social Psychology*. Alfred A. Knopf, New York, 1952.

8. Herskovits, Melville J., *Acculturation:* The Study of Culture Contact. J. J. Augustin, New York, 1938.

9. ———, *Man and His Works:* The Science of Cultural Anthropology. Alfred A. Knopf, New York, 1948.

10. Homans, George C., *The Human Group*. Harcourt Brace and Co., New York, 1951.

11. Kluckhohn, Clyde, *Mirror for Man:* The Relation of Anthropology to Modern Life. Whittlesey House, New York, 1949.

12. Kroeber, Alfred, *Anthropology*. Harcourt Brace and Co., New York, rev. 1948.

13. Leighton, Alexander H., and Dorothea Leighton, *The Navaho Door:* An Introduction to Navaho Life. Harvard University Press, Cambridge, Mass., 1944.

14. Lewin, Kurt, *Resolving Social Conflicts:* Selected Papers on Group Dynamics. Harper and Bros., New York, 1948.

15. Lindesmith, A. R., and Anselm L. Strauss, *Social Psychology*. Dryden Press, New York, 1949.

16. Linton, Ralph, *The Study of Man*. Appleton-Century Co., New York, 1936.

17. ———, editor, *Acculturation in Seven American Indian Tribes*. Appleton-Century Co., New York, 1940.

18. Linton, Ralph, editor, *The Science of Man in the World Crisis.* Columbia University Press, New York, 1945.

19. Lowie, Robert H., *Social Organization.* Rinehart and Co., New York, 1948.

20. Malinowski, Bronislaw, *The Dynamics of Culture Change:* An Inquiry into Race Relations in Africa. Yale University Press, New Haven, 1945.

21. Miller, Neal E., and John Dollard, *Social Learning and Imitation.* Yale University Press, New Haven, 1941.

22. National Research Council, *The Problem of Changing Food Habits:* Report of the Committee on Food Habits, 1941–1943. Bulletin No. 108, National Research Council, Washington, October, 1943.

23. Redfield, Robert, *A Village That Chose Progress:* Chan Kom Revisited. University of Chicago Press, Chicago, 1950.

24. Roethlisberger, F. J., and William J. Dickson, *Management and the Worker.* Harvard University Press, Cambridge, Mass., 1940.

25. Selznick, Philip, *TVA and the Grass Roots:* A Study in the Sociology of Formal Organization. University of California Press, Berkeley, 1949.

26. Sharp, Walter R., *International Technical Assistance:* Programs and Organization. Public Administration Service, Chicago, 1952.

27. Sherif, Muzafer, *The Psychology of Social Norms.* Harper and Bros., New York, 1936.

28. —— and Hadley Cantril, *The Psychology of Ego-Involvements.* John Wiley and Sons, New York, 1947.

29. "Social Implications of Technical Change," *International Social Science Bulletin,* vol. 4, no. 2, Summer, 1952.

30. Volkart, Edmund H., *Social Behavior and Personality:* Contributions of W. I. Thomas to Theory and Social Research. Social Science Research Council, New York, 1951.

31. Whyte, William Foote, *Street Corner Society:* The Social Structure of an Italian Slum. University of Chicago Press, Chicago, 1943.

32. ——, editor, *Industry and Society.* McGraw-Hill, New York, 1946.

33. Williams, Robin M., *American Society.* Alfred A. Knopf, New York, 1951.

34. Wilson, Godfrey, and Monica Wilson, *The Analysis of Social Change:* Based on Observations in Central Africa. Cambridge University Press, Cambridge, England, 1945.

INDEX

INDEX

ACCULTURATION, 138–139, 147–148, 179, 195, 203, 240, 249, 262, 277
Adair, John, 3
Administrative organization, 59, 61, 66, 110, 202, 205, 215
Adult education, 197, 242
Age roles. *See* Roles
Aggression, 239
Agricultural innovation, 55, 58, 108
Agricultural surplus, 26, 31, 38
Agriculture, U.S. Department of: extension service, 13, 35, 38, 39
Alaska, 127–148
Aleuts, 129, 138
Andrews, C. L., 139
Anthropology, 285
Apache Indians, 24
Arapaho Indians, 176
Arensberg, C. M., 282
Arizona, 23–32, 41–54, 185–207, 209–223; University of, 9
Arkansas, 240, 248
Associations: formal, 235, 268, 289; informal, 235, 289; reindeer, 127–128, 129, 134, 141, 145–146
Australia, 69–90

BARBER, Carroll, 3
Barnett, H. G., 295
Bell, W. H., 217
Benedict, Ruth, 295
Brunner, E. deS., 295

CANADA, 225–243
Cantril, Hadley, 296
Carnegie Corporation of New York, 9
Caroline Islands, 149–164, 261–280, 290, 291
Cash economy. *See* Economy
Castetter, E. F., 217
Change: acceptance of, 17–18, 122, 292; guidance of, 30, 288, 292, 294; in economy, 31, 110, 145, 191; process of, 18; resistance to, 17–18, 38, 49, 99, 122, 256, 257, 293–294; technological, 13, 69
Chesky, Jane, 27, 217
Cheyenne Indians, 176
Clan, 77, 80, 88, 102, 151, 154, 159, 172, 195, 267, 272; totemic, 77, 86
Collective ownership. *See* Ownership
Collier, John, 205

Communication, 14, 37, 58, 62, 121, 122, 236, 250, 254, 257, 260, 272, 287, 289
Community organization, 26, 29, 31, 48, 52, 60, 102, 110, 116, 121, 122–123, 133, 154, 170–173, 204, 212, 234, 250
Community solidarity, 31, 52–53, 163, 259
Compartmentalization, 17
Competition, 51, 132
Converse, E., 64
Coon, C. S., 64
Cordova, A. R., 37
Cornell University, program for research and training, 9
Cottrell, L. S., Jr., 295
Creek Confederacy, 170, 173
Creek Indians, 165–180
Crop improvement, 35–37, 56–57, 65, 110
Crop rotation, 57, 104, 108
Crops, 36, 57, 97, 100, 108, 116
Cross-cultural barriers, 15, 155
Cross-cultural change, 183, 288
Cultural bias, 144, 160–161, 162, 278, 281, 291, 294
Cultural integration, 88, 179, 191, 287, 288
Cultural lag, 14, 111
Cultural linkage, 17, 30, 33, 84–85, 86, 89, 109, 195, 200, 281, 286, 290, 294
Cultural Missions of Mexico, 13
Culture, 16–17, 286–288; breakdown of, 86, 109; contact, 70–73, 87, 176, 263; processes, 9; stability of, 87, 89, 109
Curzon, Lord, 55
Custom, 13, 286

DEMONSTRATION, 39, 53, 56, 57, 67, 108, 186, 189
Dependence, economic, 239
Dickson, W. J., 296
Diffusion, 14
Disorganization, 111
Displacement of tools, 32, 73
Division of labor, 26–27, 31, 32, 73, 74, 101, 147, 287
Dobyns, H. F., 3
Dollard, John, 296

ECONOMIC dependence, 239
Economic security, 202

Economy: cash, 110; changes in, 31; diversified, 145; subsistence, 110, 191
Elections, introduction of, 261, 266, 275
Embree, J. F., 158, 253
Ensminger, Douglas, 295
Eskimos, 127–148
Etawah Pilot Project (India), 57

Factions, 159, 167, 168, 169, 179, 276
Family counseling, 254, 255, 260
Family organization, 26, 44, 60, 76, 100, 101, 108–109, 121, 195, 212, 229–230, 231, 232–233, 239
Famine: Bengal, 55; Commission, 55
Felt needs, 38, 53, 216, 222, 292, 294
Fertilization of crops, 104, 107, 108
Food habits, 25, 38, 39, 133–134, 211, 231–232, 249, 287
French Canadians, 226–227, 240
Fryer, E. R., 196

Gardner, B. B., 295
Garrett, Annette, 125
Genetics, 285
Gillin, John, 295
Government. See Political organization

Harper, A. G., 37
Hartley, E. L., 295
Hartley, R. E., 295
Health, public, 10, 15, 217
Herskovits, M. J., 295
Holmberg, A. R., 3
Homans, G. C., 295
Hoover, F. W., 217
Hostility, 100, 105, 111, 114, 116, 120, 163, 201, 202, 237, 239, 248, 262
Human relations, 11, 256, 286

Incentive to work, 41, 146, 288
India, 9, 55–67, 290; Department of Agriculture of, 55
Indian Affairs: Bureau of, U.S., 23, 24, 97, 98, 130, 131, 185, 188, 198, 210, 215; extension work in, 56, 57, 104, 108, 111, 218, 221
Industrialization, 10
Initiation rites, 75, 84
Innovator, role of, 39, 59, 61, 62, 66, 111, 163, 223, 263, 281, 290–291, 294
International Social Science Bulletin, 296
Interviewing, 125–126, 183
Iowa, 248
Irrigation, 104, 107, 110, 113, 119
Issei, 45, 47, 49, 249, 250, 255

Japanese, influence in Micronesia, 262, 264
Japanese Americans, 41–54, 245–260, 293
Joseph, Alice, 27, 217

Keesing, F. M., 274
Kimball, S. T., 3, 196
Kinship, 76, 102, 109, 227, 232–233
Kluckhohn, Clyde, 3, 106, 196, 295
Kroeber, Alfred, 295

Labor relations, 150, 157, 289, 291
Land use, 26, 102, 105, 109, 110, 116, 120, 153, 195, 231
Lantis, Margaret, 139
Lapps, 128, 129
Leadership, 26, 38, 42, 48, 49, 52, 67, 85, 103, 110, 117–118, 120, 123, 132, 146, 150–151, 159, 161, 180, 195, 204, 206, 207, 213, 235, 237, 241, 242, 250, 259, 264, 270–271
Learning process, 286–287
Leighton, A. H., 3, 282, 295
Leighton, Dorothea, 106, 196, 295
Leisure, 82
Leonard, Olen, 37
Levy, G. E., 228n
Lewin, Kurt, 295
Lindesmith, A. R., 295
Linton, Ralph, 295
Loomis, C. P., 37
Lowie, R. H., 296

Malinowski, Bronislaw, 296
Mayer, Albert, 58
Micronesia, 149–164, 261–280, 290
Miller, N. E., 296
Missionaries, 23, 71–73, 83, 90, 128, 185, 211, 212, 227–228
Mormons, 97, 102, 105, 108
Myths, 79–81, 87, 88

National Research Council, 296
Navaho Indians, 97–111, 185–207, 293
Neighborhood, 45, 52, 54, 250
New Mexico, 17, 35–39, 97–111, 185–207
Nisei, 45, 47, 49, 248, 250

Oberg, Kalervo, 37
Ogburn, W. F., 14n
Oklahoma, 165–180, 240
Oliver, Douglas, 158, 274

Opler, M. E., 3, 64
Organization. *See* Community; Family; Political; Social
Ownership, individual vs. collective, 31, 127–128, 141–143, 145

Papago Indians, 23–32, 203, 209–223, 287–288, 293
Participation, 38, 61, 63, 67, 120, 122, 146, 203, 204, 206, 216, 218–219, 222, 242, 254, 258, 260, 262, 281, 292–293, 294
Personalness of relations, 64, 67
Peru, 9, 113–123
Physiology, 11, 285
Pima Indians, 26
Point Four, 13, 206, 207
Political innovation, 261–262
Political organization, 45, 61, 103, 117, 153, 165, 167, 170, 173–175, 176, 187, 194–195, 213, 215–216, 220, 222, 261, 264, 267–269
Power structure, 262, 264–265, 276
Prestige, 118, 120, 121, 132–133, 145, 146, 148, 191, 237, 265, 273
Property, 26, 29, 30, 31, 73, 76, 78, 109, 111, 127, 141, 144, 145
Provinse, J. H., 196
Psychological stress, 83, 89–90
Psychology, 206, 285
Public health, 10, 15, 217
Pueblo Indians, 99, 100, 291

Rainey, F. G., 139
Redfield, Robert, 296
Religion, 45–46, 79, 90, 101, 107, 109, 118–119, 121, 122, 123, 173, 174, 177, 191, 223, 229, 235, 237, 287
Relocation center, 41, 43, 95, 245–260, 288
Roethlisberger, F. J., 296
Role, 95; playing, 125–126, 183
Roles: age, 27, 83, 86, 101, 107, 108, 121, 232; sex, 27, 31, 39, 76, 79, 83, 86, 101, 102, 111, 163, 223, 232, 236, 263, 264, 267, 275, 281, 290–291
Russell Sage Foundation, 9

Sanchez, G. I., 37
Sasaki, T. T., 106
Schweitzer, J. L., 3
Selznick, Philip, 296
Sentiment system, 47, 78–81, 85, 251, 259
Sharp, Lauriston, 3, 81
Sharp, W. R., 296
Sherif, Muzafer, 296

Sioux Indians, 278
Social organization, 31, 32, 39, 54, 60, 74, 84, 85, 100, 102, 109, 116–117, 123, 161, 175, 187, 195–196, 239, 242, 263, 278, 281, 288–290, 294; lack of, 241
Sociology, 285
Soil conservation, 98, 185, 186, 189, 209; service, 186
Southwest, American, 9, 23–32
Spanish influence, 23–24, 25, 99, 191, 211–212, 262
Specialization, 14, 16, 30
Spencer, Katherine, 3
Spicer, E. H., 9
Spicer, R. B., 27, 217
Stein, William, 165
Stock improvement, 197
Stock reduction, 100, 105, 186, 189, 202, 214
Strauss, A. L., 295
Surplus, agricultural, 26, 31, 38, 98

Technological innovation, 9, 17, 28, 30, 55, 58, 72, 82, 118, 287
Technology: Australia, 69; New Mexico, 39; Papago, 26
Thailand, 9
Thomas, R. K., 3
Trade, 26, 31, 75, 77, 83, 84, 105–106, 262
Transportation, 14, 31, 87
Trust territory, 261

Underhill, R. M., 27
Useem, John, 158, 274

Values, 39, 46–47, 53, 78, 85, 118, 121–122, 145, 147, 163, 180, 202, 227, 229, 236–238, 239, 240, 242, 259, 263, 273, 287, 291, 294
Vernon, W. H. D., 225n
Volkart, E. H., 296

Wage work, 147, 150, 203, 226
War Relocation Authority, 43, 44, 45, 51, 245
Warner, W. L., 81
Whyte, W. F., 296
Williams, R. M., 296
Wilson, Godfrey, 296
Wilson, M. L., 282
Wilson, Monica, 296

Yir Yoront, 69–90